Dissertationstitel

The Right to Asylum in International Law and Legal Philosophy:
The Syrian Conflict and Refugee Crisis

Dissertation Zur Erlangung der Doktorwürde
an der Fakultät für Rechtswissenschaft der
Universität Hamburg

vorgelegt von:
(Rawan, Diab)
Aus (Syrien)

Tag der mündlichen Prüfung: 28.06.2023

Hamburg 2023 (Druckjahr)

Erstgutachter/in: Prof. Dr. Jochen Bung

Zweitgutachter/in: Prof. Dr. Nora Markard

Tag der mündlichen Prüfung: 28.06.2023

The Right to Asylum in International Law and Legal Philosophy

The Syrian Conflict and Refugee Crisis

By
Rawan Diab

TRANSNATIONAL PRESS LONDON
2023

LAW SERIES: 7
Series Editor: Özgür Heval Çınar

The Right to Asylum in International Law and Legal Philosophy - The Syrian
Conflict and Refugee Crisis

By Rawan Diab

First Published in 2023 by Transnational Press London in the United Kingdom, 13
Stamford Place, Sale, M33 3BT, UK.
www.tplondon.com

Transnational Press London® and the logo and its affiliated brands are registered
trademarks.

Requests for permission to reproduce material from this work should be sent to:
sales@tplondon.com

Paperback
ISBN: 978-1-80135-119-5
Hardcover
ISBN: 978-1-80135-249-9
Digital
ISBN: 978-1-80135-235-2

Cover Design: Nihal Yazgan
Cover Photo by Ggia, dust spots/scratches removed by Kim Hansen. Edges
cropped due to scan. Further restoration improvements using masks by Ggia. -
File:20101009 Arrested refugees immigrants in Fylakio detention center Thrace
Evros Greece.tif, CC BY-SA 3.0,
https://commons.wikimedia.org/w/index.php?curid=17437976

Transnational Press London Ltd. is a company registered in England and Wales
No. 8771684.

The Right to Asylum in International Law and Legal Philosophy

The Syrian Conflict and Refugee Crisis

by

Rawan Diab

Faculty of Law
University of Hamburg
2022

Supervisors of the Dissertation:
Prof. Dr. Jochen Bung
Prof. Dr. Nora Markard

Declaration according to § 7 Section 4 and Section 7 Doctoral Regulations
I hereby declare on oath that I have written the dissertation independently and have not used any aids other than those specified.

I certify that the text on the electronic medium is identical to the written herewith-submitted version.

Hamburg, date: 13.12.2022

Rawan Diab

CONTENTS

ABOUT THE AUTHOR

Born in Syria in 1990, Rawan Diab embarked on her academic journey in law at Tishreen University immediately following her high school graduation in October 2007. Successfully completing her undergraduate studies in 2012, Diab's academic pursuits led her abroad, where she secured a prestigious scholarship from the University of Algiers. Her dedication to legal scholarship culminated in the completion of her master's degree in public law, with a specialization in the Department of Environment and Urbanization, in 2015. Diab, later, became part of the Albrecht Mendelssohn Bartholdy Graduate School of Law in November 2016, having been granted a scholarship. Under the guidance of her supervisors, Prof. Dr. Jochen Bung and Prof. Dr. Nora Markard, she studied the right to asylum and migration studies. Her commitment to advancing understanding in these critical areas is evident in her doctoral thesis, where she rigorously investigated the right to asylum in International Law and Legal Philosophy. With a keen focus on the internal conflict in Syria and the resulting refugee crisis, Diab earned her doctoral degree from the University of Hamburg with distinction in June 2023. She has received her doctoral degree from the University of Hamburg with grade cum laude in June 2023. and her thesis is published by Transnational Press London in 2023.

INTRODUCTION

Migration is not a new phenomenon in the current century, it has existed since the individual moved from one country to another seeking to achieve some objectives or fleeing extreme poverty and other difficult living circumstances. Many migration studies have been established in the Political and Social sciences. Nevertheless, in the contemporary World, there are notable restrictions on migration that have been put in place by the States, much more than the previous obstacles in the last century.

On top of that, the differences between States widen dramatically to find a gap in many fields such as economics, politics, and so on. Migration can be attributed to the difference between the developing and developed States, which motivates needy people to leave their countries seeking to resettle in the latter, where they can live in a safe, prosperous, and democratic State. Nowadays, many States face the challenge of internal conflicts and terrorist attacks besides environmental disasters and the impact of climate change.

All these factors have contributed to increase the influx of refugees from many States worldwide, such as (Syria, Libya, Iraq, Somalia, and Azerbaijan) who appeal to the developed States and most European States, which are, in fact, their sole destination for protection mostly, because some States insist on limiting migration according to their rights of setting their immigration policies and consequently, they accept a certain number of immigrants. Kukathas has called those States "modern States" and says: "Modern States are reluctant to allow people to enter and settle within their borders at will for a variety of reasons. Security is one important consideration, though different States have different security concerns."[1]

Asylum seekers who have fled from their countries, because of persecution or internal conflict, have chosen to protect their lives by seeking a place that will be safer and more secure. More Than one million asylum seekers apply every year to resettle in rich States, but only some of them are accepted. Regarding the responsibility of those States to grant protection to all persons

---

[1] KUKATHAS, Chandran. (2004). The case for open immigration. In Contemporary debates in applied ethics (pp. 376-390). Blackwells. P.3.

3

at risk of harm, all international conventions accept a person's right to asylum, particularly under the status of persecution.

Moreover, the right to leave one's country was included in the Universal Declaration of Human Rights 1948 in Art 13, which States that every person has the right to leave their country and return to it.

The main question of this thesis revolves around the idea that, by detecting the right to immigrate in legal approaches, the reader can realize the nature of the right of individuals to leave their country. However, several serious impediments are placed in their way to obstruct their fair implementation. These obstacles restrict the right to emigrate as a human right by States curtailing people's freedom to move wherever they want to, and they are widely condemned across the international community.

One of the most common difficulties that those seeking to emigrate face is the right to stay and reside in the destination State, if the migrant enters the host country. Since he necessarily needs the permission of entry from that country, he might wait to get the permission in vain or, even if he has succeeded to enter maybe an illegal way, that person will live in camps waiting for the Court's decision which could be a refusal, and hence, he would face expulsion from the State which examined his application, and the worst is expulsion from the entire European Union.

In this thesis, I pose and address the following three questions:

1. Is there a right to stay from a global aspect?

2. To what extent does the right to leave make sense even if there isn't any sort of right to stay and resettle?

3. What is the probability of extending the right to stay in the future?

To obtain sound answers to the three previous questions, I have opted for an analytical method that can reinforce the research process by analyzing the essential documents in International Law and EU Law as well as the philosophical perspective which I use in the second section from the second chapter onwards, where I probe different philosophical approaches in detail regarding the case of open borders.

Outline of the Thesis:

The thesis is divided into three main chapters; the first provides clarification of the basic terminologies such as the definitions of the asylum seeker, refugee, and person eligible for subsidiary protection. Regarding the former, I will rely upon the UNHCR definition of the asylum seeker: "asylum seekers are individuals who have sought international protection and whose claims for refugee status have not yet been determined."[2]

An asylum seeker initially applies for international protection in the host country. A refugee was initially an asylum seeker, who originally applied for asylum in the host country. Hence, they are called asylum seekers until the final decision has been made. They are entitled to a refugee status if they fall under the provisions of the 1951 convention of the refugee definition. In this regard, both the asylum seeker and the refugee comply with the principle of non-refoulement, in addition to other provisions in the 1951 Refugee Convention.

After that, other definitions of asylum seekers according to many international bodies will be addressed. By considering the refugee definition of the 1951 Convention and how it explains the refugee, we will observe in the first section that two elements determine the persons who could be considered as such, which will also be contended in this section. A refugee is defined as: "A person, who owing to a well-founded fear of being persecuted for reasons of race, religion, nationality, membership of a particular social group or political opinion is outside the country of his nationality and is unable or, owing to such fear, is unwilling to avail himself of the protection of that country; or who, not having a nationality and being outside the country of his former habitual residence as a result of such events, is unable or, owing to such fear, is unwilling to return to it."[3]

According to many statistics, a massive number of asylum seekers do not qualify as refugees, and, instead, belong to another category and becoming "persons eligible for subsidiary protection". Alternatively, to the subsidiary

---

[2] UNHCR, 2009 Global Trends, p.23.
[3] Article 1 A (2) of the Convention relating to the Status of Refugees, United Nations, Treaty Series, vol.189, p.152.

5

protection, it is known by another name in international law: "Complementary Protection".

In the second chapter, the right to migrate will be developed by studying its basis according to the Universal Declaration of Human Rights and the International Covenant on Civil and Political Rights ICCPR, in addition to other international and European documents. First, the causes of migration and focus on the political violence that causes most large-scale forced displacement worldwide are examined. In this section, the relationship between conflict and displacement is elaborated upon, highlighting the persecution in relation to its forms and referencing the internal conflict in Syria. The UNHCR strongly asserts the relationship between the internal conflict and the increasing number of displaced people around the World. In the second part of this section, after studying the crucial reasons for migrating in our contemporary World, whether those displaced persons have the right to leave their countries of origin as a first step to seek asylum elsewhere is discussed, after studying the crucial reasons for migrating in our contemporary World. This right is examined by considering what is stated in Article 13 of the UDHR, Article 12 of the ICCPR, Article 2 of Protocol 4 of the ECHR, and Article 21 of TFEU.

This discussion leads to the investigation of the possibility of free movement and to illustrating the case of open borders in legal philosophy, which is the second section. First, it is considered whether the borders should be opened generally. Moreover, I will discuss from a philosophical perspective to what extent can a person leave his State freely and stay in another State? Here I will discuss this argument from a philosophical perspective. In the first part of the second section, different opinions concerning the case of open borders are discussed; some of them contend the State's right to lock its doors to all outsiders, while others have open borders. In this section I will focus on some of the different views on the matter, such as the libertarian and Egalitarian views. Then, I will try to find a solution to the case of open borders by studying the Cosmopolitan borders to figure out the relation between open borders and cosmopolitanism, especially when we see that borders are changing rapidly in many ways, in terms of their nature, their function, and their ownership. Furthermore, the main reason for labelling some borders "cosmopolitan" is that they are no longer only a project of the nation-State.

Borders are increasingly shaped by forms of governance beyond the nation-State, the European Union (EU) is the most obvious example, and by citizens working from the 'bottom-up'. This activity is called 'border work.' Therefore, borders are cosmopolitan because they are no longer only under the control of the State, and that entails a decisive shift from State to society. Border studies scholars have already embraced many dimensions of the changing nature of borders ('borders are everywhere', 'remote control', offshore bordering, etc.).

The third section of this chapter will focus on determining the connection between the right to leave and the right to stay to discover the logical connection between them by illustrating an argument grounded on a critical question: when a country grants the right to leave without any right to stay, does the right to leave make sense? We will then move on the next question in the third chapter. The third chapter investigates the right to stay and illustrates an essential question: Is there a right to stay in the global scene?

Overall, we must differentiate the two faces of this right, which are: first, the right of a State to grant asylum, which is well established in international law. It follows from the principle that every sovereign State is deemed to have exclusive control over its territory and, hence, all persons in it. One of the implications of this general rule is that every sovereign State has the right to grant or deny asylum to persons living within its boundaries. Second, the right of an individual to seek asylum is mentioned in several international and regional instruments. Article 13(2) of the Universal Declaration of Human Rights establishes that "everyone has the right to leave any country, including his own." Therefore, an individual's right to seek asylum is vindicated by many international bodies such as the United Nations Commission on Human Rights and the Sub-Commission on Prevention of Discrimination and Protection of Minorities, the functional commissions which are created by the United Nations Economic, and the Social Council under Article 68 of the U.N. Charter.

Then, in the second part of this section, we will study the issue of the principle of non-refoulement. The question that is especially important in this regard would be: How is the principle of non-refoulement protected under International Law and European law?

The principle of non-refoulement can be defined as "the prohibition to expel or return a person to a place where he could face persecution, torture or inhuman treatment." Then we will define the legal basis for this principle which is grounded in Article 33 of the 1951 Refugee Convention as a prohibition of expulsion or return and is enshrined in Article 3 of the UN Convention against Torture. Additionally, in this section, we will explore the implementation of the principle of non-refoulement in International and then European law to see how these two approaches have modified the principle and how the member States of the European Union respect the prohibition of expulsion or refoulement of asylum seekers and refugees.

Furthermore, the principle of non-refoulement was internationally recognized as one of the rights to which refugees are entitled. But what about asylum seekers? Are they also protected by the principle of non-refoulement? Before being granted refugee status, a person is accounted for at first under the term of the asylum seeker, who turns to an asylum process to seek protection. Then, after examining the asylum application, a person may be granted protection under either the refugee status if he qualifies as a refugee according to the 1951 Refugee Convention definition, or subsidiary protection status, if this person did not qualify as a refugee. However, he cannot return to his country of nationality or former habitual residence because he could be subject to severe potential persecution there if he did.

The second section in the right to stay aims to a future vision: how could we imagine the right to stay, should it be legitimated in the future? To analyze such an assumption, we need to search deeply into the fact of the right to stay, such as the meaning of this right, including the length of residence. For example, according to the European Convention on the establishment, the three conditions for the long-term residence of the Convention are significant: the procedural guarantees in case of expulsion, the restrictions of the grounds of expulsion, and the access to the labor market after a long residence.

Additionally, the second part of the second section will be based on a comparison of two terms (self-determination of States and self-determination of individuals), aiming for a more equitable vision of the right of asylum for refugees at the international level. Despite the failure of the European Union to adopt a concrete immigration policy placing fairly responsibilities towards the refugees, relating to the Syrian refugees in the recent decade, Germany and the Netherlands, for instance, have received the largest number of refugees, while other member States did not even open their borders to aid asylum seekers. On the other hand, what is very optimistic in this matter is that, so long as International Law continues to be dominated by justice positivism, it is difficult to conceive how human rights will be adequately protected against invasions from State authorities. However, the inevitable fact is that the Charter and the Universal Declaration reflect one fundamental truth that there is an international legal order protecting the individual and to which States are subject and, hence, which they cannot reject at will.

FIRST CHAPTER

TERMINOLOGY

The Asylum Seeker, Refugee, and Person Eligible for Subsidiary Protection

The Asylum Seeker According to the UNHCR, EU Law, and ECHR:

Initially, an asylum seeker would be any person suffering from any kind of persecution in his country who seeks to get international protection, on the assumption that if he returned to the country of origin he would be threatened, and his life would be at a real risk of being subjected to serious harm.[1]

According to the United Nations High Commissioner for Refugees (UNHCR):

There is a kind of ambiguity in the definition of an asylum seeker in the 1951 Refugee Convention. It did not establish the difference between asylum seekers and refugees. Therefore, it is common in many countries to use the term refugee to refer to an asylum seeker or even to a person eligible for subsidiary protection. However, persons who seek international protection are asylum seekers, and they could be refugees or persons eligible for subsidiary protection after studying their files. Thus, this lack of definition leads countries to set out their guidelines for granting asylum to individuals in need of international protection.[2]

The accepted definition of an asylum seeker is stated in the United Nations High Commissioner for Refugee, and according to its definition: "Asylum seekers are individuals who have sought international protection and whose claims for refugee status have not yet been determined."[3] The UNHCR was

---

[1] Bacaian, Livia Elena (2011): The protection of refugees and their right to seek asylum in the European Union Mémoire présenté pour l'obtention du Master en études européennes par Livia Elena Bacaian rédigé sous la direction de Nicolas Wisard Jurée : Master in European Studies, Geneva. INSTITUT EUROPÉEN DE L'UNIVERSITÉ DE GENÈVE. P.17.
[2] Bacaian, Livia Elena, ibid. P17.
[3] UNHCR, 2009 Global Trends, p.23.

not the only international organization that defined the term asylum seeker, other definitions were also privileged, for instance, the council of the European Union has its new developing version of the definition in "the 2003/9/EC Directive laying down minimum standards for the reception of asylum seekers" when it described the asylum seeker or (applicant) as" a third-country national or Stateless person who has made an application for asylum in respect of which a final decision has not yet been made."[4]

Therefore, a refugee was an asylum seeker initially, but correspondingly an asylum seeker is not inevitably a refugee. But he could be if he fulfilled the provisions of the Refugee Convention 1951.[5]

 Most of the definitions share the same idea that "asylum seekers are demanding justice from a diffuse, complex group of legal individuals who have exercised their rights with no consideration for the collateral damage they have inflicted" (Sheldon 2004).[6]

However, by taking a comprehensive look at the Refugee Convention of 1951, some observers confirmed that some provisions in the Convention, such as the non- refoulement principle, and revelatory applied not only to refugees but also to asylum seekers. That proves the existence of a similarity between both terms, particularly in the implementation of the Refugee Convention.

 According to data on the results of asylum decisions in the EU released by Eurostat, the statistical office of the EU:

"A decision on an asylum application means a decision on an application for international protection as defined in Art.2(h) of Council Directive 2011/95/EC, i.e., including requests for refugee status or subsidiary protection status, irrespective of whether the application was lodged on arrival at the border, or from inside the country, and irrespective of whether the person entered the territory legally (e.g., as a tourist) or illegally."[7]

Moreover, some clarifications were included in the previous data such as the

---

[4] Bacian, Livia Elena, ibid.P.17.
[5] Ibid. P17
[6] Laura Westra, Satvinder juss,Tullio Scovazzi(2015): Towards a Refugee Oriented Right of Asylum. United Kingdom, Dorset Press. P. 21.
[7] Eurostat pressrelease 75/2016 - 20 April 2016.Asylum decisions in the EU P. 6.

meaning of the first and the final decision: "First instance decision means a decision made in response to an asylum application at the first instance level of the asylum procedure. The final decision on appeal means a decision granted at the final instance of administrative/judicial asylum procedure and which results from the appeal lodged by the asylum seeker rejected in the preceding stage of the procedure. As the asylum procedures and the numbers/levels of decision-making bodies differ between Member States, the true final instance may be, according to the national legislation and administrative procedures, a decision of the highest national court. However, the applied methodology defines that 'final decisions' should refer to what is effectively a 'final decision' in most cases: i.e., that all normal routes of appeal have been exhausted."[8]

According to the concrete definitions which aimed to determine the difference between the terms refugee, asylum seekers, and other migrants, it seemed obvious that asylum seekers comprised the largest category, then the other migrants who left for economic objectives, which are considered much larger than refugees as well.[9]

Under European Union Law:

The EU Acquis regulated the asylum seekers' status in the member States when the first chapter of Annex 1 discussed the situation of asylum seekers who have abandoned their country to get international protection inside EU territories, those who had applied for asylum and were still waiting to be examined and then getting the final decision. While the application of an asylum seeker is being examined, the member State has no right to expel him so long as he exists in its territories lawfully until the decision has been made, according to Article 7.1 of the Asylum Procedures Directive (2005/85/EC). Similarly, the (Annex 2003/9/EC for EU Member States bound by the directive) in Article 6 has granted the right to give the applicant a document within three days from submitting his claim that protects him from expulsion and confirms that he is allowed to stay as long as the final decision has not been made yet.[10]

---

[8] Eurostat pressrelease, ibid, P. 6.
[9] Bacaian, Livia Elena, ibid. P. 17.
[10] Handbook on European law relating to asylum, borders and immigration. Luxembourg, Publications Office of the European Union 2013. P.43.

Under the European Convention on Human Rights (ECHR):

The European Convention in Article 5.1 has explicitly stated the necessity of personal liberty and the right to enjoy security and liberty on the one hand, and the obligation of the State in which the asylum seeker has applied for protection to govern the status of the asylum seeker in its territory after submitting the applications while they are being processed. Therefore, domestic law in the territory allows him to stay until the final decision is made. If the entry of the asylum seeker to the territory of the State was unauthorized, then the State has the right of detention to prevent his affecting the State.[11]

Article 5 (1): "Everyone has the right to liberty and security of person. No one shall be deprived of his liberty save in the following cases and in accordance with a procedure prescribed by law". Letter (f) of the same article says: "the lawful arrest or detention of a person to prevent his effecting an unauthorized entry into the country or of a person against whom action is being taken with a view to deportation or extradition." Also, Article 2 of Protocol 4 of ECHR grants the right of free movement to asylum seekers who are lawfully resident while examining their applications. In correspondence, the asylum seeker may lose his lawfulness status, which had been announced in Article 1 of Protocol 7 that provided safeguards against expulsion to asylum seekers who entered the State lawfully.[12]

The Refugee Definition:

Before the Refugee Convention 1951:

The definition of the term 'refugee' over the years has two phases, before the Refugee Convention and after it. Initially, between 1920 to 1934, there were three approaches to the refugee definition: the juridical perspective, the social perspective, and the individualist.

First, the juridical perspective: according to this approach, refugees were treated because of their membership in a group of individuals who lost their

---

[11] Ernst Hirsch Ballin, Emina Ćerimović, Huub Dijstelbloem, Mathieu Segers: European Variations as a Key to Cooperation. The Netherland Scientific Council for Government Policy (WRR). Published by Springer Nature Switzerland, 18 September 2020. P. 130.
[12] Ibid, P. 43,44.

formal protection of the State of origin.[13] Thus, in this period from 1920 to 1926, the definition of a refugee was related to State protection; therefore, refugees were people who were not protected by their governments, such as Russian refugees who were defined as persons who no longer had the protection of their State of origin (Union of Socialist Soviet Republics).[14]

Second, from a social perspective, the definition of a refugee between 1935 and 1939 was formulated according to a social approach after adopting the refugee agreements. This definitional approach has a sole task, to provide assistance and protect the persons who were subjected to social and political events. For example, the arrangements of protecting people leaving Germany. So, the essence of this approach is that the definition was related to the situation of persons suffering from social or political practices.[15]

The third perspective, the individualist perspective shows the accords of 1938-1950. According to this approach; the refugee is "a person in search of an escape from perceived injustice or fundamental incompatibility with his home State, he distrusts his authority and desires the opportunity to build a new life abroad."[16] The core of this perspective lies in the facility of the international free movement for persons who are looking for personal freedom and liberty. Consequently, the refugee definition became, however, a term that relied on the fundamental rights of individuals, and this way of defining the refugee concept established the cornerstone for the development of contemporary international refugee law.[17]

After the Refugee Convention 1951:

The term 'refugee' had a different meaning after the Refugee Convention of 1951, which became the general definition at an international level. Precisely, article 1(A)(2) described the refugee status, specifying that the term 'refugee' shall apply to any person who:

> "(1) has been considered a refugee under the arrangements
> of 12 May 1926 and 30 June 1928 or under the Convention

---

[13] James C. Hathaway (1990): The Law of Refugee Status, Canada. P. 2,3.
[14] Guys S. Goodwin- Grill, Jane McAdams (2007): the refugee in International Law. Oxford, New York. P 16.
[15] James C. Hathaway: Ibid. P. 4.
[16] Ibid. P.5.
[17] Ibid. P. 6.

of 28 October 1933 and 10 February 1938, the Protocol of 14 September 1939 or the Constitution of the International Refugee Organization."[18]

"(2) As a result of events occurring before 1 January 1951 and owing to a well-founded fear of being persecuted for reasons of race, religion, nationality, membership of a particular social group or political opinion, is outside the country of his nationality and is unable or, owing to such fear, is unwilling to avail himself of the protection of that country; or who, not having a nationality and being outside the country of his former habitual residence as a result of such events, is unable or, owing to such fear, is unwilling to return to it."[19]

The refugee definition according to the 1951 Refugee Convention has four guidelines for facilitating the way to determine a refugee status:The first element of the definition is "A person outside his country of origin or residence". The Convention has announced that any person who needs international protection against persecution and is then considered a refugee must exist outside his country overall. Thus, the person who suffers from a well-founded fear of persecution for reasons which are mentioned in the Convention but is in his country will not be considered a refugee at all. This person is considered a displaced person internally and must have international protection, but not as a refugee, it is a person suffering from the same violation of his basic human rights. In such a case, the person who is outside his country could become a refugee only if he proved that he left his country after facing well-founded fear of persecution or is outside his country because of his job or studying, etc., and then something happened in his country that instilled fear for him to return. Furthermore, the Convention means by "his country of origin or residence", the person who has been subjected to persecution outside his country of origin or the country of habitual residence because some people have no nationality but only a residency in the country in which the persecution happens. Also, they do not have another country to offer them its protection in this situation. In

---

[18] Convention, supra, note27, at Art. 1(A)(1).
[19] Convention, supra, note, 27, Art. 1(A)(2).

contrast, those people who have multiple nationalities cannot become refugees unless they prove that they cannot benefit from the protection of one of their countries of nationality.[20] The second element is the well-founded fear of persecution as a reason to live outside a person's country of origin or residence. The expression 'well-founded fear' consists of two components as well: fear, which is a subjective part that a person must prove as a real threat of persecution, and the objective part is 'well-founded', which means that only a real and serious fear of persecution can be taken into account in order to seek a refugee status. The term 'persecution' still has an expansive meaning, to encompass all "the ongoing development and up-to-date sorts of persecution in the future".

The third element is the types of persecution: the Convention recognised that a person might face the well-founded fear of being persecuted for many reasons: race, religion, membership of a particular group, or political opinion. Thus, the person should fear persecution because of one of the previous reasons, according to the convention, in order to be considered a refugee.

The fourth element of the refugee definition is the inability or unwillingness of a person to return to his country because of his fear. Most persons that have suffered from persecution do not have the will to return to their country after living in such a difficult situation, and their country has become untrustworthy to grant them protection anymore. Regarding the fear that persons have from persecution in their country, the Convention has clarified that the unwillingness because of what the person has experienced, renders the person "unable or unwilling to avail himself of State protection".[21]

The next definitions, which came after the 1951 convention for refugees, expanded on the general foundations of the refugee definition in the Refugee Convention. For instance, the definition included in the 1969 OAU Organization of African Unity Convention Governing the Specific Aspects of Refugee Problems in Africa proposed in Article I (2) that:

"The term "refugee" shall also apply to every person who,

---

[20] Bacaian, Livia Elena, The protection of refugees and their right to seek asylum in the European Union Mémoire présenté pour l'obtention du Master en études européennes par Livia Elena Bacaian rédigé sous la direction de Nicolas Wisard Jurée : Master in European Studies, Geneva, 2011. INSTITUT EUROPÉEN DE L'UNIVERSITÉ DE GENÈVE. P. 12.

[21] Bacaian, Livia Elena, ibid. P.13.

owing to external aggression, occupation, foreign domination or events seriously disturbing public order in either part or the whole of his [or her] country of origin or nationality, is compelled to leave his [or her] place of habitual residence to seek refuge in another place outside his [or her] country of origin or nationality."[22]

Moreover, article 1 in the OAU Convention affirmed the essential role of the Refugee Convention as a basic international instrument covering all provisions relating to the status of refugees. The previous definition endorsed the refugee definition in the Refugee Convention, but with some additional elements that also encompassed the person who left his country by force on account of external aggression, occupation, etc. Thus, it allowed all the persons who left their countries because of civil war or significant violation to apply for a refugee status in a party State to the OAU Convention. Hence, it was a complementary definition that a person is granted the status of a refugee under both definitions in the conventions.[23]

In 1984 there was another definition that emerged during the convening "the colloquium of government representatives and distinguished Latin American jurists" in Cartagena, Colombia, in which the international protection of refugees was discussed, and resulted in the Cartagena Declaration that endorsed the right to asylum and the right to stay in the State the person entered and not to return him to his country where he may face the serious harm (the non-refoulement principle), and affirmed that the refugee definition should include what had been defined in the 1951 Refugee Convention, which is, all the persons who left their countries because of a serious threat to their lives, safety, violence and massive violation of fundamental rights or internal conflict or disturbing public order. However, all the persons who are considered refugees, according to the refugee definition in the OAU Convention and the Cartagena Declaration, are considered refugees just as the persons who have been recognized as refugees in the 1951 Convention, and thus, they all have the same rights, and merits

---

[22]Self-study module on Refugee Status Determination (Identifying who is a refugee), UNHCR.1 September 2005. P.06.
[23] Expert Group on Refugee and Internally Displaced Persons Statistics (2018), International Recommendations on Refugee Statistics. Manuscript completed in March 2018. Luxemburg: Publications Office of the European Union (Population and social conditions/ eurostat). P.21.

without any kind of discrimination, even if the determination procedures that were applied to their status were different.[24]

Despite having several definitions of the term refugee, which emerged after the 1951 convention, there was a better definition in the Eurostat report in 2018, which encompassed the real meaning of the refugee status that was particularly determined in many international documents comprehensively in order to capture the exact meaning of the term. According to this, a refugee is:

> "A person covered by a decision-granting refugee status, taken by administrative or judicial bodies during the reference period. A refugee status means the status defined in Art.2(e) of Directive 2011/95/EC within the meaning of Art.1 of the Geneva Convention relating to the Status of Refugees of 28 July 1951, as amended by the New York Protocol of 31 January 1967. According to Art.,2(d) of that Directive, a refugee means a third-country national who, owing to a well-founded fear of being persecuted for reasons of race, religion, nationality, political opinion, or membership of a particular social group, is outside the country of nationality and is unable or, owing to such fear, is unwilling to avail himself or herself of the protection of that country, or a Stateless person, who, being outside of the country of former habitual residence for the same reasons as mentioned above, is unable or, owing to such fear, unwilling to return to it"[25].

However, to achieve the objectives of the 1951 Convention in providing international protection to persons who are really in need thereof, because of some reasons lie in the essence of the refugee status, States which are party to the Refugee Convention 1951 and 1967 Protocol play a very important role in determining the refugee status for making sure whether a person can be considered a refugee, fulfilling the obligations stated by the Refugee Convention and 1967 Protocol. Besides, those States have the mandate to

---

[24] Ibid. P. 21.
[25] Eurostat newsrelease, 67/2018 - 19 April 2018.P. 06.

respect the refugee status, and not to return them to their countries of origin where the risk of exposure to persecution or any kind of serious harm still exists. [26]

The matter is that States concerned with the refugee status have a kind of discretion in interpreting the refugee definition in the 1951 Convention to determine the applicants who should get in and qualify as such. The States apply the Convention in many ways: some of them consider any person who has faced a kind of persecution and left his country seeking protection as a refugee, while others require something else, for instance, the person must prove that "he has been subjected to violence by agents of his country"[27]. In fact, some States have accepted people as refugees because of abuse of authority when it expelled those who had expressed their political opinions for months or even two weeks. In contrast, other States do not give the refugee status to persons who have faced a civil war in their country, and whose lives were seriously in danger, just because they were not personally subjected to deprivation or violation. Similarly, in other circumstances such as famine or further reasons other than political membership, race, and nationality, which were mentioned in the Refugee Convention exclusively. The previous reasons were marginalized in the refugee definition in the 1951 Convention. Perhaps because of their nature, all human circumstances "are not absolute but relative". By revising the refugee definition, it is evident that all the statuses which were highlighted in article 1 instituted an absolute obligation to consider as refugees all those persons whose "lives were at risk" and, in principle, not all lives are equally at risk. Therefore, the content is significant and important to determine whether an asylum seeker deserves to be considered as a refugee or not. [28]

At this point, it has been observed that the Convention had a kind of contradiction in prioritizing the persons who must obtain protection as refugees by taking into account "the severity of the threat" to the fundamental human rights of the person in addition to "the degree of the

---

[26] Self-study module on Refugee Status Determination (Identifying who is a refugee), UNHCR.1 September 2005. P.09, 10.

[27] Carens, Joseph H. The ethics of immigration. 1. issued as an Oxford Univ. Press paperback. New York: Oxford University Press; Oxford Univerisity Press (Oxford political theory)2013/ 2015.P. 200.

[28] Fine, Sarah; Ypi, Lea, Migration in political theory. The ethics of movement and membership / edited by Sarah Fine and Lea Ypi. First edition 2016. Oxford: Oxford University Press. P. 257.

risk" that threats his life[29].

As a conclusion on the meaning of what a refugee is we have what was stipulated in Article 2 of the Council Directive in 2004 on the minimum standards for the qualification and status of third-country nationals or Stateless persons as refugees or as persons who otherwise need international protection and the content of the protection granted. The Article ensures that the refugee status covers two categories, the third country national as well as the Stateless person, in case of a well-founded fear of the person who is outside his country to be persecuted for the same reasons as in Article 1 of the Refugee Convention in 1951 (race, religion, nationality and ... so on), as well as the fact that, owing to his fear, he becomes unwilling or unable to return to his country.[30] Moreover, all previous persons qualify for the status of refugee by a recognition of a member State. As can be seen, the description of the refugee status in this Article is so far similar to the definition stipulated in the Refugee Convention. Although there is perhaps a sole component that makes the definition in the Council Directive more accurate in determining the categories of persons that should be included in the definition to facilitate the role of the States while studying the applications when it announced explicitly to whom the status of a refugee should be granted, which is the more accurate component [31].

The Person Eligible for Subsidiary Protection:

The most displaced people who applied for international protection "were not covered by the traditional instruments of International Law", according to the UNHCR in the global trends report in 2014. Moreover, the 1951 Refugee Convention was somewhat incomprehensive. There was a significant number of people who needed protection and they had not been given it.

Then the subsidiary protection came as a European emergency response to the historical gaps in the Refugee Convention. Some European States grant

---

[29] Carens, Joseph H. The ethics of immigration. Ibid, P. 201.

[30] Carol M. Swain (2018): Debating Immigration. Second edition, Cambridge University Press. New York, USA. P. 356.

[31] Article 2 (a),(b),(c),(d) of the Council Directive 2004/83/EC of 29 April 2004 on minimum standards for the qualification and status of third country nationals or Stateless persons as refugees or as persons who otherwise need international protection and the content of the protection granted, O.J. L304, 30 September 2004, pp. 12-23 (hereinafter Council Directive 2004/83/EC).

people subsidiary protection in the massive refugee influx to resolve the problem. After that, the European initiative was taken by the Council of Europe in Directive 2004/83/EC, which was "on minimum standards for the qualification and status of third-country nationals or Stateless persons as refugees or as persons who otherwise need international protection and the content of the protection granted". It defined the person eligible for subsidiary protection as follows:

> ' a person eligible for subsidiary protection' means a third-country national or a Stateless person who does not qualify as a refugee but in respect of whom substantial grounds have been shown for believing that the person concerned if returned to his or her country of origin, or in the case of a Stateless person, to his or her country of former habitual residence, would face a real risk of suffering serious harm as defined in Article 15, and to whom Article 17(1) and (2) do not apply, and is unable, or, owing to such risk, unwilling to avail himself or herself of the protection of that country"[32].

Also, the term subsidiary protection manifests in the first paragraph of section 4 of the Asylum Act, which emphasizes the right of every applicant to get subsidiary protection whenever he proves that he is "threatened with serious harm" in his country:

> "(1) A foreigner shall be eligible for subsidiary protection if he has shown substantial grounds for believing that he would face a real risk of suffering serious harm in his country of origin. Serious harm consists of the following:
> 1. death penalty or execution,
> 2. torture or inhuman or degrading treatment or punishment, or
> 3. serious and individual threat to a civilian's life or person

---

[32] Antonio Di Marco, The Subsidiary Protection: The Discriminatory and Limited Protection of the "New Refugees" 20 (1-2 2015). Available online at Mediterranean Journal of Human Rights. P. 183, 184, 185. And see Article 2 (e) of the Council Directive 2004/83/EC of 29 April 2004 on minimum standards for the qualification and status of third country nationals or Stateless persons as refugees or as persons who otherwise need international protection and the content of the protection granted, O.J. L304, 30 September 2004, pp. 12-23 (hereinafter Council Directive 2004/83/EC).

because of indiscriminate violence in situations of international or internal armed conflict"[33].

In this case, 'serious harm' means in this sense: "the imposition or application of capital punishment, torture or inhuman or degrading punishment or treatment, or a serious individual threat to the life or integrity of a civilian as a result of indiscrimination violence in an international or internal armed conflict"[34].

The European legislator constituted new regulations relating to the rights concerning subsidiary protection, such as Directive 2011/95/UE and the Procedures Directive (Directive 2013/32/UE), which were essential to making a kind of regulation between the subsidiary protection and the refugee status, especially in terms of rights and merits. Hence, the subsidiary protection cases had evidently become more prevalent than the refugee status, and that created some arguments against the subsidiary protection, especially with existing all the international Conventions that existed and saw to the protection of Fundamental Human Rights against any kind of violation, besides all the treaties against torture, in addition to the UN Covenant on Civil and Political Rights. So, the question: to which international instrument or international law is subsidiary protection complementary?

The first time that subsidiary protection was analyzed, was in the asylum law as a complementary protection of refugee protection. The Directive 2011/95/EU addressed subsidiary protection in a complementary way to the refugee protection as those who don't qualify as refugees but should be considered as persons who need protection because of the common ground they share with refugees, which is facing a "real risk of serious harm". Article 2(f) of the Directive included this definition of a person eligible for subsidiary protection:

> "a third-country national or a Stateless person who does not qualify as a refugee but in respect of whom substantial

---

[33] Bundesministerium der Justiz und für Verbraucherschutz, Gesetze im Internet. Asylum Act in the version promulgated in September 2008 (Federal Law Gazette 1, p. 1798, last amended by Article 2 of the Act of 11 March 2016(Federal Law Gazette1, P. 394)

[34] Jasmin Lilian Diab, International Migration and Refugee Law, Does Germany Migration Policy towards Syrian Refugees Comply? Anchor Academic Publishing. Hamburg, 2017. P. 78.

grounds have been shown for believing that the person concerned, if returned to his or her country of origin, or in the case of a Stateless person, to his or her country of former habitual residence, would face a real risk of suffering serious harm"

Thus, the subsidiary protection as a status should be given to people who did not meet all the conditions stipulated in the refugee definition, so as to be protected internationally. In these cases, they belong to an alternative and more comprehensive category than the refugee status as defined in the 1951 Convention[35]. For instance, the refugee definition is based on the assumption of persecution, which refers to a serious deprivation of a person's fundamental rights "on the grounds of race, religion, nationality, membership of a particular social group or political opinions", according to Article 1(2) of the Refugee Convention. This persecution should be faced by a person, or it might be the case that a person has a well-founded fear of it. Therefore, one of the five reasons mentioned previously should exist, and then must be linked to a persecution so that to the person is given a refugee status. If the person cannot prove the relation between the serious risk to his life and one of the reasons concerning his case, those reasons which subsidiary protection doesn't consider exclusively to grant the person international protection under its provisions, that person will not get a refugee status, but rather becomes a person eligible for subsidiary protection[36].

The most important thing to highlight here is that the subsidiary protection has a second form of protection in its role of encompassing the "new asylum seekers or extra-convention refugees", because the refugee concept, which was defined in the 1951 Convention, was very restricted and unable to fit the recent developments. Especially after new circumstances or categories of people who need international protection emerged. Therefore, subsidiary protection is an instrument of complementary protection and is different from temporary protection, which was mentioned for the first time in Thailand in 1979 when it granted temporary protection to the "mass influx" of asylum seekers who were coming from Cambodia fleeing from their

---

[35] Antonio Di Marco, The Subsidiary Protection: The Discriminatory and Limited Protection of the "New Refugees" 20 (1-2 2015). Available online at Mediterranean Journal of Human Rights P.187,188,189.
[36] Ibid. P. 191.

dictator regime at that time. This case showed a lack of response to a "broader class" of persons in need of international protection when the Convention did not consider such a situation as a "mass influx" of persons. Afterward, the UNHCR issued a note in 1994 on international protection, which defined the gaps in international protection for refugees in the 1951 Convention and its Protocol in 1967 and looked for legal solutions in its provisions. It described the temporary protection that:

> "In situations of mass outflow, for providing refuge to groups or categories of persons recognized to require international protection, without recourse, at least initially, to individual refugee status determination. It includes respect for basic human rights but, since it is conceived as an emergency protection measure of hopefully short duration, a more limited range of rights and benefits offered in the initial stage than would customarily be accorded to refugees granted asylum under the 1951 Convention and the 1967 Protocol".[37]

On the other hand, there is a kind of overlap between the temporary protection and subsidiary protection when it comes to "mass influx," especially when the asylum system cannot solve this problem, then the temporary protection is granted as a solution to protect all persons who are in need. But the point is that temporary protection, which is granted to the mass influx of displaced persons who exist in a certain State legally, is merely a political decision of the European Council without grounding on the effectiveness of the asylum system, and without examining every individual claim to get protection. Instead, it is based on the mass influx elements regarding "the group legal basis" in such circumstances, where the objective conditions of those people being at risk of serious harm in their origin country exist[38]. For instance, the European Council is mandated to grant emergency protection in case of a mass influx for a limited period of time, which means temporary protection to those persons who fled from non-EU countries and were unable to return to their countries without processing

---

[37] Ibid. P. 196. and see Note on International Protection 1994, UN Doc A/AC.96/830 of 7 September 1994 [46].
[38] Ibid. P. 220.

each case separately, but it is considered adequate to ground such protection on the group legal basis[39]. Besides, temporary protection is a practical tool manifested as an obligation of the States to provide immediate emergency protection to persons against refoulement. It also encompasses the extension of residence visas or permits to stay in the non-convention States as a wider scope of its application.

So, subsidiary protection has had a very important role in the development of international protection, and it could somewhat extend the range of international protection in defining unprotected categories.

According to the previous definition of subsidiary protection, it requires the person to prove "substantial grounds" that he would face the risk of serious harm in his country of origin, which could be a threat to a person's life in internal or international armed conflict, regardless of the reasons for persecution that should be proved in the person's claim for a refugee status. This way, subsidiary protection helped a new category of persons who were in need of international protection, thus, it contributed to filling the gap of the 1951 Refugee Convention[40]

The Relation between the Asylum seeker, Refugee, and Person Eligible for Subsidiary Protection:

By defining the three terms (asylum seeker, refugee, and person eligible for subsidiary protection) in the previous section. A general Idea of entitling a person to each of these statuses in fundamental conditions has been established in our minds.

Initially, when the asylum seeker applies for protection in the host country, he is immediately considered a person who has the right to stay in this country, so long as his application is still being studied, and hence, the principle of non-refoulement is applied in this case as a fundamental principle in the International Law. After, this person is either considered as a refugee under the refugee status or granted subsidiary protection if he could face serious harm, such as torture, violence due to international or internal

---

[39] Expert Group on Refugee and Internally Displaced Persons Statistics (2018), International Recommendations on Refugee Statistics. Manuscript completed in March 2018. Luxemburg: Publications Office of the European Union (Population and social conditions/ eurostat). P. 22,23.
[40] Antonio Di Marco, ibid. P. 221, 222.

conflict, the death penalty, etc., upon returning to his country. [41]

---

[41] Bacaian, Livia Elena (2011), The protection of refugees and their right to seek asylum in the European Union Mémoire présenté pour l'obtention du Master en études européennes par Livia Elena Bacaian rédigé sous la direction de Nicolas Wisard Jurée : Master in European Studies, Geneva. INSTITUT EUROPÉEN DE L'UNIVERSITÉ DE GENÈVE. P. 20.

SECOND CHAPTER

IS THERE A RIGHT TO LEAVE?

Introduction:

The sovereignty of a State refers not only to its territories but, also, to the live of all the people living within its borders. Moreover, sovereignty gives the State the power to exercise authority over civilians or persons, including its territory, and to intervene those people's behavior. That gives the individual right to migrate or move across international borders under the State's control[1]. Consequently, though the right to leave has been recognized by the Universal declaration of human rights 1948 (UDHR), and the International Covenant on Civil and Political Rights (ICCPR), it is constrained by the State's control. The UDHR ensures in Article 13 that: everyone has the right to freedom of movement and residence within the borders of each State. Everyone has the right to leave any country, including his own, and to return to his country. Thus, UDHR was the foundation for respecting and admitting individual liberties and freedom[2]. Furthermore, there is a similar definition according to the ICCPR in article 12, which affirms that: "Everyone shall be free to leave any country, including his own". Besides, this article has mentioned that "the right to leave and free movement shall not be restricted, except the rights which are provided by law for protecting national security, public order, public health, or morals or the rights and freedoms of others and, are consistent with the other rights recognized in the present Covenant"[3]

The Human Right to Migrate

The massive influx of immigrants around the World is caused by internal conflict, political violence, environmental, and economic reasons. Especially when people face political violence in their countries, they have just two choices: attempting escape or living with the consequences of the internal

---

[1] Brian Opeskin, Richared Perruchoud, Jillyanne Redpath cross, Foundations of International Migration Law, Cambridge University 2012.P. 124
[2] Ibid. P. 126.
[3] Ibid.P.127

conflict. However, the prevalent response would be escaping from their countries, in most cases, attempting to reach a safer place.

A critical question that comes to mind is, how could the movement of migrants be imagined across international borders? Is there a basic right to leave in legal approaches?

Overall, people can lawfully choose their places of residence within a State's territory, so they have this kind of freedom in their countries (internal movement). Thus, to what extent do migrants have the freedom to move externally across international boundaries?

The open-borders standpoint can be defended, regardless of the assumption that there is a right to immigrate. In other words, borders should be open by giving equality of opportunity or by showing the inability of the States to exclude migrants. [4] That means if the right to migrate could be established, then it would eliminate all restrictions that could hinder free migration. [5] Thus, first we need to clarify the meaning of the right to migrate as a human right to be a comprehensive tool against the discretion of the State in preventing people from entering its territories. According to David Miller, the right to migrate would be achieved when the other human rights of the migrants were protected in the host country. Moreover, the right to migrate must be efficient, it should guarantee to enter not only a certain State or a few States, but it should also be a right to move from one country to another and the system should give people the choice to pick a particular State in which they decided to live.[6]

Therefore, the right to migrate is a right that should be established along with the other human rights that are recognized in that State, such as political rights, civil, economic, and so on. Regardless of how different migrants' rights might be from civilians, the issue depends on having some degree of flexibility when treating migrants. The essence of the right to migrate lies in the actual protection of the previous right given by the State to all migrants living within its territories.

---

[4] Maurice Stierl: Migrant Resistance in Contemporary Europe, edited by Jenny Edkins and Nick Vaughan-Williams. New York: Routledge, 2019. P. 196.
[5] Fine, Sarah; Ypi, Lea (2016): Migration in political theory. The ethics of movement and membership / edited by Sarah Fine and Lea Ypi. First edition. Oxford: Oxford University Press. P. 13.
[6] Ibid. P. 14, 15.

In any case, migrants may need assistance and protection from an armed conflict they might be facing in their countries, or even in the country they traveled to before reaching their destination. However, migrants are legally protected by International Humanitarian Law (IHL), regardless of them being either in their countries or in a different country where there is an armed conflict. This chapter will also provide an overview of the protection granted by International Humanitarian Law (IHL) to migrants as civilians in international and non-international armed conflicts.

The Root Causes of Displacement:

What kind of circumstances do migrants live in their countries of origin where their lives could be threatened by serious harm? And how can this serious harm be used as a general approach for forced migration?

Originally, serious harm means that a lack of protection leads any kind of persecution that may cause people to suffer and forces them to leave their home, seeking to live in another country where they can be protected against anything that could threaten their lives.

That means, regardless of the other causes for fleeing from one's country of origin such as persecution, internal conflict, and civil wars, especially as serious harm, could be the most important factor for this phenomenon.

Moreover, the UNHCR announces explicitly that the causes of displacement are strongly related to internal conflict. This kind of relationship between internal conflict and migration is evident, especially in cases, such as the migration crisis after the armed conflict in Syria, the situation in Iraq, Libya, Rwanda, Somalia, and so on. Therefore, this section aims to identify the main cause of migration nowadays, highlighting the Syrian migrant crisis.

Persecution as the Main Cause:

Refugees have left their countries for the first time because of the religious persecution that occurred in their societies, then they had to flee extreme persecution, intending to live their lives in a simpler, safer way, without any kind of violence or injustice.

What exacerbated the situation is that persecution almost always leads to internal conflict, which carries oppressing results as well. Many people and their family members died sadly in such conflicts. Perhaps the Second World War was the cause of the biggest number of displaced people and refugees that had ever taken place. Therefore, there was a need to establish an international agency has emerged that had the task of protecting people and providing different types of goods and supportive activities by following the refugees' situation from the moment they flee their homes until they arrive to the host country which will offer them asylum, Another task was to find the best solutions for refugees which were compatible with their circumstances by providing the assistance for governments to facilitate the assimilation of refugees in the new countries on the one hand, and, on the other hand, to help the refugees in encouraging the repatriation to their countries of origin in some cases. That is precisely the mission of the United Nation High Commissioner for Refugees. It coordinates and organizes all actions for protecting refugees and safeguarding their rights at an international level.

Thus, the UNHCR was completely created in the 1950s to be the sole agency that deals with all the affairs related to refugees from that moment onwards. Regarding the previous purposes that it sought to achieve, the office firmly ensured that everyone could exercise the right to seek asylum and find safe refuge in another State and return home voluntarily[7].

According to the UNHCR global appeal, today, there are more than 67 million people around the world who are divided into four categories; refugees, returnees, Stateless people, and internally displaced people (IDPs) under UNHCR protection who have been affected by internal conflict or any kind of persecution. Most of them fled to neighboring countries, but the others decided to go away to European countries, where they could get a better life. Germany has hosted the highest number of refugees in Europe, which gave protection to more than 16% of the refugees around the world.

As in previous years, the EU has proved its capability to carry on international responsibility through fruitful efforts to protect a huge, displaced population globally. Besides, it became clear to the international community that it is impossible to fulfill civil developing world and peacebuilding objectives without facing and challenging the displaced people crisis and the forced

---

[7] UNHCR Global Appeal 2018- 2019. P.2.

migration, which are grounded on persecution, conflict, or even on any kind of violation[8].

Thus, how can those goals be achieved with the incredibly increasing number of displaced people over the past three years? For instance, there were about 12.6 million displaced Syrian people at the end of 2017 due to the civil war in Syria which broke out initially in 2012. And this number continued to be the largest one in terms of displaced population worldwide[9].

To determine particularly whether some particular actions are considered as persecution, it should be clear literally what persecution means. In its most common form, "it has been defined actually as an abuse of human rights committed by organs of the State, such as the police or the military".[10] Consequently, any person, in this case, does not have any sort of national protection, and another thing which makes the situation harder is that the government authorities commit such violations of fundamental human rights. For instance, when the Syrian demonstrations started in March 2011, people wanted to gain a new, better life. Then they demanded to overthrow the regime after realizing that it was the sole obstacle that prevented them from having their new lives. However, the regime did not accept the simple rights of the citizens, but rather it resorted to inhuman ways and oppressed the people with many kinds of violations, detention, tortures and so on. [11]

This is, of course, considered an essential factor in seeking asylum in another country, fleeing from the most damaging consequences of persecution. It is featured, for instance, in Article 14 of the Universal Declaration of Human Rights in 1948, which States that:

(1) Everyone has the right to seek and to enjoy in other countries asylum from persecution[12].

However, persecution has not been defined in any international instruments, including the Refugee Convention of 1951, except for article 31 and 33 of it,

---

[8] Ibid, P.14.

[9] UNHCR Global trend 2017. P.6.

[10] James C. Hathaway, Michelle Foster (2014): The Law of Refugee Status. Cambridge University Press. P. 125.

[11] Basem Mahmud: Emotions and Belonging in Forced Migration, Syrian Refugees and Asylum Seekers. Routledge Advances in Sociology, First published. New York 2022. P.50.

[12] Fine, Sarah; Ypi, Lea (2016): Migration in political theory. The ethics of movement and membership / edited by Sarah Fine and Lea Ypi. First edition. Oxford: Oxford University Press.

which refers to people whose lives or freedom was threatened or would be so.[13] In addition to this definition, "persecution as a crime in International Law was literally recognized in many trials after the Second World War. Article 5 of the Statue of the International Criminal Tribunal related to former Yugoslavia which conducted the legal proceedings against those who were responsible for persecutions on political, racial and religious grounds in an armed conflict"[14]. Moreover, persecution is a common concept that has featured in a lot of examples around the world, which is depicted as inhuman behavior towards another person, and has been defined in some known behaviors.

While the UNHCR provided a more comprehensive definition of persecution with the term (Well-founded Fear of Persecution), which is a fundamental cause for obtaining international protection by elaborating the substantial elements of the persecution that should be present, that term divided persecution into two main elements: the subjective element, and the objective element. [15] However, we will explain all the elements of persecution more precisely, so that a person could not be in fact recognized as being persecuted without meeting all of these requirements.

Elements of Persecution:

1) The subjective element: is the fear that the applicant experienced in his country of origin. This fear of persecution has been defined by the UNHCR fear as "a State of mind and hence, a subjective condition, which will depend on the individual's personal and family background, his or her personal experiences, and how he or she interprets his or her situation"[16]. However, this facilitated the procedures that the displaced people need to do for applying to be legal refugees in case there is an unwillingness to return to his or her country, which if expressed explicitly by the applicant, then it would be sufficient to prove the fear element. But if that is not possible; in other words, if the applicant does not express that their fear is caused by some objective reasons, he will be almost recognized as a refugee only when he

---

[13] Guys S. Goodwin- Grill, Jane McAdams (2007): the refugee in International Law. (Third Edition). New York, Oxford University Press. P 90.
[14] Ibid. 94 P.
[15] UNHCR Protection Training Manual for European Border and Entry Officials Session 3 Manual UNHCR on 1 April 2011. P.5,6.
[16] Ibid, P.06.

applies for a refugee status.

2) The objective element: It means a well-foundedness related to the situation of the applicant's country. The Immigration and Nationality Act (INA) relied on the existence of a well-founded fear of persecution as an essential element of an asylum claim which should be grounded on past persecution or risk of it in the future.[17] In this case, it is not a required of the asylum seeker to prove the cause of their fear in their country of origin. It is simply left to the adjudicator's discretion, who should consider the credibility of the applicant's fear, in other words, whether the applicant would face real harm if he returned to his country of origin or even to his country of habitual residence [18].

For instance, not every threat to a person's human rights could be considered a well-founded fear related to persecution that would require a need for protection. There are certain fundamental rights that every person should have in his country, and countries cannot restrict them legitimately. Those are called non-derogable rights, such as the right to life, the right to freedom from torture or cruelty, the right to freedom from slavery or servitude, the right to freedom of thought, conscience, religion, and more. Thus, any serious violation of fundamental or non-derogable rights will be considered persecution[19].

Otherwise, even though the concept of "persecution" was not defined in 1951 and it has no precise definition in INA either, it could be defined according to the UNHCR in relation to certain types of behavior that are categorized as persecution. In each case that adjudicators will determine whether the applicant faced persecution or not, considering that courts have defined persecution as "a threat to life or freedom on account of race, religion, nationality, political opinion or membership of a particular social group"[20].

3) The failure of State protection as an element: This element also should be present when the applicant claims that he is persecuted and then needs international protection. Basically, Refugee Law is imposed on the State,

---

[17] INA; Asylum Basics: Elements of Asylum Law
[18] UNHCR, ibid. P.06
[19] UNHCR, ibid. P. 07
[20] INA; ibid.

which is a member of the Refugee Convention, to provide protection to every person facing well-founded fear on its territories. However, refugee law is not a system that facilitates all the circumstances to enable the person to flee from his country whenever he faces a serious fear; rather, he must be given protection by his country as it is its official duty.[21]

Therefore, "the general purpose of the Refugee Convention is to enable the person who no longer has the benefit of protection against persecution for a Convention reason in his own country to turn for protection to the international community"[22]

According to the Directives, 2011/95/EU of the European Parliament and of the Council of 13 December 2011, the actors of protection when a person faces persecution or serious harm are:

"(a) the State; or (b) parties or organizations, including international organizations, controlling the State or a substantial part of the territory of the State; provided they are willing and able to offer protection in accordance with paragraph 2".

Furthermore, it ensures in paragraph 2 that: "Protection against persecution or serious harm must be effective and of a non-temporary nature. Such protection is generally provided when the actors mentioned under points (a) and (b) of paragraph 1 take reasonable steps to prevent the persecution or suffering of serious harm, inter alia, by operating an effective legal system for the detection, prosecution and punishment of acts constituting persecution or serious harm, and when the applicant has access to such protection"[23].

Obviously, refugee law will intervene to grant the international community protection in a substitutional manner, which means it will provide such protection to persons "in situations where there is no reasonable expectation" to enfranchise national protection in the present or even in the

---

[21] James C. Hathaway, Michelle Foster (2014), The Law of Refugee Status. Cambridge University Press. P. 288.

[22] Harvath v. Secretary of State for the Home Department, 2001. 1AC, P. 495. Ibid. P. 288.

[23] Council Directive 2011/95/EU of 13 December 2011 on standards for the qualification of third country nationals or Stateless persons as beneficiaries of international protection, for a uniform status for refugees or for persons eligible for subsidiary protection, and for the content of the protection granted (2011) OJ L 337/9 (December.20. 2011), Article. 7 (1), (2).

future. It comes thus just as a response to a lack of national protection[24]. Moreover, the decision of whether a person faces the risk of being persecuted is linked to the ability of the State, or even its willingness, to protect the person who suffered serious harm. Besides, the risk of being persecuted implies some conditions to be existent such as persistence, inescapability, and relentlessness, in addition to the unwillingness or inability of the State to respond and protect the person. So, the decision to protect a person against persecution must merely depend on two factors; the nature of the risk and the nature of the State response, in other words, when there is indeed a risk of serious harm and failure of the State to protect, a person could be considered as persecuted according to the refugee status in the Convention, and thus, that person undoubtedly deserves international protection[25].This makes it necessary to explain the two situations of the failure of State protection separately:

> The unwillingness of the State to protect is rated as almost
> the clear and simple aspect of the failure of State protection.
> This one could have occurred in three situations.

In the first situation, if the State itself is responsible for the serious harm that person faces, as to be pursuance for infecting sanctions or implying general laws in a discriminatory manner. Persecution in this situation may be imposed by central organs in the State or civil servants, military, or any armed force[26].

The second situation is when the government of the State condones persecution exercised by "subordinated or localized arms," for instance, members of an unofficial military or others who are local officials in the central government.

The third occurs when the State's tolerance or encouragement of the non-State actors to persecute persons can intervene to prevent such persecution, but it chooses not to do so. Then this reaction from the State to condone persecution towards segments of the community could be devoted by law or administrative discretion. For example, violence and discrimination against some people may be tolerated by the State; therefore, it will not do anything

---

[24] James C. Hathaway, Michelle Foster (2014), The Law of Refugee Status. Cambridge University Press. P. 292.
[25] Ibid, P. 293.
[26]Ibid, P. 297.

to protect them[27].

> The inability of the State to protect: this situation is embodied when "the risk of serious harm is deliberated by non-State actors, where the State has the willingness to protect, but it is, in effect, unable to respond. Alternatively, when central institutions in the State have collapsed, or State's authorities have broken down totally, such as what happens to the State during a civil war."[28]

But how can we determine whether the risk of serious harm committed by the State, is tolerated, and condoned by the State, or is serious harm but not tolerated and condoned? In other words, how to distinguish between both cases? whether the State failed to protect its civilians from harm due to the unwillingness or capacity of the State?

When serious harm is not tolerated or condoned by the State, it simply coincides with the failure of protection because it was incapable of offering protection, because there is no effective function of the State, or there was no State in concept. Consequently, when there is no State to prevent persecution, then there is a genuine need for international community protection[29].

Reasons for persecution:

There are many reasons establish the risk of persecution that could cause serious well-founded fear by depriving someone of the Fundamental Human Rights and that could threaten a person's life in many forms of discrimination, because of race, religion, nationality, membership of a social group, and holding a political opinion. We will discuss each of them very briefly.

1) Race, which is one of the most prominent categories worldwide, could refer to various kinds of ethnic characteristics that should be perceived. For example, the mixed marriages of a person from a minority group and another one from a majority group, what would be more likely in this relation is that

---

[27] James C. Hathaway, Michelle Foster (2014), The Law of Refugee Status. Cambridge University Press. P. 298, 299.
[28] Ibid, P. 304.
[29] Ibid, P. 306, 307,308.

the minority will be oppressed by the majority. But the opposite might just happen when the majority is persecuted by the minority in other situations. In any case, situations that involve people from different racial backgrounds may lead to persecution if problems arise, that in turn leads to the denial of citizenship and loss of some rights as a consequent.[30]

2) Religion means that right based on the freedom of choosing a religion which is

a non-derogable right, while international human rights law permits certain restrictions on the right to manifest one's religion. Examples of this type of persecution are when a person faces a serious restriction on his right to religious freedom, such as the prohibition of being a member of a specific religious caste, or even practicing his religious rites. Moreover, persecution because of religion may be perceived as discrimination against a religious practice or membership of a religious community[31].

3) Nationality as a reason for persecution could entail many forms such as citizenship, especially for refugees or even other people who are defined by their religion, culture, race, and language perceived as relating to their nationality.

4) Membership of a particular social group or holding of a political opinion: The first case happens when a person who belongs to such a group has a specific ideology or common characteristics such as sex, caste, or even sexual orientation.

Persecution could be grounded because of political opinions as well, which includes engaging with any political party or holding of a different opinion from the government's opinions. regarding some considerations such as whether this opinion that person holds is tolerated in his country or not, and if there is a well-founded fear of persecution as a result of this political opinion[32]

---

[30] UNHCR Protection Training Manual for European Border and Entry Officials Session 3 Manual UNHCR on 1 April 2011. P.07.
[31] Ibid. P. 07.
[32] Ibid. P. 07.08.

Forms of persecution:

Detention and arrest:

This kind of procedure is an official action carried out by the police or other mandated custody in the country of the persecuted person. It is considered a violation of an internationally guaranteed human right when it is established on a ground of arbitration, in other words, detention and arrest could amount to the risk of persecution and harm only if they are arbitrarily forced and they are not based on any valid law.

In any case, even though the detention and arrest were lawful, without any kind of arbitration, they must be compatible with the assumption that governments take over a task to prove that all people who are deprived of their liberty have been treated with respect, dignity and humanity. Therefore, States try to make detentions or arrests permissible actions that are a consequence of the conditions that States consider. Thus, there is going to be a harsh risk of a "breach of the International human rights norms," and then this situation requires protection from persecution.

However, in all these cases, courts must estimate from all the circumstances around detentions or arrests whether there is, indeed, a persecution taking place in the persecuted person's country. Furthermore, although these considerations and conditions that help to detect persecution evidentially through detention, most of the decision-makers conclude that an "absolutist approach" can be taken in all cases because there are some exceptions that motivate the States to apply some kinds of procedures that deprive someone of their liberty, or even to order preventive detention as a way to protect their national security, safeguarding the public order from the emergency, so the government may arrest people in accordance with their duty to protect their population almost by lawful procedures grounded on the criminal authority in their States. Besides, States are obliged to order detentions and arrests in a real legal framework. They also must take into account that detentions and arrests should not be arbitrary actions, giving a humanitarian and respectful treatment to the detained or arrested persons. Only while complying with all these international conditions, would detention and arrest not be proof of risk of persecution.[33]

Prosecution:

In this form of persecution, harm excludes those people who committed an offense according to the common law and intend to flee from prosecution or punishment under the pretext of facing the risk of serious harm in their country of origin. This situation of facing legitimate prosecution for violating the criminal law has not been recognized as a refugee status. Especially since refugees are supposed to be "victims of injustice, not fugitives from justice."[34] Prosecution can take many faces so that it can seem an act in the criminal law. Nevertheless, it is not actually a violation of rights. Consequently, the prosecution here could not be considered as a risk of being persecuted.[35]

The first scenario is when a person faces prosecution because of an action that is not a genuine violation of his country's laws. In this case, the punishment determined by the State's authority is considered as a risk of prosecution because there are some cases in which a conviction is not within the State's legitimate process; thus, it could not be in fact a breach of ordinary criminal law, which would not make it a clear threat for the person to face persecution.

The second one may happen when there seems to be a risk of jeopardizing hindering the criminal law enforcement in the country of the persecuted person, and this implementation may cause serious harm by infringing International Human Rights Law.

And the third face is when the criminal law punishes a person who did not commit any actual offense, but is punished just because of adopting a political opinion. In other words, applying the criminal law in a certain way can be an act of discrimination or be disproportionate.[36]

Internal Conflict:

This term means political violence happens inside the borders of the applicant's country of origin, which has a serious consequence on the general

---

[33] Hathaway, James C.; Foster, Michelle (2014): The law of refugee status. Second edition. Cambridge United Kingdom: Cambridge University Press.P. 240, 242, 243.
[34] Ibid. P. 243.
[35] Ibid. P. 244
[36] Ibid, P. 243, 244, 245.

situation in that country. At the same time, the induced crisis will not be a sustainable situation that requires decision-makers making efforts to take necessary measures to reduce the impacts of the internal conflict and its implications, especially those related to forced migration and causing displacement when people resort to fleeing from of their country as a natural response to the internal conflict.[37]

That is what the United Nations ensured as well. It placed an unequivocal meaning to internal conflict, which is defined as an "armed conflict within States for political reasons involving citizens fighting for internal change, some are secessionist movements, generally spearheaded by a group of people, more often than not a minority within a community, who take up arms to fight for the establishment of either an autonomous entity within an existing State or an entirely new and independent State of their own."[38]

In addition to this definition, armed conflict within States may be caused by a group of armed people fighting to take over the main power of the State, and money could be the reason behind that. These militias or armed civilians seek to eradicate all the State's institutions, especially the police and judiciary, as well as create a situation of chaos and banditry inside the State, which are all considered adequate reasons to drive civilians to flee all these kinds of horrible catastrophes.[39] However, enforced migration because of internal conflicts is not considered a new phenomenon, even though the numbers have changed and increased continuously since the First World War till now. If we looked, for example, at the period during the Cold War, we can see that the whole world has suffered from an influx of huge numbers of displaced persons across the borders because of internal conflict, seeking peaceful asylum.[40]

Internal conflict has led to a shift in the causes of displacement because the main reasons were the differences in economic developments between the southern and northern countries, which created an evident gap and led thousands of people to migrate seeking better living conditions. This way, the

---

[37] Fiddian-Qasmiyeh, Elena; Loescher, Gil; Long, Katy; Sigona, Nando (2014): The Oxford handbook of refugee and forced migration studies. First edition. Oxford: Oxford University Press.P. 317, 318.
[38] United Nation, Armed Conflict, and their Consequences. (2001), chapter XV. P. 203.
[39] Ibid, P. 203.
[40] Crawley Heaven, Castles Stephen, Loughna Sean, States of Conflict: Causes and Patterns of Forced Migration to the EU and Policy Responses. Report 2003. P. 20.

notions of internal conflict and displacement hold a potential transformation in the root causes of migration since the late 1990s.[41]

By recalling the theories of conflict induced-migration, we can see that most of these theories rely on two categories of causes, which are root causes and proximate causes. Both of them must be combined to motivate migration; otherwise, if root causes have existed in a State such as political oppression, or inequality but did not combine with proximate causes such as ethnic cleansing, riots, or war, they could not develop and exacerbate the situation in the State to a genuine output migration.[42]

The question here, which could be at the core of internal conflict as a cause of immigration, is why do people not always flee when they live in real misery due to internal conflict in their countries?

Some people do not have the ability to adapt to another community, therefore, they prefer to stay and succumb to all miserable circumstances in their country of origin. While others can do so and simply decide to leave. Thus, there must be several conditions that determine why they decided to stay or to leave. Moreover, the researcher Sarah Kenyon Lischer says that besides the relationship between the refugee crisis and regional politics, there are many types of conflicts that influence people to leave, such as internal war, ethnic conflicts, and fleeing from authoritarian and revolutionary regimes. Especially when these circumstances coincide with other factors that could make the conflict surpass the country's borders to subsequently force migration and a huge number of refugees fleeing their countries because a weak party in a conflict has many allies in a neighboring country, for example, or the conflict may be caused by refugees themselves, etc.[43]

According to the UNHCR, internal conflict is the main cause of displacement of most of the refugees around the world. More than half of them are from Iraq, Afghanistan, Somalia, and Syria, where the large-scale displacement with more than half of the Syrian population has become refugees since the beginning of the conflict (UNHCR Global Appeal report 2018-2019).

---

[41] Alexander Betts (2011): Global Migration Governance. Edited by Alexander Betts. First edition. Oxford University Press. P. 299.
[42] Fiddian-Qasmiyeh, Elena; Loescher, Gil; Long, Katy; Sigona, Nando (2014), ibid.P. 319.
[43] Ibid.P. 321.

In that sense, the UNHCR has ensured its working in situations of conflict more than ever before because the causes of displacement are increasingly related to internal conflict. Therefore, all these alarming developments in the conflict zones encouraged the UNHCR, non-governmental organizations, and other international humanitarians to support refugees and other vulnerable people in many aspects.

Internal conflict has changed these days to mean not only violence between a State and non-State actors who demonstrate the territory and people, but it has also exceeded its traditional meaning to involve other actors who could be members of international ideological movements or terrorist groups whose purposes of controlling territories or lands make them active parties of conflict could exercise criminal violence in order to achieve their goals. Thus, the real challenge for International Humanitarian Law in the conflicts nowadays is the "distinction between combatant and civilian". Then, many people find themselves facing with the sole solution, which lies in displacement and fleeing their countries to another destination where they can live in a safe asylum.[44]

And this kind of change that came up with conflict had many effects, especially on humanitarian operations, which made the mission of aid workers harder than before by adding difficulties in conflict zones, such as restricting access to humanitarian aid to people who are really in need and other obstacles, such as threatening workers' security. [45]

Even though humanitarian aid in an environment of violence could not be an efficient tool to resolve the internal conflict as a cause of displacement in these situations, at least it can help by enhancing the role of "legitimate institutions, governance, and international justice as well against those who threaten civilians.

In such conflicts, the UNHCR and other non-governmental organizations may have to cooperate with local governments to complete their mission of protecting vulnerable people and supporting them in various aspects.[46]

There are many examples embodied in the case of internal conflict-induced

---

[44] UNHCR (2012): The State of the World's Refugees. Oxford University press. P. 6.
[45] Ibid. P. 6-8.
[46] Ibid, P. 8.

forced displacement. However, I chose to focus particularly on the armed conflict in Syria and its impacts, particularly that it has given rise to fleeing millions of Syrians abroad since it started in 2011 until now.

The armed conflict in Syria and displaced people:

With more than eight years in the Syrian war and all the terrible circumstances that people experienced in their daily lives, they can tell countless stories about how they suffered from oppression, were deprived of fundamental rights, intimidation, death, and desolation. All they want is to get a new asylum safer than theirs. Therefore, leaving has been decreed. A lot of Syrians have resettled in neighboring countries, which had the majority number of Syrian refugees between 2011 and 2019, with more than three 3,684,982 registered refugees in Turkey, which hosted the largest number of Syrian refugees, besides Lebanon which has estimated the actual number of Syrians living in the country to be 1,5 million. Iraq hosted about 228,851, as well as more than 660,000 Syrian refugees in Jordan, according to the UNHCR.[47]

This massive migration because of armed conflict represented about half of the Syrian population, which is currently a huge number, and represents a real crisis for the whole world, even though the conflict may end for any reason in the future. In any case, it has affected all generations of Syrians in different fields, particularly the health care that every Syrian person should have wherever he might live. As well as the children's right to education, including those who are in camps in neighboring countries. Especially since many of them do not have access to the most basic health services, and most children have been deprived of access to education on account of the destruction of a lot of schools within Syria and wading through residence procedures and registration while living in other countries as well.[48]

However, the World Health Organization (WHO) plays an essential role in collaborating with international frameworks to advocate for refugee's human rights and employ the principles and priorities for enhancing the health care for refugees, as the Global Compact for Migration (GCM) ensured the importance of establishing concrete guidelines to fulfill better and healthier

---

[47] Samer N. Abboud (2016): Syria. Polity press, Cambridge CB2 1UR, UK. P. 211-213.
[48] Ibid. P. 213.

lives for refugees and migrants [49]. Specifically, the Objectives for Safe, Orderly, and Regular Migration include objective 15 (e) in the Global Compact for Migration which seeks to provide access to basic services for migrants and says: "Incorporate the health needs of migrants in national and local health care policies and plans, such as by strengthening capacities for service provision, facilitating affordable and non-discriminatory access, reducing communication barriers, and training health care providers on culturally-sensitive service delivery, to promote the physical and mental health of migrants and communities overall, including by taking into consideration relevant recommendations from the (WHO) Framework of Priorities and Guiding Principles to Promote the Health of Refugees and Migrants."[50]

Furthermore, the Global Compact for Migration has imposed a commitment to giving access to migrants to education systems in the hosting countries through the same objective 15 in action (f): "Provide inclusive and equitable quality education to migrant children and youth, as well as facilitate access to lifelong learning opportunities, including by strengthening the capacities of education systems and by facilitating non-discriminatory access to early childhood development, formal schooling, non-formal education programs for children for whom the formal system is inaccessible, on-the-job and vocational training, technical education, and language training, as well as by fostering partnerships with all stakeholders that can support this endeavor."[51]

The nature of the armed conflict in Syria from 2011 until 2019:

At the beginning of the Syrian conflict, there was a massive backlash against spreading the protests in many areas of Syria, especially in Daraa city. When regime forces failed to suppress the protests in 2011, they resorted to using violence against protesters, which caused a clash between protesters and regime forces. This violence was repeated every time that protests broke out. Therefore, the international community has pursued several efforts to subside the situation and inhibit any attempt to use violence, but it quickly

---

[49] Nefti-Eboni Bempong, Danny Sheath, Joachim Seybold, Antoine Flahault, Anneliese Depoux and Luciano Saso: Critical reflections, challenges and solutions for migrant and refugee health, 2nd M8 Alliance Expert Meeting. Public Health Reviews, meeting report (2019). P. 4,5.

[50] Global Compact for Migration, Global Compact for Safe, Orderly and Regular Migration, Final Draft (11 July 2018). P. 23.

[51] Ibid. P. 23.

turned to regional and military forces to face the conflict. For instance, Qatar, Turkey, Saudi Arabia, and Arab States, which are powerful regional States and made diplomatic efforts through the League of Arab States (LAS) to find a solution, and then they indeed brought a solution in 2011 condemning the violence and immediately calling to have an open dialogue.[52]

Moreover, based on the recommendation from Saudi Arabia and Qatar, (LAS) suggested constituting a National Coalition and recognizing it as an official participant in all political discourses. In contrast, the regime in Syria was obviously against the peace plan that was displayed by (LAS) after its initial acceptance. That was evident when regime forces rejected the withdrawal of its Army from cities, despite what the plan had determined, there were others (LAS) that required the Syrian regime to release political prisoners, have a political dialogue with the Syrian National Council (SNC), and give access to the observer mission to entry into Syria to evaluate the situation inside the country. After a few months of this plan failing, (LAS) had a new peace plan which was acceptable to the regime as an idea to gag the protesters of the regime. Effectively, the regime agreed to the entry of the observer mission into Syria in December 2011, but all these attempts to halt the harsh violence failed as well, and (LAS) announced explicitly the failure of the mission in 2012. Thus, this forced (LAS) to make important decisions such as suspending the membership of Syria LAS, besides imposing economic sanctions against Syria and other sanctions to constrict Syria's trade, especially with Gulf countries. [53]

On the other hand, there were some Arab countries that did not agree to these sanctions on Syria, such as Algeria and Iraq, which considered all the measures taken by (LAS) as illegal interventions in internal affairs.[54] And correspondingly, Qatar was not merely a simple actor in (LAS). But in addition to that, it was at the forefront of the participants to armed opposing groups, so it gave them and shipped weapons in mid-2012. These weapons were almost entirely acquired from west Europe and Libya and were received by Turkey and Qatar intelligence to redistribute them to the opposition groups in order to not have all the weapons in a single group. Turkey, Saudi

---

[52] Samer N. Abboud (2016): Syria. Polity press, Cambridge CB2 1UR, UK. P. 120, 121, 122.
[53] Ibid. P. 122.
[54] Ibid. P. 123.

Arabia, and Qatar had the same perspective, so they created a kind of cooperation to support the armed opposition because they shared interests in overthrowing the regime in Syria at that time. To achieve their objective, they inserted themselves in the internal conflict in many ways, for example, Qatar had more effective relationships with certain factions in the Syrian National Coalition (SNC), such as the Muslim brotherhood to dominate the SNC, which included different fractions of that time, but they actually succeeded in splitting it into many factions, some of them working for Saudi Arabia, others working for Qatar, as well as other factions which are considered as nonaligned actors. But what happened later was that those who worked for Qatar and Saudi Arabia used their plan to cultivate mistrust among the members that, in turn, contributed to a negative role and caused a massive failure in the SNC's task of attempting to find a solution for the conflict in Syria.[55]

Regarding Russia's role in the armed conflict, one will immediately see that Russia was the strongest ally of the Syrian regime. It supported Syria in all international events, and it did not waste the opportunity to stand by the regime when the United Nations Security Council Resolution decided to impose economic sanctions on Syria to push the regime to make a political transition, but Russia has blocked all the efforts of the UNSCR.

In a more specific manner, Russia's support had three main reasons for getting involved in Syrian affairs: geopolitics, economics, and domestic reasons.

The first reason could be summarized in Russia's fears of the spreading of Salafist- jihadist extremism in the region, especially in the Caucasus region, which would directly threaten its internal security, especially if ISIS or Daesh launched a strong attack to take the Syrian -Iraqi desert and to reach Kurdistan and that would in turn increase the danger of extremism reaching this region. And because of Russia's mistrust of the west's intentions. Therefore, it pursues a rejection policy of any kind of international intervention in Syria. This contrasts with the intervention in Libya in 2011. Even though the crisis in Syria has evolved in a similar manner, it justifies the international community to take prompt actions to halt the blood-shedding

---

[55] Ibid. P. 124,125.

in Syria.[56]

Moreover, Russia was fighting the United States over some regional matters, and the Iranian nuclear issue was one of them. So, Russia continues to oppose the USA by vetoing Syria at the UNSCR to prevent imposing economic sanctions and ensuring the necessity of respecting the principle of (non-intervention in the sovereign affairs of Syria). Besides this, there is another reason that makes Russia supports the Syrian regime, which is exemplified by the relations between Russia and Iran, especially since Iran is Syria's major ally in the region. Russia wanted to maintain a good relationship with Iran going well because Iran is Russia's main arms purchaser, where it helped develop its nuclear technology, in addition to another shared interest, which is Iran's fear of Salafist Fighters spreading over the region, which would also destabilize Iran.[57]

The second reason is the domestic one: Russia has many intensive investment projects in Syria, where Russian companies conducted investing contracts and a lot of them have been affected by the conflict, which represents many losses for Russia regarding existing contracts. Additionally, its dominance on a naval base in Tartus on the Syrian coast could be threatened as well, if the regime changed in Syria. Particularly, it did not want the Libyan scenario in 2011 to repeat, when it lost more than 2 billion dollars in contracts agreed upon by the Gaddafi regime, which became invalid after the regime was overthrown.[58]

Also, Iran's role in the Syrian armed conflict was supporting because it was alongside the regime from the beginning, and it had an important dominance in making decisions in Syria. This was the case because the regime depends on Iran for many issues, such as financial and military aspects, informing that Iran provides military suppliers and strategists to work for the regime in the conflict, it increases the training and draws most of the plans that National Defense Forces execute in the battlefield. So, its military got involved in the regime fighting rebel forces. Although Iran pretends as if it wished for the conflict to continue, it has played an important role in the ceasefires because

---

[56] Karim Atassi (2018): Syria, the Strength of an Idea, the Constitutional Architectures of Its Political Regimes. Preface by Jean Marcou. Translated from the French by Christopher Sutcliffe. Cambridge University Press first published. P. 435.
[57] Samer N. Abboud (2016): Syria. Polity press, Cambridge CB2 1UR, UK. P. 126.
[58] Ibid. P.127, 128, 129.

its leadership believes that it could be a gradual solution which could be a political transition if Iran's conditions were applied. Iran intends to maintain its allies which are Iraq and Hezbollah, in case the conflict's consequences reach them. In addition to that, if we take into consideration reducing the oil prices, especially since Iran has suffered sanctions, and a decline in oil prices as a reaction from the international world for Iran's rejection to make any nuclear deal a grand bargain and to cease any support to Syrian regime and other allies, Syria cannot rely on Iran in military and financial aspects for long. That requirement was the result of international negotiations conducted between Iran and other States (USA, Russia, China, UK, Germany), and Iran did not respond to any of the previous terms. But what is the reason behind all these rejections and its strong insistence on being an actor in the Syrian conflict? Maybe it is Iran's desire to exercise a kind of control on Hezbollah's weapons to serve its interests.

Thus, Shiite Iran, with its support to the Syrian regime deepens the conflict and enhances the sectarian tensions in Syria and over the region in general, which would cause a kind of war against Sunni Saudi Arabia based on the sectarian division between Sunni- Shiite 'rivalry[59]. Additionally, the Russians' main objective lies in the Syrian internal conflict to continue, so as to prevent Qatar and Iran from installing gas pipelines across the Syrian territory that could reach Europe.[60]

Turkey has hosted numerous Syrian refugees and provided humanitarian aid for them, besides its role in opening its border to enter the army defectors from the Free Syrian Army. It has also coordinated the external opposition and made the representative of the Syrian uprising legitimate to intervene in Syrian affairs. Furthermore, it had been set on establishing a safe zone in the northern parts of Syria, and in fact in 2014 it demanded to set up a 4,000- or 5,000-Kilometer safe area safe from any kind of terrorism. In fact, Turkey had made such a demand to ensure its need to set up a safe zone in the area which would be very important for humanitarian reasons, but Russia replied then that this demand needed an acceptance from the UNSC. After about two weeks of Russian intervention in Syria in 2015, Turkey failed in

---

[59] Ibid. P. 130, 131, 132.
[60] Kamilia Rostom: Integrating Syrian Refugees in Eastern Germany. A Cultural Textbook. New York. Peter Lang, 2020. P. 63.

overthrowing the Syrian regime for many reasons: firstly, Turkey's policy was somewhat trying to make a balance between Turkey and regional powers, and these regional relations led, in turn, to enervating Turkish aspirations and goals in facing the conflict.[61]

For the European States, the western States do not have any significant or effective role concerning the armed conflict in Syria, except for imposing economic sanctions on the Syrian regime and official institutions at the UNSC to pressure the regime and force it to comply with a political compromise. But not surprisingly, Russia has used the right to veto to hinder all the international community's efforts. Thus, western States, through their sanctions, have failed in changing the regime, but in contrast, that led to more intensive sanctions, which have obscenely affected the Syrian people. While the European Union has also imposed four phases of sanctions, the first three of them were around the period between the outset of the conflict in 2011 and 2013, which were against State's institutions and Syrian trade. The European Union is the most important market for Syrian oil, and it thought that these economic sanctions and banning of all Syrian oil exports would affect the regime. The fourth phase of these sanctions was implemented in April 2013, which embodied a transition in the EU policy against the conflict through facilitating executing sanctions in providing military and political support to the opposition in Syria, such as enabling the opposition to sell Syrian oil outside the regime areas. Without any doubt, the European Union's sanctions failed in finding a solution to cease conflict or even changing the regime in Syria, which is no longer its purpose at all. In many examples, the western States failed to adopt policies to alter the course of the Syrian conflict because its allies did not let them achieve their aims.[62]

Furthermore, there were many attempts to resolve the conflict in Syria, manifested in three external processes: Geneva1, Geneva2, and Moscow process.

Firstly, Geneva1 was initiated by Kofi Annan, who was the UN envoy at that time and started his mission as an observer to Syria in April 2012. In fact, he could invite different parts that represented the conflict, in addition to the

---

[61] Samer N. Abboud (2016), ibid. P. 134.
[62] Ibid. P. 136.

UN, UK, US, Russia, Turkey, France, China, Kuwait, Iraq, and Qatar, to international negotiations aimed at implementing a plan for a political transition by means of new elections, which would lead to a non-sectarian government with perfect standards of "transparency and accountability". [63] There was a conference between the opposition and the regime to agree on some terms to wrap the conflict up. However, the Syrian regime did not accept the participation of parties of the opposition in the political process, and, correspondingly, the opposition insisted on the necessity of al-Assad submitting his resignation as a precondition for implementing the political plan. This initiative failed entirely, and its collapse led to Anan's resignation when he declared: "It is impossible for me, or anyone, to compel the Syrian government in the first place, and also the opposition, to take the necessary steps to begin a political process." After that, the UN appointed Lakhdar Brahimi as the new UN representative in Syria.[64]

What happened in the Geneva2 process in January and February 2014, was not very different from the last scenario in Geneva1, but the difference during the process was attending representative actors of the Syrian regime and the opposition as well, unlike Geneva1, along with several armed factions as the Islamic State of Iraq and the Levant (ISIS), and others which have been known as radical jihadist fronts. That led the Western States to accelerate the process with the aim of finding a solution to the conflict. The opposition group had no clear agreement. It was simply incapable of reaching unanimity of all its members and the armed factions on a political solution. Some of them rejected the propositions while others were supportive, and this kind of clash was proof of an unstable situation. Eventually, the failure to reach a real solution to ending the conflict through the negotiations in the Geneva 2 process reflects the inability of the international efforts to halt the conflict in Syria and to make a political change that would satisfy all parties.[65]

In late 2014 there were active negotiations between the Syrian regime and the opposition in what was called the Moscow Process, which was based on an official invitation from the Russian Foreign ministry to all conflict's parties as a serious attempt to reach a compromise to end the conflict because all

---

[63] Karim Atassi. Ibid. P. 444.
[64] Samer N. Abboud, Ibid. 150- 152.
[65] Ibid. 152, 153.

previous attempts had failed miserably, including the initiatives of de-Mistura and Russia in 2015, which were alternatives to the Geneva processes.

However, the Moscow process took place in the same year and consisted of both the regime representatives and the opposition, which was, in fact, an internally loyal opposition group. Contrary to what the Russian Foreign Ministry assured that the Moscow process was going to be the "initial Geneva communique," it was indeed disappointing, for two main reasons: first, there was no representation of any part of the external opposition group who are the genuine actors in the conflict against the regime, unlike the internal opposition which is "the other face of the regime."

Second, the Moscow process did not provide a serious solution for ending the conflict. In fact, it was nothing more than fake narratives that the regime used to talk about the nature of the conflict. Therefore, all the basic opposition and the armed factions besides the armed groups rejected all the suggestions and requirements proposed by the Moscow process, which the "internal opposition" demanded and were far from what the major opposition really wanted.[66]

Later on, there were more discussions between the Russian Foreign Ministry and the Secretary of the US at that time, John Kerry, about the future of Syria and new international efforts aimed to eradicate the armed conflict, especially because all the previous initiatives had faced complicated obstacles. Nevertheless, despite this new diplomatic initiative, there could not be a serious prospect for reaching a resolution pledging to halt the conflict, or even the possibility of implementing such a resolution on the ground. For example, if the negotiations reached a resolution to ceasefire, it would be mandatory for all the armed groups to comply with it, including the regime forces where its main allies (Russia, Iran) have no efficient control on this regime to enforce it engaging in an actual peace process. Similarly, the allies of armed groups, which are Saudi Arabia and Qatar, could not promise that all the armed factions would carry out the resolution, even after placing all the pressure tools on them[67]. Perhaps, according to the researcher's opinion, all the allies' countries for both the regime and the armed factions are happy

---

[66] Ibid. P. 158, 159.
[67] Karim Atassi, ibid. P. 454, 455.

to continue fighting until Syria is destroyed completely.[68]

Until December 2018, De Mistura conducted a series of steps to establish a transition in the government, but all these efforts could not be beneficial without a legitimate recognition of the necessity of a ceasefire, and an actual implementation on the battlefield from the two combatants, the regime and the armed opposition. De Mistura said about his resignation in 2018 that: "I felt the war territorially was leading to an end and having really fought against what happened in Aleppo, in Idlib, in Daraya, I could not be the one that is shaking Assad's hand and saying malesh (an Arabic word means do not worry)"[69]. Then, in January 2019, the secretary General appointed Geir Pedersen as the new envoy. Nevertheless, the question that comes to mind now is, which international measures could help to resolve the crisis in Syria, and are the UN political initiatives since 2011 until now considered the right choice? or does the situation really require military intervention to end the conflict and adopting the roadmap of the future of Syria? Especially since most Syrians prefer finding a political solution without any kind of external intervention, and they hope that Syria will hold itself together and must be managed by a liberal, authentic political regime.[70]

Migration to Europe and the Syrian crisis in Germany:

Considering the complicated circumstances that Syrian people have experienced due to the armed conflict in their country, they do not but two choices: either stay at home awaiting the time of their death, which could be predictable at any time and, in case they survived, they would be worried all the time for the lack of basic things such as gas, electricity, daily sustenance, especially those who live in hot spots, or leaving their country and searching for asylum wherever that might be. Based on this illustration, "the refugee resettlement is about protection"[71]. Thus, all the Syrian refugees need is only protection from the serious harm that they will certainly experience in their country after the armed conflict broke out in their territory.

---

[68] Samer N. Abboud, ibid. P. 160, 161.
[69] https://www.theguardian.com/world/2019/nov/05/ex-un-syria-envoy-says-he-quit-to-avoid-having-to-shake-assads-hand
[70] Karim Atassi, ibid. P. 461, 469.
[71] Basem Mahmud: Emotions and Belonging in Forced Migration, Syrian Refugees and Asylum Seekers. Routledge Advances in Sociology, First published. New York 2022. P. 7.

Overall, most of the Syrian migrants fled to Europe, particularly to Germany, which has changed its migration policy recently to be compatible with the most dangerous crises around the world, from the Yugoslav wars in (1991-2001) to the Syrian civil war which started in (2011), for instance, Germany has received 79% of the Syrian asylum seekers who came to Europe in 2016.[72]

At the outset of Syrian migration to Europe, which started in 2013, all the migrants had requested asylum applications, but only 30% percent were approved. However, this number increased in 2014 when about 127,000 asylum seekers registered in Germany, where more migrants from Syria in 2015 and 2016 (about one million persons) who came seeking asylum were accepted. Germany has been considered the most important host country in Europe for Syrian migrants[73]. In addition to the huge number of refugees with admission in Germany in 2017, when more than 2,455 Syrian refugees came from Turkey to resettle in Germany, over 60.000 visas for Syrian families were issued. Thus, Germany advocated all forms of admission to it, such as facilitating the reunification procedures for families and granting international protection for their relatives as well, especially after the Christian Democratic Union party (CDU) won the election in 2017. Chancellor Angela Merkel organized an agreement between the CDU and Social Democrats for a renewed grand coalition that recognizes the international and national protection of refugees but restricts the reunification of the families of people under subsidiary protection to 1,000 cases per month[74]. This initiative to receive the Syrian refugees in 2015 by Chancellor Merkel was considered a clear transformation in Germany's policy, from the pure "nation-saving" to an accepting foreigners and newcomers' policy. The first policy manifested in the nation-saving principle in which the State's main purpose was to "involve the membership control", and then to protect the native generations in Germany because otherwise, the national system would be likely to collapse, whereas the new integrating policy depends on granting almost the same citizens' rights to the refugees and accepting them in the society as a first step to fulfill the integration and

---

[72] Kamilia Rostom: Integrating Syrian Refugees in Eastern Germany. A Cultural Textbook. New York. Peter Lang, 2020. P. 63.
[73] Vicki Squire: Europe's Migration Crisis, Borders Deaths and Human Dignity. University of Warwick. New York, Cambridge University Press, first published 2020. P. 89.
[74] The UN Refugee Agency, Country-Update GermanyQ1 2018:https://www.unhcr.org/dach/wp-content/uploads/sites/27/2018/03/Factsheet_Germany_O1_2018.pdf.

reject any kind of antisemitism.[75]

As seen in 2016, according to the UNHCR, about 362,000 refugees fled to Europe crossing the Mediterranean Sea. Additionally, 181,400 persons arrived in Italy and 173,450 in Greece but, on the other hand, an estimated 2,700 persons registered either died or went missing in 2017. Those migrants decided to leave facing many risks on the way, aiming to benefit from financial and social assistance that the German government grants.[76]

Between 2018 and 2019, Syrian migrants were rated as the main asylum seeker citizens in six of the EU member States. Approximately 16.200 persons were complete number of the Syrian applicants who sought asylum in the European Union, 57% of them resettled in Germany.[77]

However, what was different was the perseverance of migrant's influx into European countries in 2019, for their main countries of their origin are Syria, Afghanistan, and Venezuela. These migrants were hosted by about four main countries. Germany hosted the most, then France, Spain, Greece, and the UK.[78]

The European Union made more efforts to develop an asylum system, including its main legislation related to the European Union as a protection area called 'the common European asylum system' (CEAS) to be more compatible with the current crises of migrants' influx into Europe. Further, it included more facilities in hosting procedures, and accommodation conditions as a serious response to supporting displaced people seeking asylum. This system guaranteed protection for all those people fleeing from their countries because of persecution or serious harm, in other words, the refugees and people under subsidiary protection who were at risk of facing serious harm whenever returned to their homes, and therefore, in need of protection.

---

[75] Kamilia Rostom: Integrating Syrian Refugees in Eastern Germany. Ibid. P. 41-44.

[76] The UN Refugee Agency, Europe Situation: https://www.unhcr.org/europe-emergency.html.

[77] Asylum quarterly report, Statistics Explained: https://ec.europa.eu/eurostat/statistics-explained/pdfscache/13562.pdf. P. 6.

[78] European Commission: COMMUNICATION FROM THE COMMISSION TO THE EUROPEAN PARLIAMENT, THE EUROPEAN COUNCIL AND THE COUNCIL 481 final, Progress report on the Implementation of the European Agenda on Migration. Brussels (2019): https://ec.europa.eu/home-affairs/sites/homeaffairs/files/what-we-do/policies/european-agenda-migration/20191016_com-2019-481-report_en.pdf.

In the CEAS, all the European Union members commit to granting the required protection for refugees within their open borders; thus, the refugees have the right to move freely and have fair processes anywhere in the EU. All the members pledge to examine all the cases of applicants for asylum in a similar manner, wherever they have applied within the EU borders.[79]

Furthermore, the CEAS has determined two principles as fundamental rights, which are also emphasized in both the Refugee Convention 1951 and its protocol 1967. These are the right to asylum and the principle of non-refoulement. These principles are firmly adopted by the European Court of Human rights (ECHR), and the Court of Justice of the European Union (CJEU), both stand by refugees almost in issues related to detention, the conditions of reception facilities and such cases where they find that any of the EU members committed a violation in its legislations. The CJEU has a critical mission in safeguarding the implementation of the right of asylum as a fundamental right in the Charter of Fundamental Rights of the European Union in Article (18), besides other rights which all the EU members are obliged not to infringe, such as the right to protection in the event of removal, expulsion, or extraction in Article (19), the right to an effective remedy and a fair trial in Article (47).[80]

All the European countries were forced to host the Syrian refugees, who were fleeing from the armed conflict to comply with the CEAS. By having all the facilities and assisting tools to allow the refugees enter the borders, the European countries established an organized cooperation with each other for asylum seekers in which they can resettle in any European country they choose. For national reasons, some European Countries restricted this policy towards asylum seekers to prevent them from entering through Greece, Italy, and Hungary. That led the EU to decide to transfer asylum seekers from those countries to others in the EU, although this decision has not been widely used, it was limited to execute on the part of the whole number of asylum seekers.[81]

As a result of these obstacles that hindered the implementation of the EU

---

[79] Common European Asylum System, Migration and Home Affairs: https://ec.europa.eu/home-affairs/what-we-do/policies/asylum_en.

[80] Jasmin Lilian Diab (2017): International Migration and Refugee Law: Does Germany Migration Policy towards Syrian Refugees Comply? Hamburg. Anchor Academic Publishing. P. 39. 45. 46.

[81] Ibid. P. 41.

Policy, the EU made a deal with Turkey to control the movement of asylum seekers to prevent them from reaching Europe. As a result, the EU has promised Turkey to support the refugees and to provide them with financial assistance, in addition to facilitating visa procedures to enter Europe among other things. Nevertheless, this deal between the EU and Turkey was not managed adequately because of the inability of the Turkish government to control its borders. As a result, there were a lot of irregular migrants who reached Greece in 2016, which returned about 750 asylum seekers to Turkey when the Greek courts considered Turkey to be an unsafe country. This reflects the controversial attitudes of European Countries towards refugees.[82]

However, the EU still supports many countries, such as Lebanon, Jordan, and Turkey, where there are numerous Syrian refugees who prefer to stay nearby their country in order to be able to go back to their homes whenever the circumstances in Syria allow them to. They can stay on countries nearby thanks to financial aids given by the United Nations to refugees. Although Lebanon and Jordan did not sign the Refugee Convention, both countries received huge numbers of Syrian refugees and retained them temporarily in their territories based on the non-refoulement principle as one of the other obligations established in other conventions and treaties that both countries signed related to refugees. This way, they comply with the non- refoulement principle as a fundamental principle in the Customary Law to protect the refugees from arbitrary return.[83]

Additionally, the EU guarantees applicants' rights after entering the European borders, which includes procedural rights starting from the moment the asylum applicant enters European borders until registering in the asylum country and applying for a refugee status.

a) The concept of a safe third country:

The concept of a safe third country means that asylum seekers should apply for protection in the first safe country that they reach. They can register in this country where they find asylum after fleeing from persecution or armed conflict that they faced in their country of origin.

---

[82] Ibid. P. 42.
[83] Anne Marie Baylouny: When Blame Backfires: Syrian Refugees and the Citizen Grievances in Jordan and Lebanon. Cornell University Press. First published. Ithaca, New York, 2020, p. 39.

The concept is set out in the Refugee Convention, precisely in Article 31(1), which says:

> "The Contracting States shall not impose penalties, on account of their illegal entry or presence on refugees who, coming directly from a territory where their life or freedom was threatened in the sense of article 1, enter or are present in their territory without authorization, provided they present themselves without delay to the authorities and show good cause for their illegal entry or presence."

Thus, this article excludes from penalization the asylum seekers who entered any of the member States illegally if they come directly from a territory where they faced serious harm threating their life or freedom. In this case, asylum seekers do not resettle in a safe third country before entering another country where they want to get international protection. In contrast, they come directly to the asylum-providing country. Therefore, the member States comply with the concept of non -refoulement that has been established in Article 33(1) of the Refugee Convention on the basis that returning the asylum seeker to his country will put him at risk of serious harm that threatens his life or freedom. On the contrary, according to article (2) the asylum seeker cannot benefit from the non-refoulement principle if his residence poses a danger to the asylum country's 'security because, for instance, he committed a crime.[84]

The concept of 'the safe third country' was enshrined in the Asylum Procedures Directive (APD), which declared in Article 27 the "possibility for member States to apply the safe third country concept". That means, according to the APD, that member States can send the applicant to a safe third country if there is nothing that threatens his life or his liberty in the third country and all the following principles are respected in the third country:

1. The principle of non-refoulement in accordance with the Geneva Convention.

---

[84] Mariana Gkliati (2017): The EU-Turkey Deal and the Safe Third Country Concept before the Greek Asylum Appeals Committees. Movement- journal.org. P. 214. / UNHCR. The 1951 Convention Relating to The Status of Refugees.

2. The prohibition of removal, in violation of the right to freedom from (torture, cruelty, inhuman or degrading treatment) as laid down in International Law.

3. The possibility of requesting a refugee status in accordance with the Geneva Convention.

Therefore, member States may apply the concept of the safe third country when its competent authority ensures the achievement of these conditions in the safe third country. All conditions should be considered, as the UNHCR emphasized, and it added additional conditions as well, such as the need for the applicant to be connected to the third country, and it would not be enough and then accounted as a close link if the applicant just has an opportunity to be granted protection in the third country. Also, the third country must permit the applicant to challenge all the dangers set out in article 27 of the APD in its national legislation.[85]

However, the concept of the safe third country prompted criticism regarding its implementations in some European countries such as Greece, Slovenia, and The Netherlands. The gap lies in their national legislation and how they determine whether the third country is considered safe or not. Despite that, concerning the Syrian refugee issue, as a legal application of the EU- Turkey Statement of March 2016, Turkey is a key partner for the European Union. Turkey is considered a safe third country. Consequently, Greece, as one of the member States, has the right to apply the concept of the safe third country in returning the Syrian refugees who entered Greece through illegal migration to Turkey, which is a safe third country according to EU decision. Then, all asylum applications submitted in Greece should be unacceptable, and then all applicants should be returned to Turkey, where they must request international protection. Greece rejected all the asylum applications without checking whether Turkey was, in fact, a safe third country or not. And then, it merely relied on the assumption that Turkey is a safe third country to be able to make such decisions against asylum seekers.[86]

---

[85] Asylum Procedures Directive, Directive 2005/ 85/ EC of 1 December 2005: https://www.asylumlawdatabase.eu/en/content/en-asylum-procedures-directive-directive-200585ec-1-december-2005

[86] Maurice Stierl: Migrant Resistance in Contemporary Europe, edited by Jenny Edkins and Nick Vaughan-Williams. New York: Routledge, 2019. P. 111, 192.

Later on, this decision had positive reactions from many international human rights organizations besides the European Commission, which exerts efficient efforts to support resettlement and returning procedures as well[87]. Furthermore, the German concept of Safe Third Country does not contradict the Refugee Convention of 1951, established on the assumption that all countries that share the boundaries with Germany by land or sea comply with this conception which, according to Article 16 (a)(1), (2) and (5) of the German Federal Constitution entails:

(1) Anybody persecuted on political grounds has the right to asylum.

(2) Paragraph 1 may not be invoked by anybody who enters the country from a member State of the European Communities or another third country where the application of Convention for the protection of Human Rights and Fundamental Freedoms is assured. Countries outside the European Communities that fulfill the conditions of the first sentence of this paragraph shall be specified by legislation requiring the consent of the Bundesrat. In cases covered by the first sentence, measures terminating a person's sojourn may be carried out irrespective of any remedy sought by that person.

(3) Paragraphs 1 to 4 do not conflict with international agreements of member States of the European Communities among themselves and with third countries which, with due regard for the obligations arising from the Convention relating to the Status of Refugees and the Convention for the Protection of Human Rights and Fundamental Freedoms, whose application must be assured in the contracting States, establish jurisdiction for the consideration of applications for asylum including the mutual recognition of decisions on asylum[88].

Thus, all countries that share borders with Germany are considered safe third countries, according to the second paragraph of the previous article. Additionally, the Federal Constitutional Court outlined the meaning of the safe third country legislation in the German Federal Constitution and the limits of the concept. The court set provisions based on a "normative ascertainment of safety in a third State", and it combined several conditions

---

[87] Mariana Gkliati. Ibid. P. 215.
[88] Rosemary Byrne, Gregor Noll and Jens Vedsted -Hansen (Eds) (2002): New Asylum Countries? Migration Control and Refugee Protection in an Enlarged European Union. Kluwer Law International. Netherlands. P. 33.

that should be met for a country classify as a Safe Third Country. For instance, it should comply with the 1951 Convention and its Protocol 1967, and the ECHR as well. Besides, the country must be bound by the principle of non-refoulement, in other words, its legal order includes the obligation of providing protection to the asylum seeker and ensuring that he will not be returned to a fourth country, and more conditions[89].

Therefore, Germany, as a member State of the EU, was obliged to declare Turkey as a Safe Third Country, and did not object to Greece's decision when it returned Syrian refugees to Turkey.

b) The reception of asylum seekers:

When an asylum seeker enters the European territories and applies for international protection, he must comply with all obligations and EU legislations concerning asylum, so he can benefit from all the rights in the country of asylum under Directive 2013/33/EU of the European Parliament and of the Council of June 26, 2013, regarding the reception of asylum seeker standards for providing international protection to the applicant that requires it in accordance with the EU law. Also, Member States must register the applicants under international protection without any delay[90]. The Directive prescribes that the applications for international protection should be filled and registered within three days after filing. This period could be extended to an additional three days in case the applications were made to authorities that do not have the competence to force the registration, with the possibility of extending the registration period up to ten days if the competent authority faces numerous numbers of applications that need more time to be filled.

International protection has been defined as "a request made by a third country national or a Stateless person who seeks refugee status or subsidiary protection".[91] Other regulations have been imposed on all asylum seekers, and Syrian migrants complied with these regulations, for instance, the EURODAC regulations, which were set out for the first time on July 20, 2015. It was carried out in a centralized fingerprint database for all applicants. Perhaps, this procedure has played a very essential role in recognizing all

---

[89] Ibid. P. 34, 35.
[90] Directive 2013/32/EU of the European Parliament and of the Council of 26 June 2013. Official Journal of European Union (27) P. 3.
[91] Jasmin Lilian Diab, Ibid. P. 47, 48.

Syrian asylum seekers, especially those who are underage. Also, it facilitated the mission of national authority of attesting if the applicant is a third-country national or a Stateless individual because it would be difficult to qualify him, especially because vast numbers of those migrants entered European territories in an illegal manner. Therefore, all member States have committed to executing the regulation of taking fingerprints of all applicants to grant them international protection. The national authorities take all the applicants' fingerprints and submit them to the Central Unit to be uploaded to the central system in Europe.[92]

Furthermore, to prevent the applicant from registering in more than one member State in the EU for international protection, the member State is obliged to review the applications that asylum seekers submit in accordance with the Dublin Regulations, which were enforced in 2014. Article 3 States the following: (1) the procedure for examining an application for international protection:

"1. Member States shall examine any application for international protection by a third-country national or a Stateless person who applies on the territory of any one of them, including at the border or in the transit zones. The application shall be examined by a signal Member State, which shall be the one which the criteria set out in Chapter III indicate is responsible"[93].

Besides other measures in which member States are responsible for asylum seekers, such as integration of refugees that was emphasized by the 1951 Convention related to the status of refugees, the convention established social and economic rights that all member States should avail to refugees, as well as the note of the UNHCR's executive committee which ensured the necessity of refugee's integration in the host country as "a principle of durable solution for refugees in the industrialized world". The UNHCR has placed assessments in many European countries to eliminate most obstacles that refugees face on the way to integration, such as the lack of knowledge of the host country's language, suffering from discrimination and disrespect against

---

[92] Ibid. P. 49.
[93] Ibid. P. 50. Official Journal of the European Union (29. 06. 2013), Regulation (EU) No 604/ 2013 of The European Parliament and if The Council of 26 June 2013, General Principles and Safeguards Article 3(1), chapter II.

refugees, limited access to rights for persons with subsidiary protection, etc.[94] The UNHCR was keen on implementing the integration policy on the refugees because the office asserted that this policy would be more effective if it was applied to refugees without extending it to encompass all asylum seekers. The integration policy aims to reduce the isolation and separation of those asylum seekers who have been recognized as refugees or persons under subsidiary protection in hosted communities. This policy relies on many measures such as serving effective language, assisting in accessing employment, and providing vocational skills development.[95]

In that sense, Germany has pursued an evolution in its migration policy, for it supplied several facilities which are qualified in different aspects as supporting refugees by providing the essentials: food, accommodations, health care, and offering advanced assistance to help them access the national market after learning the local language of the host country as an important step to integrate the refugee into the society. Thus, Syrian refugees have benefited from the integration policy which Germany considered as an implementation of the Geneva Convention Relating to the Status of Refugees 1951, where the German policy towards refugees derived from article 1(A) of the Convention, which defined the term 'refugee' and, consequently, mentioned this term in section 3 of the German Asylum Act. Therefore, the number of refugees which have been hosted in Germany increased in 2014 considerably, and most of them came from Syria after the outbreak of the armed conflict in their country. Even now, it still comprises the largest number of refugees in Germany until 2018, and the rest of the refugees came from Iraq and Afghanistan.[96]

Germany had allocated several facilities to Syrian asylum seekers since they arrived at the borders until settling inside the country. They can choose either to register as asylum seekers on the borders or to apply for asylum application inside Germany. Then they get the certificates that are lodged by the competent reception authorities, which prove the admission of being asylum seekers. After, authorities take over the mission of appointing the German State to be responsible for the processing of the applications and distributing

---

[94] UNHCR, Note on the Integration of refugees in the European Union. Unhcr.org/463b462c4.pdf. P. 1,2.
[95] Ibid. P. 3,4.
[96] Jasmin Lilian Diab, ibid. P. 72. The UNHCR Global Appeal 2018- 2019, 104.

asylum seekers in German States compatible with the EASY system, with considering the capacity of the State for absorbing the numbers of refugees, which is why some German States received only a small number of refugees. As a result, the federal office for Migration and Refugees has its considerations in registering asylum seekers and granting them international protection. For instance, it deems ineligibility to claim asylum for asylum seekers that came from a Safe Third Country, and Germany has the right to return them to that country.[97] On the other hand, the Asylum act and Residence Act regulate the process of asylum claims in Germany, where the Asylum Act organizes the process after granting or rejecting the asylum claim, while the Residence Act sets all the rules regarding settlement, staying, exiting, and working. Thus, the asylum seeker has two possibilities: a) the first one is being considered under a refugee status or subsidiary protection if he fled from his country for any kind of political persecution or other humanitarian reasons and needs international protection and then staying in Germany, and, as a result, he gets a three-year residence permit.

b) The second possibility is being deported from Germany. If his application is rejected, then he must leave Germany. Deportation usually happens if any of the following reason has been met: when the application is considered as "unfounded or manifestly unfounded", there is no prohibition against deportation, the application is withdrawn, or the asylum application was rejected because of the responsibility of processing the application of another EU member State as an implement of Dublin procedure. In this case, he has a specific period for deportation which is thirty days if his application was rejected with kind of merits, or only one week to leave Germany if the application was inadmissible and without merit.[98]

Because of the numerous numbers of Syrian refugees that were flowing into Germany between the period of 2015 and 2017, which created a genuine crisis, Germany has made many legal amendments to its laws regarding the refugees' handling procedures. These amendments encompass the following laws:

-   The Act on the Acceleration of Asylum Procedures came into

---

[97] Ibid. P. 74, 75. P. (low case) 74f.
[98] Ibid. P. 77-79.

force on the 24th of October 2015. This Act aimed to accelerate the procedures of asylum for asylum seekers, such as accelerating the process of handling the applications, granting accommodations and financial aid to refugees, and providing free language courses and other learning lessons to prepare them to access the labor market. In addition, it sought to reform integration policies for refugees and categorizing Albania, Kosovo, and Montenegro as secure for accelerating asylum procedures to facilitate granting work visas for their citizens after returning to their countries because this Act relies on the assumption that the applications which are lodged by nationals of the Western Balkan countries are "manifestly without merit", thus, they must leave Germany within a week. Then, they can apply for a work visa instead of applying for asylum.[99]

- The Act on Improving the Housing, Feeding and Care for Unaccompanied Minors, which entered into force on the 1st of November 2015, aims to support minors and adolescents by receiving them in all German States and improving housing care. After this Act, there have been many developments to help this type of refugees in many ways, such as basic care, health, and housing. And as a consequence of this Act, the age of legal capacity to act in an asylum procedure has been raised from sixteen to eighteen years. Otherwise, all applicants under eighteen years mandatorily need a legal guardian to act on their behalf in all the phases of asylum procedures.

- The Data Sharing Improvement Act, which came into force on February 5, 2016, besides, The Act on the Faster Expulsion of Criminal Foreigners and Extended Reasons for Refusing Refugee Recognition to Criminal Asylum Seekers, which came into force on March 17, 2016.[100]

- The Act on Introduction of Fast Track-Asylum Procedures on March 17, 2016.

- The Integration Act of the 6th of August 2016, which aims to

---

[99] Jasmin Lilian Diab, ibid, 79, 80.
[100] Ibid. P. 81-82.

establish a link between the individual organizations and procedures in the phase of arrival and registration, as well as taking all procedures to integrate refugees into German society. Based on this, it is possible to anticipate that the Syrian refugees in Germany will not be returned to Syria, at least until now. Especially those who are integrated into society where they got acceptance from the native people and have new dreams in Germany and are working hard to achieve them. Otherwise, the others will return to the third countries if their country has not been yet announced as a safe country.[101]

- The Act on Combating Child Marriage, July 22, 2017.
- The Act to Improve the Enforcement of the Obligation to Leave the Country, which came into force on July 29, 2017.[102]

The Right to Leave in International Law and EU Law:

The primary purpose of this section is to conclude whether there is initially a right to leave in the European and International instruments because this right is considered the first essential component of the right to immigrate. In contrast, the right to stay, which will be articulated in the third chapter, comprises the second component. Thus, the section will cover most of the International and European documents that explicitly list the right to leave as a recognized right and address this right in the freedom of movement that they enshrined in general.

The Right to Leave in the UDHR:

The main document of human rights asserts that everyone has the right to freedom of movement and residence within the borders of each State.[103] While the right to leave has been recognized firmly according to its instrument, the right to stay was partially absent in Art. 13 of the declaration in which the right to stay was mitigated somehow.[104] However, recall to Art.

---

[101] Kamilia Rostom (2020): Integrating Syrian Refugees in Eastern Germany. A Cultural Textbook. NewYork. Peter Lang, p. 238, 239.
[102] Federal Office for Migration and Refugees. Germany, Institutional Framework for immigration and asylum Policies. European Migration Network, EMN. (ec.europa.eu). P. 1.2. and Jasmin Lilian Diab, Ibid, 79-83.
[103] Article 13 (1), UDHR.
[104] Maurice Stierl: Migrant Resistance in Contemporary Europe, edited by Jenny Edkins and Nick Vaughan-Williams. New York: Routledge, 2019. P. 196.

14, it is observed that this article has mentioned implicitly the right to stay in a State that is supposed to be the asylum destination, but did not provide any guarantees enforcing countries to grant refugees this right. In other words, Article 14 States the right to seek and enjoy asylum in another country. However, it did not totally affirm whether the right to stay is indeed obligatory and whether all countries should be compelled to execute it without objections.

The Universal Declaration of Human Rights of 1948 enshrined the right to leave in Article 13 (2), which says:

> (2) Everyone has the right to leave any country, including his own, and to return to his country.
> This specific instrument in the UDHR ensures the right to migrate and includes an international guarantee encompassing the right to leave one's country for another as well.

So long as Human Rights are recognized in many international agreements conducted between countries, to protect all rights included in controversial documents and ensure implementation of those rights in applied domestic laws and within jurisdictions of the countries, therefore, the right to leave as one of the Human Rights has been recognized and defined : "the right to depart from a concrete State to go somewhere else where the same Human Rights may or may not be guaranteed."[105]

In other words, the right to leave is a half right, it encompasses part of the right to migrate, which has been addressed as a human right for every person who wants to reside in any State, and this State could not deny it. A researcher interpreted how the right to migrate can be recognized through such arguments. For instance, the right to migrate would be fulfilled if the other human rights of the migrants in the host State were preserved, and it must be applied by opening the borders of any State, not only to a few States. The researcher says that the right to migrate cannot be obtained as an outcome of the right to leave, even if the reasons for the right to leave could be used as justifications for the right to migrate. On the other hand, "the right to leave a specific country does not entail the right to stay in any State of one's

---

[105] Council of Europe, Commissioner for Human Rights: The right to leave a country. P.9

choosing."[106] Therefore, there are three strategies that affect justifying the right to migrate as a human right.

> A) First, the direct strategy. It stands on the supposed fact that all human rights are justified because they serve fundamental human interests, and the right to migrate could be justifiable by advancing the interests of human beings. So, the right to migrate will be justified similarly to the existing rights.
>
> B) Second, it is an instrumental strategy. According to this strategy, the right to migration could be recognized, and its recognition constitutes an instrumental argument for other human rights that are already on the canonical list. And if the right to migrate is not recognized, then the other human rights will not be recognized as well because the instrumental argument would be gone. Thus, this new right guarantees other human rights in accordance with the instrumental strategy.
>
> C) Third, the cantilever strategy. It means that the right to migrate could be recognized as an expansion of human rights. When the right of free movement within the State is evidently recognized as a human right, then the right of free movement across the boundaries of the State must be recognized because of its nature as an extension of the previous right. Therefore, according to this strategy, it should not be hard to recognize the right to migrate, so long as it is an extension of another right which is considered a fundamental source for the new one.[107]

Article 13 of the Universal Declaration of Human Rights has obviously addressed an insufficient right to migrate, where it articulated that the right to leave as a human right should be available for any person to leave any country, as well as their own, to settle in another one. However, the obstacle in executing this right is when a person is, in fact, prevented from departing

---

[106] Fine, Sarah; Ypi, Lea (2016): Migration in political theory. The ethics of movement and membership / edited by Sarah Fine and Lea Ypi. First edition. Oxford: Oxford University Press. P. 14.
[107] Fine, Sarah; Ypi, Lea (2016): Migration in political theory. The ethics of movement and membership, ibid. P. 15,16.

his country, despite the extension in article 15 that has supported the general meaning of the right to leave in article 13. Article 15 declares the right for everyone to maintain his nationality and at the same time to get another nationality after his resettlement in a country outside his own. It says: "No one shall be arbitrarily deprived of his nationality nor denied the right to change his nationality."[108]

Recalling the right to leave mentioned in article 13, there is an argument that this right is almost executed in such a specific situation in which citizens regularly migrate from their State according to the State's considerations. Then, they can be regulated migrants only under some terms the State addresses. However, the right of a person to leave his State can become a control strategy when a State decides to prohibit the person from departing its territories, treating him like State property to look after its interests. Then, according to this Act, the State has overridden the essence of the right to leave as a human right enshrined in the UDHR, and aims to achieve purposes related to the person.[109] Nevertheless, by analyzing the right to leave, there are three interpretations of this article:

> A) The first interpretation focuses on free movement, the right to leave established on the ground of a person's claim to travel abroad without any restrictions of his origin State; thus, it treats the movement with one country. Therefore, a person has access to developing his own life when he moves forward and exits his State to access another country, deal with another society, and experience new opportunities in many fields.[110]
>
> B) The second interpretation, the right to leave is established on a claim to relocate and move between two countries. It says that everyone has the right to reside within the borders of each State, so, the article also outlines the claim to relocate permanently to another country when the person leaves his own, then the right to leave here is grounded on the claim to change residence from the destination State. In other words,

---

[108]http://www.un.org/en/documets/udhr.
[109] Fine, Sarah; Ypi, Lea. Ibid. P. 57.
[110] Ibid. P. 59.

the person has, in this case, an extraordinary interest in fulfilling specific purposes to improve his life in a good way, which is why he decided to seek asylum. The person fleeing from persecution in his country probably considered that whenever he gains a new residence in the destination country, he becomes a citizen after some time. Then, he has the right to get the nationality of the destination country, and then he becomes a citizen. This leads to the third interpretation of the article.

C) The third interpretation of Article 13 involves the right to exit. The right to leave here is grounded on a claim to abandon the national obligations of citizenship in the country of origin and being free from restrictions of allegiance to a person's State if he has a serious intention to leave his State and thus, he becomes immune to coercion to comply with his national obligations. However, this interpretation of the right to leave has been established on the assumption that a person has the whole freedom to consent to national obligations in his State or to renounce them without any influencing role by the State in his right to self-determination.[111]

The Right to Leave in the International Covenant on Civil and Political Rights (ICCPR) 1966:

The International Covenant on Civil and Political Rights proposed a similar form of the right to leave to the one defined in the Universal Declaration of Human Rights. The (ICCPR) has endorsed the right to leave explicitly in article 12.2 when it says: "Everyone shall be free to leave any country, including his own." Then the International Covenant on Civil and Political Rights provides the right to leave to every person as a fundamental right, and an "indispensable condition for the free development of a person" related to other rights in the covenant. The right to leave must be analyzed thoroughly in all its paragraphs to find references in this article.

The first paragraph of Article 12 asserts a person's right to move freely within

---

[111] Ibid. P. 59, 60.

the territory of his country. In other words, the article has enshrined the internal free movement for every person as a human right, and it confers this right to all persons who live in the country, whether civilians or even foreigners equally.

Article 12.1."Everyone lawfully within the territory of a State shall, within that territory, have the right to liberty of movement and freedom to choose his residence."

Fundamentally, everyone existing in any State has the right to choose anywhere to live inside this State, according to this part of article 12. Mainly it considers internal movement within the territories in the State for the foreigners whose status when they entered the State is legal or has become legal, in addition to the civilians. Thus, this kind of freedom is guaranteed by the law once the foreigner is lawfully in that State, and it requires to justify its actions when dealing with foreigners in a different way from that of civilians.[112]

The second paragraph of the article has gone further as it includes another type of movement when a person leaves his country and moves across borders, regardless of the reasons and purposes of leaving. Besides that, the article had not determined a period for a person's residence outside his country. The UN Human Rights Committee in 1999, in its General Comment No. 273 mentioned instructions on what article 12. 2 intended, clarifying that the right may not be dependent on any specific purpose or on the period the individual chooses to stay outside the country.

Consequently, this paragraph of the article concluded that all travelers abroad, and immigrants for a permanent time have the right to choose their destination. It entitled to all persons who are lawfully in the State, such as civilians or legal aliens, in addition to the persons who faced expulsion for any reason from the State and the State guarantees the total discretion to them in choosing their destination as well.

Furthermore, this paragraph has firmly imposed obligations on the State of nationality. On the one hand, the State of nationality must issue a passport

---

[112] Human Rights Committee: General Comments Adopted by The Human Rights Committee Under Article 40, Paragraph 4, of The International Covenant on Civil and Political Rights. CCPR/C/21/Rev.1/Add.9. 1 November 1999. P. 2.

for the person who lives in the destination State, or prolong it to enable him to leave the State of residence or to move abroad wherever he wants. Moreover, on the other hand, the nationality State cannot even argue that the person can return without a passport to its territories. In other words, it should not deprive any person of enjoying his right of free movement because of his passport, nor place obstacles in the way of a person seeking to leave. Paragraph 2 of article 12 says: "Everyone shall be free to leave any country, including his own."

The third paragraph of article 12 discusses the restrictions on the right to leave, which were practical exceptions in which States can restrict the rights in paragraphs (1) and (2) of the article, only when the rights are not compatible with the public order or national security, or if they threaten the public health, other people's rights and their freedom. Thus, the restrictions served and protected the aforementioned purposes.

This paragraph establishes a condition for the State, in which all these restrictions must be provided by law and must not impair the essence of the right. Then States must prove the conformality between their restrictions and the requirements mentioned in article 12. Also, applying these restrictions should be consistent with the other rights guaranteed by the ICCPR, as well as with the general principle of the right of equality and non-discrimination. Paragraph 3 of article 12 of the ICCPR: "The above-mentioned rights shall not be subject to any restrictions except those which are provided by law, are necessary to protect national security, public order, public health or morals or the rights and freedoms of others and are consistent with the other rights recognized in the present Covenant"[113].

The fourth paragraph of article 12: "No one shall be arbitrarily deprived of the right to enter his own country." This paragraph involves two important elements: the first is a person's right to enter his country, whether he was a broad and decided to return to his own country or even if he was born in another country and has never visited the country of his nationality and then wanted to return to it (this right has very important implications for refugees who seek voluntary repatriation). The term "his own country", which was used to refer to the country of nationality, either by birth or by conferral, as

---

[113] Ibid. P. 3,4.

well as the country of nationality which has been given or transferred to another entity. In this case, the individual still has ties to his country despite this transfection, and he cannot be considered a foreigner. However, the second element of the right to return is when a person faces enforced expulsion to other countries but, in this case, the right to return to his country mentioned in the article protects him[114]. When Paragraph 4 mentions the right to enter one's own country, it emphasizes that it should be applicable to all persons without any kind of discrimination, and also that no one may be deprived of the right to enter his own country or stripped of his nationality or even expelled him to a third country[115].

The Right to Leave in the ECHR:

The European Convention on Human Rights has titled the right to leave with the same orientation towards liberty as Article 12 of the ICCPR had previously addressed it. It is intended for persons who are lawfully in the territory, that have the right of free movement and of choosing their residence within that territory; hence, unlawful persons are not considered according to this provision as eligible persons to get such right according to this point. The restrictions on this right could be imposed with a kind of discretion on unlawful persons. However, there could be some issues concerning article 8 of the ECHR arising in this case, which enshrined the right to respect personal autonomy except for unlawful persons in contrarily with the provision in Article (1) that requires all contracting parties in the ECHR to respect and ensure the rights and freedoms of all persons within their jurisdiction, without distinguishing between lawful and unlawful persons. Moreover, a person's lawfulness "refers to the domestic law"; for instance, when this law establishes some requirements, then the person has to meet them all according to the State's domestic law, in order to benefit from the provision of Protocol 7 of the Convention (which guarantees the person's right against expulsion if he is a lawful resident in the State). Otherwise, he will be considered an unlawful person that cannot stay within the territory because, for example, he did not submit a refugee request to the State's authority when repealing his residence permit. Correspondingly, the States have no right to classify a person unlawful in their domestic law, thus

---

[114] Ibid. P. 5.
[115] Ibid. P. 6.

enjoying any guaranteed right in international law, such as the right to asylum from persecution.[116]

Article 2 of Protocol 4 of the European Convention on Human Rights:

> "1. Everyone who is lawfully within the territory of a State shall, within that territory, have the right to liberty of movement and freedom to choose his residence.
>
> 2. Everyone shall be free to leave any country, including his own.
>
> 3. No restrictions shall be placed on the exercise of these rights other than such as are in accordance with the law and are necessary in a democratic society for interests of national security or public safety, for the maintenance of order public, for the prevention of crime, for the protection of health or morals, or for the protection of the rights and freedoms of others.
>
> 4. The rights set forth in paragraph (1) may also be subject, areas, to restrictions imposed in accordance with the law and justified by the public interest in a democratic society[117]."

Art 15.2 of the ECHR "No derogation from Article 2, except in respect of deaths resulting from lawful acts of war, or Articles 3, 4(1) and Article 7 shall be made under this provision".

Neither Article 15.2 of the ECHR nor Article 4.2 of the ICCPR[118] are applicable under Article 6 of protocol (4) which proscribes a derogation from the right to leave.

The Right to Leave in the Treaty on Functioning of European Union (TFEU):

The Treaty on Functioning of the European Union was one of the European initiatives for ensuring a person's right to leave his country, which was supposed to be a European country, and resettle in another country that is

---

[116] Nuala Mole, Catherine Meredith, Asylum, and the European Convention on Human Rights. Council of Europe publishing, 2010. P. 175,176.

[117] European Convention on Human Rights: echr.coe.int/documents/convention_eng.pdf. P. 37.

[118] Article 4.2 of ICCPR says: "No derogation from articles 6, 7, 8 (paragraphs I and 2), 11, 15, 16 and 18 may be made under this provision". International Covenant on Civil and Political Rights, United Nations Human Rights, Office of The High Commissioner. (ohchr.org/en/professional interest/pages/ccpr.aspx

also a member State of the European Union.

Article 21 (1) of the TFEU says that: "Every citizen of the Union shall have the right to move and reside freely within the territory of the Member States, subject to the limitations and conditions laid down in the Treaties and by the measures adopted to give them effect"[119].

The article has announced how any member State must deal with the situation of a European asylum seeker leaving his country and crossing the borders of a member State to reside within its territory. Thus, there is obviously a missing situation that this article hid not discuss: when persons can leave their countries of origin regardless of whether those countries were member States in the European Union or not. Perhaps, Art 21 should be extended to comprise not only the citizens of the EU but also every person who is subjected to internal conflict or persecution.

On the other hand, at least Art 21 of the TFEU has addressed the right to leave as one of the most important rights that all European citizens should enjoy without any restrictions. However, the article, in the second and third paragraphs, has given the necessary powers to the European Parliament and the Council to adopt provisions to facilitate the practicing of the right to leave that the first paragraph mentioned. Furthermore, it provided the power to take measures related to social security or protection to the Council, in accordance with a particular legislative procedure after consulting the European Parliament for the same objective mentioned in the first paragraph.[120] Moreover, the Consolidated Treaty on the Functioning of the European Union TFEU in Art 78 went further regarding the right to leave in Article 2, so as to justify the right to asylum in the European Union as well. Art 78 legitimated the right to asylum in the European Union, and it also affirmed the need of developing the standard policy of the European Union on asylum, subsidiary protection, and temporary protection to provide the required protection to any third-country national in accordance with the Refugee Convention of 1951 and its Protocol in 1967, while maintaining the

---

[119] Consolidated Version of the Treaty on the Functioning of the European Union, Official Journal of the European Union, 2012. C 326/57.
[120] Ibid. Article 21, Paragraphs 2,3. C 326/57.

non-refoulement principle.[121]

Conclusion

After examining the essential documents in International Law, in addition to European Law, this section reached the conclusion that the right to leave is, in fact, present in legal approaches, specifically in Art. 13 of the Universal Declaration of Human Rights does indeed grant this right to every person in general as a response to the vital interest of moving freely. Moreover, the right to leave is legitimated by the States as well, grounded on its nature of being a human right, which is why it deserves to be protected internationally. Besides, States have no right to set up restrictions on a person's right to leave his country, as well as the right to seek and enjoy asylum, which is also recognized in Art. 14 of the UDHR, as long as the armed conflict or persecution is still present in his country, for he would be subject to a risk of being persecuted again if the host State did not grant him protection and instead decided to return him to his origin country, that if the host State has such a right at all, because the Court of Justice of the EU and the European Court of Human Rights asserted to offer international protection to those people who are subject to a risk of being persecuted in their country.

The Case of Open Borders in Philosophical Approaches:

The potential question coming to mind is, what would happen if the whole World's borders were open? Can we exceed the current boundaries and get just a united body to affect free movement?

The notion of free movement is strongly connected with the principle of self-determination of the legitimate States, also the freedom of association and, consequently that makes this freedom an integral component of self-determination. There is no doubt there will be different opinions regarding the State's willingness to deal with foreigners or to refrain from this treatment. There are obviously different perspectives and essential aspects in the debate on the case of open borders. Most of the philosophical discussions elaborate on the conditions that migrants should comply with and the right

---

[121] Bacaian, Livia Elena, The protection of refugees and their right to seek asylum in the European Union Mémoire présenté pour l'obtention du Master en études européennes par Livia Elena Bacaian rédigé sous la direction de Nicolas Wisard Jurée : Master in European Studies, Geneva. INSTITUT EUROPÉEN DE L'UNIVERSITÉ DE GENÈVE, 2011. P. 22.

of migrants to stay in the host county on the one hand, and the State's right to exclude those persons who pose real danger or threaten its order, security and public health or any other consideration according to the State, on the other hand.

The Egalitarian and Libertarian Cases of Open Borders:

This section consists of two different legal and philosophical overviews to answer the question of whether there is a right of free movement crossing the borders of countries or whether the borders should be closed although there are people who are persecuted are desperately in need to leave their countries of origin because they require international protection elsewhere abroad.

The Egalitarian Case of Open Borders:

Initially, egalitarians advocate a general principle that all persons are equal in deserving merits and moral considerations, "the equality of opportunity."[122] Thus, if a person has been born in a certain country that will hold a lot of consequences and would be significantly affecting his life in many aspects, in other words, a person does not choose where to be born, so a person who is born in a poor part of Norway ,for instance, has a better life than a person born in a poor part of any African State. Hence, the latter person could wish to leave his country to resettle in Norway, although that would not be acceptable for Norway, which will hinder this kind of migration. Consequently, egalitarians deny this fact and affirm that all people should enjoy free movement in this regard. Also, the freedom here should be correspondingly compatible with the right of the State to exclude that person. Nevertheless, egalitarians argue that open borders should be prioritized in this arrangement and pushed up because it is more critical than the presumptive rights of the State because, for them, the most important thing is poor people surviving poverty that they did not even choose for they did not choose to be born in a certain country. [123]

Thus, egalitarian considerations are so basic such as undeserved poverty in

---

[122] Carol M. Swain (2018): Debating Immigration. Second edition, Cambridge University Press. New York. P. 288.

[123] Wellman, Christopher Heath; Cole, Phillip, Debating the ethics of immigration. Is there a right to exclude? / Christopher Heath Wellman and Phillip Cole. New York, Oxford: Oxford University Press, 2011.P. 57, 59.

this example, then they can override the right of the States to control their borders and seek to promote certain policies concerning immigration in order to eliminate an unjust situation and to achieve a kind of international equality.[124]

Wellman illustrated many opposing critical views in his book, and he considered them plausible when they denied the egalitarian argument. One of them is that wealthy countries help poor countries in many ways without being committed to opening their borders. So, wealthy countries can shirk from any obligation to resolve poverty in the World without being forced to open its borders. He explained a point about economic equality that says the people who are agree with equality in moral considerations insist that not all inequality in the world should be eliminated. Thus, some faces of equality are not considered of "moral importance," such as economic equality, which implies that every person should have enough and, therefore, this does not mean having the same economic status. In other words, is everyone had enough, it would be "morally problematic" because some have more than others, and those people who have more, have not done anything more important than those who have less, they were just lucky enough to have been born in a wealthy country. Consequently, some defenders of the egalitarian approach of open borders (luck egalitarians) affirm that the equality they aim to reach in the economic aspect is not possible. If we take a look at Norway's high economic status, for example, we could say that it may be the result of its efforts and its hard-working people, on the one hand, but there is also the key factor of how the people born in Norway have a greater chance, but their efforts are rewarded, which is something that does not happen in an African country. This, in turn, creates a situation of undeserved inequality on the other hand.[125] As a result, the inequality between the Norwegians and the poor people in Africa could be morally significant just because this comparison is merely grounded on luck. So, not every inequality is considered to be morally significant, but the undeserved good fortune is inequal and unjust.[126]

On the other hand, some people are against the "egalitarian luck" and their

---

[124] Ibid. P. 59.
[125] Carol M. Swain (2018): Debating Immigration, ibid. P. 288, 289.
[126] Wellman, Christopher Heath; Cole, Phillip, Debating the ethics of immigration, ibid. P. 60.

notion of inequality and said that what is more important is that inequality is only relevant when it oppresses those are less well-off.

According to Wellman, he concludes about the relationship between Norwegians and Chadians that if Norway should open its borders to poor foreigners such as the Chadians as a commitment to eliminate the inequality that would be "morally problematic" according to the egalitarian perspective. He says that "undeserved inequality needs not to be unjust as long as it does not give rise to oppression."[127] Thus, relational egalitarianism considers that when there is no relationship between two different parties, such as the Norwegians and the Chadians, this lack of relationship cannot create oppression or even domination. Consequently, if there is not any kind of oppressive relationship between two parties, then it would not be the duty of the wealthy State to contribute to distributive justice and open its borders to those who are poor.

However, some egalitarians defend their opinion of open borders that although there is inequality between the wealthy State (Norway) and poor State (Chad), people shouldn't prefer luck egalitarianism over relational egalitarianism because relational egalitarianism can reduce the wealth disparities between the different States. Although, they still claim that wealthy States, like Norway, have duties in terms of distributive justice towards the poor States in the World.[128] Thus, according to Wellman, the relationship between countries in our World today with increasing globalization impacts has become more "interconnected" and, hence relational egalitarians have to admit that with globalization the problem deepens deepened because it makes somehow the Norwegians dominate Chad and Chadians, and that leads us to absolute worrying about the Chadians. Then, wealthy States must play a restitutive role to the poor people abroad but despite this Wellman says that nothing could affect "the legitimate State's right to set its own immigration policy, and whatever duties of distributive justice that wealthy States have to those abroad, they need not be paid in the currency of open borders." [129]

---

[127] Wellman, Christopher Heath; Cole, Phillip. Ibid. P. 64.
[128] Carol M. Swain (2018): Debating Immigration. Second edition, Cambridge University Press. New York. P. 300.
[129] Wellman, Christopher Heath; Cole, Phillip, ibid. P. 64,65,66.

Contrarily, David Miller has a different view of open border. He considers that when rich countries open their borders to poor foreigners to assist them and to eliminate the inequality that egalitarians seek to achieve, that may lead to a problem that could be significantly worse than inequality, which is the brain drain, that means depriving poor countries of the most qualified people that go somewhere else in search of better opportunities, then making it poorer at the time it is extremely in need to those people to improve itself. Miller asserts that the best way to help is when rich countries aid the poor by sending aid to where they live, without needing to open their borders.

As we have seen, the duties of wealthy States of distributive justice can be carried out in many ways, not only through opening their borders and thus "retaining their rights to freedom of association."[130]

Wellman explains that he agrees with the defenders who opt for "separate but equal" arrangements. To clarify this, he used as an example the relation between Martians and Earthlings, where the latter are poor only in comparison with the former. However, Earthlings are not 'absolutely poor' when there is no comparison, which is why the Earthlings' situation is similar to Norway in the sense that Earthlings are satisfied with their lives and hence, Martians can choose to recoil from distributive justice duties. Furthermore, they are not forced to admit the Earthlings to live with them. Wellman claims that separate but equal, or even separate and unequal, are not considered unjust so long as that doesn't lead to oppressing poor persons by the well-off ones, especially because both sides share "the significant relationship of being fellow citizens.

The egalitarian case of open borders has faced many objections. Perhaps the most decisive one stems from the political State, which will be illegitimate if it demands its citizens to renounce their citizenship and banish themselves, elsewhere outside its territories. The State must not make such nonconsensual coercion of the people who are in its territory, otherwise the State will not be able to justify acts, such as compelling any citizen to relinquish his citizenship and going abroad.

However, the right of the States to set their migration policy is still crucially considered as potential ground for admitting outsiders or even expelling them

---

[130] Ibid. P. 68.

from their territories. States are not obliged to accept persons coming from abroad to resettle in their land for two reasons:

> a) The first one is nonconsensual coercion, which means that the State has no right to force foreigners to give a share in its political community. Hence, its citizens will not be imposed to associate with the newcomers who need an admission to stay and live in the host State. The State would not be justified politically if it required its citizens to cover unreasonable costs because it should provide essential benefits and secure those benefits, such as protecting human rights. Therefore, it will not be justified or legitimated if it forced its citizens to supply those benefits.[131]
>
> b) The second reason is that the State avoided responsibly imposing unreasonable costs on both the citizens as well as foreigners. Thus, it remains a relevant right not to allow the immigrant to enter its territories and forcibly evict its citizens, which deprives them of their membership and thus of being considered a political subject.[132] In both situations, the State is responsible not to make any "unreasonable demands" on its citizens. In addition to that, evicting citizens is much more of an imposition than denying entry to ordinary immigrants. Therefore, the State can make a plausible distinction between both previous situations.[133]

Moreover, liberal egalitarians have different opinions on justifying the case of open borders, such as Joseph Carens, who attempts, as all liberal egalitarians do, to ensure that all persons are free and equal and insists that all the constituted borders between States set obstacles on the fulfillment of equality and enhancing freedom. Thus, some liberal egalitarians consider coercion an explicit infringement of the principles of the liberal egalitarians, which is applied when denying people's freedoms. In addition to that, Carens discussed the interest of free international movement grounded on the link between both, free internal movement, and free international movement. The

---

[131] Wellman, Christopher Heath; Cole, Phillip. Ibid. P. 76.
[132] Carol M. Swain (2018): Debating Immigration. Second edition, Cambridge University Press. New York, USA. P. 287.
[133] Wellman, Christopher Heath; Cole, Phillip. Ibid. P. 76.

latter, in his opinion, promotes a basic interest and, hence, it needs to be protected by a right. Based on this, he considers this basic interest a fundamental human right, and he calls to adopt the libertarian egalitarians 'principles to support his theory about open borders and non-limiting immigration. [134]

In this regard, Carens has illustrated three arguments that justify open borders:

The first argument is that the States 'control by limiting immigration would limit the people's freedom to move wherever they want because this right is "an important human freedom in itself." He justifies that by considering freedom as "a prerequisite" to other kinds of freedoms. Thus, every person should have the right to go wherever he wants, so long as that is not inconsistent with the other people's legitimate claims. Moreover, he emphasizes that freedom of movement is essential for its role in "individual autonomy," and opening the borders up would reinforce that freedom. This argument supports the liberal egalitarians' theory about open borders because Carens also argues that freedom of movement will always be constrained, but these restrictions must be justified morally by taking into account both, the interests of the outsiders as well as the ones of the people inside, in order to make these restrictions equitable to all persons.[135]

The second argument is that freedom of movement is very important to achieve "equality of opportunity," so that democratic States shall respond to the need of acknowledgment. In this sense, the standards which have to apply to a person, whether a person deserves to live in a developed society or not, depend on the skills or a person's efforts and, hence, they should rely on the person's capacity and not on the "unchosen birth related characteristics like race, class" and so on.

Carens also affirms that the equality of opportunity is inherently related to the concept of "equal moral worth," which considers that "there are no natural hierarchies of birth that entitle people to an advantageous social position", and persons should be able to go wherever they want to in search

---

[134] Carens, Joseph H. (2013 // 2015). The ethics of immigration. 1. issued as an Oxford Univ. Press paperback. New York: Oxford University Press; Oxford Univerisity Press (Oxford political theory). P. 227.
[135] Ibid. P. 227.

of better opportunities.[136]

According to Carens, an example of the relation between free movement and equality of opportunity is "feudalism," because: "under feudalism, there was no commitment to equal opportunity." He ensures that in our world today or under feudalism, equality of opportunities according to the social order in every State is constituted as a right that should be given to everyone who lives there, and because of the closed borders between the States, equality of opportunities cannot prevail. So, the opportunities will be much different between the States. Thus, social circumstances determine a person's opportunities because the States have the total discretion to control immigration and close their borders, which is why there cannot be equal opportunities. In this sense, freedom of movement and open borders are essential prerequisites for equal opportunities.

The third argument is that freedom of movement is a key factor in declining the current social, economic, and political inequality. Carens has argued that open borders could lead to equal economic opportunities for people in poor countries, if they were free to move to rich countries legally in order to benefit from more opportunities and so achieve freedom and equality for all.[137]

Carens justification for open borders has had some objections regarding his perspective on the right to movement as a fundamental human right, and how restricting immigration infringes the "ideal of moral equality."

Let's start with the first objection. David Miller says that Carens overstated the moral value of free movement when he tried to justify it as a genuine human right. Miller has referred to the importance of distinguishing between two types of human interests: basic and bare interests. Basic interests, according to Miller, should be vital and, therefore, they need to be protected by rights. In contrast, bare interests are "a legitimate interest" and so they do not require protection. Carens considers freedom of movement as a basic interest when he deems free movement to be at the same level as internal movement, which is a basic interest, and would therefore need to be

---

[136] Ibid. P. 228.
[137] Carens, Joseph H. (2013 // 2015). The ethics of immigration. 1. issued as an Oxford Univ. Press paperback. New York: Oxford University Press; Oxford Univerisity Press (Oxford political theory). P. 228.

protected.[138] In contrast, Miller agrees that free movement is at the same level as internal free movement and, hence, is a basic interest only in the case of people who are in desperate need to leave their countries of origin because of persecution, in which immigration is the only way out . However, he says that, in general, we cannot consider free movement a basic interest when it is, in fact, a bare interest because many people wish to leave their countries and resettle somewhere else to get a better life. Despite that, they all have their basic rights in their countries of origin, safeguarding by their government to give them opportunities. Therefore, the right of international free movement could be a "remedial right" to those people whose basic rights are not protected in their countries, but it is not a basic right. However, the following discussion will address Carens's justification in the libertarian case for open borders, in which he elaborates on why he favors open borders from a libertarian perspective.[139]

The second objection by Michael Blake was on Caren's presumption that when a State restricts immigration, it infringes the "ideal of moral equality" Michael Blake bases his objection on the nature of citizenship, which Carens considered morally irrelevant. Blake finds citizenship is "morally significant" because it delimits the boundaries and thus, the authority of every State, which means that the State has an authority over all its citizens that it does not have over foreigners. Liberal States, whose authority should be justified to the citizens, cannot control those who are outside their borders, so that Liberal States are not forced to justify depriving foreigners of some rights as moral equals.[140] Thus, only when the State coerces those under its power, must it provide justification and guarantees. Liberal States do not need to justify their authority or to expand those rights, which include the right of free movement to foreigners. Consequently, Blake argues that liberal States can legitimately limit immigration and do not open their borders to foreigners.[141]

Liberal egalitarians sought to endorse open borders and make this mandatory,

---

[138] Shelly Wilcox, Journal Compilation, Philosophy Compass 4/1 (2009). The Open Borders Debate on Immigration. San Francisco State University. Blackwell publishing. P. 4.
[139] Ibid. P. 4.
[140] Carol M. Swain (2018): Debating Immigration. Second edition, Cambridge University Press. New York, P. 297.
[141] Shelly Wilcox, ibid. P. 5.

at least in ideal circumstances. However, because the circumstances that we experience in our World today are not ideal at all, they reject closed borders and suggest to just "curtailing open borders", at least under provisions, to maintain the principle of equality which has taken on a new meaning in these circumstances. Liberal egalitarians make an interesting suggestion with which I agree, which is implementing porous borders, that is to say, opening the borders more than they currently are.[142]

I relation to this, Abizadeh asked the following question, how had the liberal egalitarians justified the restrictions on the open borders in a manner consistent with their values? To answer this question, he provides five arguments elaborating on the justifications as follows:

The first argument is the current global economic inequality, similar to what Carens said regarding "the industrialized liberal democratic regimes", if they open their borders to immigration dramatically, this will negatively influence the capacity of their societies to deal with all these numbers and, consequently, this would destroy the public order. Carens argues that open borders can pose a serious threat to public order in the host country's society. Therefore, it could be more reasonable to curtail the freedom of movement provisionally, based on guaranteeing freedom and equality to everyone. Otherwise, if the public order is destroyed, everyone would do worse in both, welfare and liberty.[143]

The second argument is manifest in the current global inequalities. When the wealthy industrialized States receive an influx of poor immigrants, this could damage their economy and collapse it completely, which would be worse than limiting free movement, and would seem not very urgent when compared to the breakdown of countries' economics.[144]

Carens retorts to this argument that "like the argument of public order, it gets much of its power from the assumption of discussing open borders in our world now without reducing the inequality between States." Thus, it would be a big incentive for poor people to move to rich countries. In addition to that, he asked whether this argument of the welfare State would grant justified

---

[142] Arash Abizadeh, 2006, Liberal Egalitarian Arguments for Closed Borders, Some Preliminary Critical Reflections. Ethics and Economics, 4 (1), Department of Political Science, McGill University. P. 1, 2.
[143] Ibid. P. 2,3.
[144] Ibid. P. 3.

objection to open borders, even in a "more egalitarian world." To answer that, he said that there are some States that prefer to have extensive welfare, whereas others are rich. If the borders were opened, some people from the rich States would want to move to one that has extensive welfare. That might be subject to discussion to justify the restrictions that democratic States would set on immigration, but Carens affirms that open borders as an issue would have positive effects, but welfare would also be a large incentive. We need to take "measures short of discretionary closure" for solving the stemming problems. For instance, the "generous welfare State" can specify certain waiting periods before entering immigrants into its welfare program.[145]

The third argument lies in the fact that hosting a countless number of immigrants, who are from another cultural background, would hinder the "democratic capacity to effect socio-political integration". This argument is based on the normative premise of social disintegration. There are other similar opinions concerning this argument, such as the view of the political philosopher Will Kymlicka, who is one of the most important supporters of the lack of egalitarianism. He assures the need of cultural nationalist policies to achieve the socio-political integration required in liberal democracy. This constitutes a kind of cultural homogeneity that we could not remove if the borders were not closed. However, his view was controversial, for two reasons: First, they say that liberal democracy does not need to have a sole national culture to make social integration. Second, in case the liberal democracy was established on a minimum level of what is called cultural homogeneity, and thus some members of the homogeneity group demanded "State-sponsored policies of integration", these policies are not grounded mainly on closed borders but, in contrast, they are applied in the federal States in which the borders are open. They mentioned Canada as an efficient example to prove that the industrial liberal democracy has the highest number of immigrants from almost all cultures around the World because its migration policy is based on open borders. Canada is today, according to the global relevant indicators, one of the best liberal democracies that has

---

[145] Carens, Joseph H. (2013 // 2015). The ethics of immigration. 1. issued as an Oxford Univ. Press paperback. New York: Oxford University Press; Oxford University Press (Oxford political theory). P. 280, 281.

succeeded in its integration measures.[146]

Fourth, admitting large numbers of immigrants is a consequence of open borders, and thus, that will threaten the "domestic liberal democratic institutions" because of the anti-liberal immigrants who have vandalistic political intentions. This argument has placed all foreigners in a single category without distinction, it is based on the illiberal immigrants who have subversive intentions and want to destroy the liberal democratic institutions. This argument tried to justify controlling the borders and setting some restrictions on those who have such political intentions by only preventing them from entry. It is maybe an "empirical sociological claim" and could be based on exaggerated fears. However, it can be controlled, even with fewer restrictions on open borders than the current ones.[147]

The fifth argument is that open borders could compromise the capacity of the State to provide welfare to all residents, including its citizens. According to this argument, any wealthy country responsibly provides benefits and welfare to all citizens, but with open borders, there would be others who would have resettled in its territories and, hence, it should provide welfare to those new residents, which would collapse the completely, establishing "the controversial empirical premise that industrialized liberal democratic countries domestic welfare regimes will completely collapse if they opened up their borders", which is the "strong version." Therefore, those countries, such as America, have a duty to put up some restrictions on entry.[148] The argument made a straightforward comparison between freedom of movement (open borders) and wrecking welfare completely. If we agree with the idea that the freedom of movement is not a "basic liberty" but "a socio-economic good", the losses due to the collapse of welfare clearly overwhelm the gains of free movement which would justify closed borders because that would rescue welfare to achieve global justice on the grounds of "consolidation and gradual expansion of existing liberal democratic welfarist institutions".[149] Thus, this argument depends on curtailing the range of the

---

[146] Arash Abizadeh, 2006, Liberal Egalitarian Arguments for Closed Borders, Some Preliminary Critical Reflections. Ethics and Economics, 4 (1), Department of Political Science, McGill University, ibid. P. 3, 4.

[147] Ibid. P. 4.

[148] Carol M. Swain (2018): Debating Immigration. Second edition, Cambridge University Press. New York, USA. P. 276.

[149] Arash Abizadeh, 2006, ibid. P.4,5.

people who effectively benefit from domestic welfare. It deems the restrictions on the open borders might be for a short term. In addition to that, it entails a condition to accompany with policies that are able to cover any losses that could result from closing the borders by providing a serious contribution to expanding global welfare. However, the collapse of this argument presumes that borders could be more open than they are at the current time, and that would not lead to welfare. In this sense, the porous borders policy was the safest alternative of this argument, and not closed borders.

On the other hand, the strain of the welfare argument is based on the assumption that if we make borders more open, that will surely overwork the institutions of the State in terms of providing welfare to all its citizens. It intended to justify the closed borders by assuming that the citizens have a "special responsibility" to their fellow citizens because of their welfare. This responsibility is basically the result of rescuing the poor domestic citizens, and this special responsibility is clearly much more significant than the general responsibility regarding the welfare of the global poor with open borders.[150]

This argument has met many criticisms. Some liberal egalitarians have adopted the following argument in which they agree with closed borders.

They say achieving equality for all persons' interests requires relying on relations between all citizens or even between moral agents that should be impartial to the moral agents or the citizens. They have implied that these relations result in special responsibilities regarding those people with whom we have a relationship. This special responsibility has two forms.[151]

First, when we have a special responsibility for having special considerations. This is considered an associative duty to our "near and dear".

Second, when we can give such special considerations according to associative liberties. Hence, according to Samuel Scheffler, the relations should be "independent sources of reasons for action", and then they would be considered non- instrumental relations. Consequently, there will be special responsibilities that are consistent with the moral integrity of "equal worth"

---

[150] Ibid. P. 5.
[151] Ibid. P.6.

regarding all the participants of the relation, as well as a vital constituent of moral agency or human welfare. But this opinion has been criticized because the norm is to determine whether the relation of citizenship is a necessary constituent for the moral agency or if it is, in fact, a potential constituent of human welfare. Robert Goodin argues that the special responsibilities are "devices whereby the moral community's general duties get assigned to particular agents" because this assignment is considered an efficient way to "discharge the general duties globally."[152] Additionally, Scheffler claims that even if the special responsibilities of the citizens to their fellow others in a certain State were justified in being a way to reach "equal moral worth" (as liberal egalitarianism requires), the special responsibilities would still be open to two kinds of objections:

The first is the "voluntarist objection," which means that when a person merely participates in a relation, that will not imply any commitment or special responsibility to each other. However, only "voluntary undertaking" allows them to acquire such duty, which is proceeded by general duties that all persons comply with voluntarily.[153]

The second objection is the "distributive objection," which affirms that since the special responsibilities respond to the interests of the insiders according to their citizenship, then it would be unjust if these responsibilities generated a kind of inequality in distributing the welfare to others (outsiders). Furthermore, this requires closing the borders and not letting outsiders enter. That describes the global inequality in our World today because he argues that "special responsibilities could be forced only with open borders." The objection outlined that the relationship that participants constitute, serves their distinctive interests and also entails special responsibilities towards one another, but if it forces them not to admit outsiders in their society, this responsibility of giving special preference to each other would be subject to objections.

On account of that, the responsibilities could be justifiable for closing borders only in two cases: if the special responsibilities required closing borders to be effectively fulfilled, or if the requirement of the special

---

[152] Ibid. P. 6. 7.
[153] Ibid. P. 7.

responsibilities does not negatively affect the general responsibilities towards the outsiders.[154] The latter case devotes distributive objection when the State closes its borders coercively against outsiders. This act of coercion needs a reasonable justification, and this should be compatible with the principles of justice that liberal egalitarians mention in their argument (equality and freedom), especially since there are persons (outsiders) who require free movement and the State has restricted their freedom by force. Consequently, the State will try to justify its coercion as it was trying to fulfill special responsibilities towards its citizens, which would not be possible if the borders were open. Hence, the outsiders could not object to its justification.[155]

The Libertarian Case of Open Borders:

Libertarians have different ideas about migration and open borders. Their opinion is based on the principle of self-ownership and, hence, the right of property, which is at the core of their argument for open borders. There are two types of Libertarian stances: the right-libertarian, and the left-libertarian. Right-libertarians believe in "full self-ownership" as they do not consider the idea of redistributive welfare justifies legitimate actions. Besides, they have a different interpretation of John Locke's provision. They assure that people would do worst in a State that does not allow its citizens to use its natural resources. Thus, they believe in the free-mixing of persons' properties with natural resources, to turn "common property into private property," Robert Nozick had his own opinion in this regard. He argued that redistributive welfare would cause an "Anarchy State", and Utopia.[156]

However, left-libertarians have their own interpretation of Lockean proviso, they consider the natural resources in the State as property of all citizens, so individuals have "egalitarian claims" on them. They think of redistribution of resources between all individuals as an effective way that allows them to share incomes, properties, and more. Hiller Steiner was famously known as one of the left-libertarians.[157]

However, libertarians such as Robert Nozick and Hiller Steiner, precisely

---

[154] Ibid. P. 7,8.
[155] Ibid. P. 8.
[156] Todea, Diana Virginia. "Libertarianism and Immigration ". Libertarian Papers2, no.30 (2010). P.3.
[157] Ibid. P.3,4.

determine the role of the libertarian State in the "protection of property and contractual rights." They see that both claims of the State and the individual controlling their territory are based on the same idea of the right to control who can enter the territory and who cannot. Nozick, as a right libertarian, has not stated explicitly whether libertarians agree with allowing open borders or not, and has not discussed the case of asylum seekers who need to go to a safe society either. He has only outlined his arguments regarding hosting foreigners from the perspective of protecting the rights of property, and also the issue of an "anarchy State" as well as the right of individuals or a State to exclude foreigners, which will be discussed in more detail later.

Simultaneously, Hiller Steiner, who represents left-libertarians, has talked about his view on immigration and the case of open borders. His main argument is based on the transnational migration. He considers that every community should have the right to accept or reject foreigners based on "mutual consent", so individuals in a particular community can simply accept the immigrants if they want to. There is not any contractual commitment that forces them to do so. On the other hand, the State has no right to coerce its citizens to accept the immigrants because it would be an unjust interference with their personal rights.[158] Some critics have asked him to elaborate on his argument and specify the nature of the right of property in this argument so that it is more explicit, as to include only the citizens who have legitimate rights of property (which implies denying the rights of property of those who have obtained their properties in illegal ways). According to his argument, if foreigners want to join the liberal community, they should apply to the members of that community, and then, the members have the right to accept the foreigners or to refuse them, according to their own immigration policy.[159] However, there were some positive opinions regarding Steiner's concept of immigration (contractual rights), such as Onora O'Neill's stand on "the pure property rights of individuals and the freedom of contract independent of State powers". He objected to the libertarians' idea of absolute individual property rights because the State only legitimizes and safeguards those rights. In addition to their claims of individual moral rights, libertarians grant legitimacy to the State. O'Neill has two essential claims

---

[158] Ibid. P. 7, 8.
[159] Ibid. P. 9.

concerning Steiner's perspective. First, he assures the importance of Steiner's requirements of rejecting more inequitable restrictions on immigration than the current ones. The second claim is about the Libertarians' "foundational myth" and the State of nature. O'Neill agreed with Steiner when the latter articulated that the legitimate restrictions on free movement stem only from individual property rights, otherwise they would not be legitimated. Besides, he thinks that our World would be worse and more restricted than it currently is if there were no migration policies.[160]

Joseph Carens, who is known as one of the prominent supporters of the libertarian case, provided an example that reflects the libertarians' view on open borders with "the farmer from the United States who wanted to hire workers from Mexico. The government would have no right to prohibit him from doing this, or to prevent the Mexicans from coming, for this would violate the rights of both the American farmer and the Mexican workers to engage in voluntary transactions."[161]

This example shows how State' restrictions on migration would prevent both the insiders and outsiders from achieving their interests because these policies would deny the insider' right to act freely in his property, as well as the outsider's right of free movement while seeking a better life. Thus, there are two different approaches of the libertarian case for opening the borders:

The first one is property rights. They think that these rights could justify opening the borders because States cannot restrict immigration without reducing the authority of its constituents on their lands and, hence, the rights of the citizens in inviting foreigners to their properties, for this would be affected if the State prohibited foreigners from entering their political territories and then those properties.[162] Therefore, the State limiting immigration affects the property rights of insiders, in addition to the outsiders' rights of free movement. It would essentially be a deprivation of the owner from his sovereign rights over his property, according to the libertarians' perspective.

---

[160] Ibid. P. 10.
[161] Wellman, Christopher Heath; Cole, Phillip, Debating the ethics of immigration. Is there a right to exclude? / Christopher Heath Wellman and Phillip Cole. New York, Oxford: Oxford University Press. P. 79.
[162] Ibid. P. 79.

The second approach concerns freedom of association, so they object to the State closing borders and, hence its position on "restricting people's freedom to associate" (As Chandran Kukathas mentions). They assert that the State should respect the rights of its citizens as individuals and prioritize these rights over the collective right of the State regarding freedom of association because if this right to freedom of association is a collective right, it only benefits the State, and the citizens would not have any role. Contrarily, they would find themselves complying with that collective right. In other words, if the State decided to limit immigration as a collective political right, then individuals could not invite foreigners to their property unilaterally. Consequently, libertarians have chosen the rights of the individuals over the rights of the State, including the collective right to freedom of association.[163] Wellman called this situation a "conflict between a State 's right to control its political territory and an individual property owner's dominion over his land." Although some arguments advocate that the State must allow individuals to claim their rights of property because individual rights will overwhelm the State's rights so long as the individual rights are general and absolute, Wellman refuses to prioritize the "property owner's perfectly general and absolute dominion over his property" over the rights of the States to control their territories because, in his opinion, that would lead to "anarchism." Besides, he believes that property rights shall not be respected somehow when the State recognizes individual property rights but, at the same time, does not allow them to override the State's rights. Thus, property rights in this regard could only be curtailed by the State. Willman further elaborates his opinion by assuring that the most appropriate solution is to favor "the limited property rights and the statism over the unlimited property rights and then anarchism". He reached those conclusions after considering the following: if the State's policies deal in a kind of stability and justice to protect people' properties rights which should also be general and absolute, there would not be any qualms in terms of rights of property. But, if the State is not able to protect people's property rights in the case of "territorial contiguity", the State will find itself biasing its right to control the whole territory against the individual's property rights because contiguity implies

---

[163] Ibid. P. 80.

controlling all within State's territories.[164]

However, libertarians such as Nozick turned to another argument filled with individual self-determination, because if their main objective of protecting the property rights of individuals in their theory of self-ownership, which is one of its basic principles.

Nozick used the principle of self-ownership to explain his opinion on immigration and whether the minimal State would be justified if it closed its borders and restricted immigration. He has not answered this question directly, but it can be inferred that, according to him, the State has the right of coercing its citizens, as well as of providing and protecting their basic rights, simply because they are under its authority. Nozick claims that every person has a right to make some exchanges with others as individuals, but not as citizens. Therefore, the State has no right to interfere with this exchange if the individuals did not infringe on another individual's right. Later Nozick stated his position on immigration and saying that the State has no right to restrict it by closing borders, on the contrary, it must comply with individual self-determination. Nozick's view could be briefly summarized as the idea that the States should support immigration effectively by at least not restricting it.[165] In addition to that, Carens has asked if Nozick's approach provided any ground for the State, or even the individuals, to exclude aliens. Regarding this, he does not provide any ground for both entities: First, individuals can act freely on their interests, they can refuse to hire foreigners, feed them, grant them assistance, but they cannot force their fellow citizens not to hire foreigners and so on, because they have the right to exclude individuals as such, but not as "members of a collective."[166]

Secondly, regarding the State limiting immigration, as a collective action. Nozick has mentioned the distinction between States and small communities. If individuals choose to consolidate their properties and then decide, by a collective decision, not to admit any foreigners, they can limit the membership to their collective property. But, if collective ownership as a notion justifies not admitting the foreigners, this collective ownership may

---

[164] Ibid. P. 81.

[165] Carens, Joseph H. (1987): Aliens and Citizens: The Case for Open Borders. 2nd ed. 49 volumes: Cambridge University Press. P. 253.

[166] Ibid. P. 253, 254.

also distribute income or the property itself, if the majority decides that. In the second case, Nozick elaborates on whether the State has a right to restrict immigration by saying that the State is not a collective property for its citizens. Thus, States would not be able to control who can enter the individuals 'properties and limit the right of its citizens to exercise freely depending on the principle of self-ownership. Consequently, he asserts that nothing would 'legitimize' this act, and therefore, it cannot restrict immigration.[167]

Wellman argued a similar perspective and went further when he asked, "why do you think that the individual's interest in freedom of association should prevail over the State's collective claim to design an immigration policy?" He based his answer on relational egalitarianism to say that the political community cannot make the choice of admitting foreigners to deal with them "as second-class citizens". It is crucial to be sure that no one will be subject to "political oppression", which could happen if some of the voters for opening borders in the collective State, were unable to vote because of a lack of material resources to make their voice operative, or did not have the legal right to vote. [168] Therefore, "the insiders in the political community, whether nationals or even immigrants, have the right to vote and have to admit all the newcomers as free and equal citizens." On top of that, they must redistribute the income and share it with the newcomers. In conclusion, he affirms that when an individual invites someone from outside to his property, the inviter establishes a moral requirement to all insiders of engaging in the "equal political status" with newcomers in the political community. Thus, this individual expressed his opinion of what is called "the costs of extending the benefits of equal political membership", as an essential value of the freedom of association.[169]

Perhaps, according to Wellman's opinion, the political community would be the best status to determine the immigration policy, because the individual cannot invite a foreigner to his property unilaterally. However, the owner can host foreigners on his land for a short visit and under some conditions that the owner's State requires, so that he will be "constrained by the State's

---

[167] Ibid. P. 254.
[168] Wellman, ibid. P. 83.
[169] Ibid. P. 84.

collective control over immigration policy". Nevertheless, the owner who invites outsiders with permission of the whole collective group to live permanently inside the State can do so without being constrained by it.[170]

Going back to Carens, he tries to prove that the right of free movement is a genuine human right, and when States constrain the freedom of movement across borders, they seem to contradict the "deepest democratic values." He has sought to defend the need of open borders as a way to contribute to human freedom. His argument rests on the assumption that the ability to move freely across borders is a "vital interest", therefore, it deserves to be protected insofar as all fundamental human rights require this protection. This argument can be divided into two claims: the first one devotes the "logical extension", as he called it, on which he constructed a democratic basis for free international movement as a human right, depending on the recognition of the internal freedom of movement. The second claim of Carens' argument focuses on justifying freedom of movement within a State as a basic human right, depending on the normal democratic understanding.[171] In the first claim, he begins his argument with the acknowledgment of how persecuted persons have the right to seek asylum grounded on a basic interest, as David Miller had previously justified, and thus, they can enter and resettle in the host country, so long as their country is still unsafe. However, Carens asserts that Miller's retort of what the latter called a "cantilever strategy" was based on a misunderstanding, since Carens does not mean to justify why he favors opening the borders up, but rather, he refers to human rights just as "a starting point." He assumes that the right of internal free movement is, in fact, recognized as a human right in all democratic States, as it is established in international documents such as Art 13 of the UDHR and Art 12 of ICCPR. Thus, this right is a stable ground to develop the right of free international movement as an extension. Carens says that whatever reasons made internal free movement sufficiently logical and justified as a vital interest to be a human right, both internal and international movement have the "same rationale". Both are vital interests to people for the same reasons. Consequently, international free movement should also be

---

[170] Ibid. P. 86, 87.
[171] Carens, Joseph H. (2013 // 2015), The ethics of immigration. 1. issued as an Oxford Univ. Press paperback. New York: Oxford University Press; Oxford Univerisity Press (Oxford political theory). P. 236,237.

recognized as a human right.[172]

The second claim of Carens' argument denies the reasons that make internal free movement a basic human right, as opposed to international free movement. In this claim, he challenges "the moral status of basic human rights", or in other words, the vital interests which lie in internal movement to be recognized as a human right, because human rights protect vital interests. He has used many examples to assert that free international movement could be a more vital interest than the internal one. He illustrated that internal movement, which may be someone going from New York to Los Angeles, would not be justified just because of vital interests, for what vital generic interest can a person fulfill in Los Angeles and not in New York as both are big and rich cities? However, the person can move easily within the State's borders, and it is justified as a basic human right. On the other hand, when a person from Fiji, which is a very small and poor island, has the vital interest of being able to move freely within Fiji, this person would have an even more real vital interest in moving to rich and industrial States, but this real vital interest is not considered a basic human right. He is deprived of one of the most significant interests, as democratic States close their borders without any reasons.[173]

In conclusion, regarding the basis of libertarians' argument for open borders, some opinions criticize that the libertarian position on open borders and migration as not being clear, which means that not all libertarians favor opening borders. However, the positive position of Libertarians does not demand an explicit commitment of the States to open their borders as a response to the absolute and general individual rights of property, thus preferring them over statism. Instead of that, libertarian argue that the State must recognize individual self-determination and then comply to prevail individuals' rights in the case of "freedom of association", not restricting their freedom of movement.

Cosmopolitan Borders:

The cosmopolitan law, according to Kant's theory in the world citizenship, is based on the right to hospitality proceeding from the right of the State, as

---

[172] Ibid. 238, 239.
[173] Ibid. 244, 245.

well as individuals, to institute relations with other States and individuals, which doesn't mean that individuals have the right to enter and resettle in other territories. Also, the State can refuse foreigners without damaging their lives in order to prevent any kind of intrusions. The cosmopolitan law deals with individuals and not citizens of a State, but rather as human beings. It seeks to provide asylum to refugees and, at the same time, protect the State 'territories from imperialism.[174]

Kant considers that all human beings and States have cosmopolitan rights as world citizens, which might establish a new branch of public law concerning communications across borders and deal with all types of migration. Kant tried to explain the situation through the perpetual peace when a State cannot prohibit a person from entry and resettling in its territories if that threatens this person's life, and at the same time, the State has the right to deny a person's entry as long as it does not do so violently, based on its national sovereignty which implies setting some limits on the entry of world citizens. The right of hospitality or "perpetual peace," according to Kant, is a right to approach, not to enter.[175] In other words, Kant affirmed that one of the potential implications of cosmopolitan law is providing protection to individuals in some circumstances such as starvation, fatal disease, or even internal conflicts, as well as allowing them to resettle in the host State.[176] In this case, the State must admit these individuals because it cannot legitimately return the person to his country where he may perish, just because the State does not let him resettle and have protection within its territory for any reason related to its own interests. Therefore, the State should at least provide residency to individuals if there is a threat in their country. In addition to this implication of the cosmopolitan law, Kant did not mention explicitly other situations based on racial grounds, such as religion or skin color. These issues can be widely interpreted as kinds of "destruction" and harm that could affect the person that Kant considered in his theory of cosmopolitan law as a basic reason for admitting persons to resettle in the host State. Therefore, States cannot refuse persons who belong to a certain religion or skin and admit

---

[174] Pauline Kleingeld, Kant's Cosmopolitan Law, World Citizenship for a Global Order. Washington University, St Louis. Kantian Review, Volume 2, 1998. P. 72-74.
[175] Ibid. P. 75,76.
[176] Edward Shizha, Rosemary Kimani-Dupuis, Priscilla Broni (eds): Living Beyond the Borders. Essays on Global Immigrants and Refugees. Peter Lang. New York, 2018, p. 73,76.

others.[177] Kant was extremely fond of hospitality, for he finds it an obligation of all States towards the persons who need it in their territories without any kind of discrimination. However, he did not say that every person has the right to resettle wherever he wants, but he affirmed that States have no right to deny or to expel persons who are indeed threatened in their countries of origin. Thus, all States must welcome asylum seekers and provide the required protection as a first step to aid persons whose life is exposed to destruction if they have been expelled. Besides, he embraced the complete discretion of the host State to determine who really deserves permanent residence as a national member, or who is a migrant for a certain period that can then arbitrarily be returned if it finds no necessity to resettle in its territory.[178]

However, there were some cosmopolitans, who are closer to contemporary cosmopolitanism, and who disagree with Kant and his overview of open borders for all persons, for this would mean having this merit without any restrictions on the migrants 'rights. They think that the right to migrate and resettle should be a person's right to be a member of the host country, according to the world citizenship notion. Thus, it can be traced back to the "basis of residence", separately from the political or even social rights. All States should implement the same universal principles. If they admit individuals based on moral equality and global justice for all human beings, then they should grant all admitting persons the political and social rights of full citizens. Nevertheless, migration policies do not develop the classic idea of the rights of migrants just as economic migrants, so they cannot be treated like national citizens and then given permanent residence.[179]

This debate concerning the meaning of hospitality is still articulated in contemporary political philosophy. Some contend that hospitality means granting only some of the social and political rights to foreigners, and others claim the necessity of granting them the same rights that all citizens have.

Based on Kant's theory, there is a discussion of the genuine nature of borders and to what extent they have been changed to become cosmopolitan borders, so that the notion of openness becomes very important to illustrate the "four

---

[177] Pauline Kleingeld, Kant's Cosmopolitan Law, World Citizenship for a Global Order, ibid. P. 76, 77.
[178] F. Boucher, I. Aubert, S. Guérard de Latour. Approches to Cosmopolitanism, Review Essay on Their History, Analysis and Application to the EU. Paris University1. Novamigra D4.1. September 2019, p. 19.

[179] Ibid. P. 19.

cosmopolitan dimensions of borders" which comprise "vernacularization, multiperspectivalism, fixity/ unfixity, and connectivity," according to what Rumford outlined in his usage of the term "cosmopolitan border". Rumford attempts to explain how borders have changed in many aspects, such as their function, location, or even their ownership. That leads to the idea of enhancing connectivity in our World in a much better way than what globalization does. Cosmopolitan borders might open a debate about the State's power that aims to dominate and organize mobility, especially across borders. However, if we take a closer look at the idea of the cosmopolitan borders, they have in fact a more straightforward and more perpetual task manifested in embracing opportunities stemming from cosmopolitan encounters and connective interactions between individuals worldwide.[180]

The European Union is considered a perfect example of cosmopolitanism concerning hospitality and the right to migrate, for the citizens of the member States can travel wherever they want within the EU countries to stay and work abroad in much better circumstances than those in their country of origin. Nevertheless, some argue that not all persons in the EU have the same rights as Europeans themselves since there are various co-citizens in the EU who are initially migrants although they live in the EU territories. These migrants do not have the same protection as EU citizens, or in other words, they might be granted protection, but, mostly, it is not equal to citizens' protection.[181] In addition to this, there might be a big obstacle for equal cosmopolitan borders, not only in the EU but in general, which addresses in the possibility of guaranteeing this kind of equality in spite of the inequality between States regarding their welfare status. In some case, there are rich persons in a certain State who live under very good circumstances, while others do not have the basic infrastructure. This institutes a gape in the conditions of the equal citizenship of all persons that hinder them from achieving the essence of cosmopolitanism (global citizenship) where there are no borders and all States merge into a single world State.[182] Regarding this, some cosmopolitans, who are in fact moral cosmopolitans, focus on the

---

[180] Chris Rumford, Cosmopolitan Borders. Department of Politics and International Relations, Royal Holloway, University of London, UK: Palgrave Macmillan 2014. P. 1-3.
[181] F. Boucher, I. Aubert, S. Guérard de Latour. Ibid. P. 30.
[182] Edward Shizha, Rosemary Kimani-Dupuis, Priscilla Broni (eds): Living Beyond the Borders. Essays on Global Immigrants and Refugees, ibid, p. 72.

"strong form" of cosmopolitanism to justify the open borders based on "global egalitarianism", which their claim is "global distributive justice, democracy and free movement or migration" while others embrace the weak form of cosmopolitanism and seek fundamental human rights for everyone. Some think that the national agents can enhance transnational democratic practices as well as transnational forms of citizenship to achieve the cosmopolitan goals by decentering the civic practices in society. In contrast, institutional cosmopolitanism affirms the need of transnational or global political institutions. Other cosmopolitans believe that cultural identities, because of their hybrid nature, can shape the cross-cultural identity of the people in cosmopolitanism[183].

The four dimensions of cosmopolitan borders, which have been mentioned above, explain the possibility of changing borders in some ways, particularly if we elaborate on each of those dimensions separately.

The first dimension is vernacularization, which focuses on transforming the State's border into societal borders through the idea of bordering activity, that does not stem from national security concerns anymore. In other words, the shifting study here is articulated on the changing of the State's borders regarding the "external borders,"[184] which determine the limits of the State geographically into the society in which citizens are responsible for making or eliminating the borders for facilitating the movement. This is called "Border work," according to Rumford, and it means "the activity of ordinary people" to make or dismantle borders by their own agencies without any intervention from the State.[185]

Therefore, according to this concept, "borders are everywhere," which means that they are derived from the activity of society in unconventional assumptions because, as we know, borders used to be established for fulfilling conventional assumptions of the State's affairs. Borderwork in this sense takes a new form in globalization, which requires a broader range of borders

---

[183] Ibid, P. 38,39.

[184] Maurice Stierl: Migrant Resistance in Contemporary Europe, edited by Jenny Edkins and Nick Vaughan-Williams. New York: Routledge, 2019. P. 23, 24.

[185] Chris Rumford, ibid. P. 17, 18, 23, 24. And see Beck, Ulrich. (2000). The cosmopolitan perspective: Sociology and the second age of modernity. British Journal of Sociology, 51(7), 79–105.

and actors as well. [186] Thus, involving people at borders' study in borderwork is essential for instituting "new political opportunities" by a cosmopolitan agency in border studies, as well as providing security and safety to people in a globalized society and its effects, when it gives people a significant place of study which motivates them to adapt borders like anything in their lives manifested in vacation abroad or a business trip or whatever the reason for crossing borders was, people should be aware when to facilitate moving or when to constrain it in accordance with finding a safe form of borders and open cosmopolitan borders at the same time based on every situation separately. Thus, borderwork can be applicable in different levels, particularly when people initially set up borders and constraints on mobility to limit drug smuggling or to protect against terrorism or any illegal action that could be prevented by controlling the borders, which is why this type of borders require a degree of control to protect national security. On the other hand, Borders will be used freely and without any limits for other purposes such as mobility, migration, work, etc.[187]For this reason, this function of border working might seem "national, supra-national, societal, or local from the perspective of people's activity. In other words, borders can take different forms if they are studied by focusing on the unconventional uses of them. Rumford has given examples to explain how borders take new forms of political resources because of people's activity (vernacular practice).

He distinguishes between the physical borders on the one hand, and the border work of constructing or even dismantling borders on the other hand, focusing on the latter. The concept of border work highlights the citizens' involvement in the border process and enables them to make or eliminate all borders. Rumford has illustrated some instances, such as the dismantling of the Berlin Wall in Germany and the peace wall that was built in Ireland. Thus, the process of borders is in fact included in acts of citizenship, and both border work and citizenship are widely comprehensive terms. They are not exclusive to the citizens, but they can expand and include non-status persons as well, because the power of the people manifested in borderwork is considered a political activity "transnational in nature."[188] Rumford has also

---

[186] Edward Shizha, Rosemary Kimani-Dupuis, Priscilla Broni (eds): Living Beyond the Borders. Essays on Global Immigrants and Refugees, ibid, p. 75.
[187] Chris Rumford, ibid, p. 25.
[188] Ibid. P. 26,27.

used Berwick-upon-Tweed as an example, which is an English town that has historic borders with Scotland and is now considered more as a "non-border". Although many activities have bordered this town over the years, but no one succeeded in bordering it. Especially since its residents have chosen to consider themselves neither Scottish nor English, they do not consider themselves to belong to Northumberland, which has the English identity, and do not find themselves inside the Scottish borders. Thus, after conducting a referendum, they decided to be a unique people that are a part of Berwick, a European town, but separate from Scotland and England. Berwick's political activity concerning the bordering process reflects the borderwork that enables its people to illuminate the different kinds of scales within their "everyday practices." Consequently, borders can be transforming gates for people, and they can mentally account for them as a gateway, national edges, or even transnational places without playing any role in the State's 'issues. Similarly, the very different borders that Berwick-upon-Tweed town chose to have by broadening the normal concept of borders facilitate transnational connecting and increase the "networking opportunities" of all people.[189]

The second dimension of cosmopolitan borders is multiperspectivalism, which refers to the need of adopting different perspectives to study cosmopolitan borders. Borders can be invisible to some and thus, can lose their effectiveness. Borders may not be adequately recognized if they have been interpreted from a single privileged perspective. But they may have different interpretations if we see them from another perspective. Although we have witnessed the effects of globalization in our World in recent years besides transnational trades, which are supposed to have more open borders globally, what we have seen is a kind of "plethora" of borders, which is similar to the idea of "borders are everywhere." Thus, borders demonstrate "a multiplicity of sites" that sneak into everyday life. Moreover, this concept of "borders walls" is increasing despite preventing the idea that "borders are everywhere." This notion of borders is no longer related to places or national areas, instead, they have been transformed to refer to a new form manifested in an intense bordering process instead of just borders.[190]

---

[189] Ibid. P. 28-32.
[190] Chris Rumford, ibid. P.18, 19, 40

Of course, the State institutes borders and regulates the bordering process, but it is still the sole classic predictable justification if we look at another perspective far from the conventional assumptions and securitizing borders, which are interpretations of borders from the State perspective. There are other perspectives that justify bordering if we see borders in local activities with the purpose of regulating mobility and preserving peace and security, and not only as tools in the State's hands for the "service of the State." This can be the prime factor to justify borderwork, which necessarily means in this context networking throughout society and people who can play a role in bordering. In this sense, constructing, or dismantling borders includes all these considerations.[191]

Another point is that borders can be invisible for some of the people who are living within them and do not see the borders from the outside, so borders effectively work to enhance the status of movement and organize this movement in its territories. Consequently, borders are invisible but not completely if we think of them from the perspective of the people who aspire to migrate and cross them. This is similar to the EU borders, which are designed in a way that cannot be seen by the people living within, in a very selective principle for the majority of those people. At the same time, those borders will be visible to the people who are bordered out when they think of crossing seas to reach Europe. In other words, borders must not be totally invisible for everyone, because this would make them lose their function of protecting society from illegal migrants, terrorists, etc.[192]

The most crucial argument in the discussion of borders is that there are other types of borders, not only the "State borders," which is surely the classic or conventional frame. Those new types would be constructed by relying on other assumptions, dispensing with the State's framework, where the studying of borders takes on another interpretation with a multi-perspectival study. This is why focusing on illegal migration, which is deemed "a geopolitical perspective", cannot add anything to the multi-perspectival border study. In contrast, studying borders from the perspective of cultural encounters would be an efficient frame. Particularly, if this perspective has

---

[191] Ibid. P. 41.
[192] Ibid. P. 41-45. And see Willem van Schendel. Spaces of Engagement, How Borderland, Illegal Flows, and Territorial States Interlock. 2005. P.3,4.

been disseminated in society and by people to reframe borders as "sites of cultural encounters". Then, borders should be recognized according to the new cultural assumption, although seeing borders from a divisionary perspective, that is just as "mechanisms of division" for those who are concerned, is still the consensus assumption and considered a big impediment on the way of developing a multi-perspectival borders study.

The consensus assumption which is the classical definition of border study is evident in situations dealing with the common borders of two States, such as the case of the US and Mexico. Whose governments have armed forces along the borders. Overall, this type of border, which creates a divided world frame, is strongly considered the demonstration of the geopolitical perspective of borders.[193]

It is important to mention that border studies based on a multi-perspectival approach require leaving aside the assumption that borders are invisible only in their function, since: "a country which is easily seen can be easily protected." This idea shows the empire's perspective, which supports the security of the State but stays at the same time in "global spaces" (borders) to accomplish a modern imperial framework that complies with all the conditions of globalization.[194]

A multi-perspective study of borders refines the whole idea of the invisibility of some borders only for those persons who are located within, and not for the persons who are outside. The way we see borders is obviously a selective experience that can be different from person to person and the standard here is to see from the border and like a border, not like a State. All we need to do, according to this perspective, is to place ourselves in border sites and think like borders. Berwick' borderwork is a perfect example of multiperspectival borders study because the bordering between both countries, Scotland and England, is the best instance of "consensus bordering", and what the town has chosen is for the border between the two countries to remain invisible, and hence open to connect globally with the "wider world."[195]

---

[193] Chris Rumford, ibid. P. 45, 46.
[194] Ibid. P. 49.
[195] Ibid. P. 50, 52.

Multiperspectival border studies have created a new method different from the conventional one, constrained by the State, to analyze the function of borders and who constructed them, as well as their purpose. All these aspects are reframed in a multiperspectival study instead of the frustrating monoperspective one. Nevertheless, this study is still in its infancy and needs further development over the coming years. The aim of multiperspectival borders study centers on the inadequacy of recognizing "contemporary borders" (as borders are everywhere, it is so but not for every person). Therefore, a multiperspectival study does really helps to understand the global connecting sites (borders), involving persons individually in the bordering process as well as realizing the idea of "borders are everywhere" for some and invisible for others.[196]

The third dimension of cosmopolitan borders is the fixity or unfixity of borders. This is particularly relevant in our World nowadays and the increasing desire for migration. Even more so because there are so many difficulties that hinder people from getting a visa to live in their destination country. This situation has contributed to exacerbate the problem of illegal migration. In this case, there might be a failure in fulfilling the borders' function, which can affect negatively and reduce the permanence of borders entirely. This would make them somehow 'unfixed', and that determines if borders get to be "institutionalized or not." In this context, borders do not mean exclusively guards, walls, passengers, etc., but rather they embody all acts related to trafficking, lines where the passports can be checked, and all the mobility is organized by the State's power to regulate movement and prevent illegal migration and terrorism, or any other threat that could affect the national security of the State. The study of the fixity and unfixity of the borders makes them incomplete or "provisional". Although borders must be established on "a regular basis" in case they do their function effectively, and despite the fact that some borders are highly fixed, unfixity is still possible. For instance, the common border between the US and Mexico. Despite being the most efficient policed border worldwide on the US side, with infra-red sensors in addition to the high wall, they are still incapable of prohibiting illegal migrants from passing the border and entering American territory. Thus, the fixity cannot be fully achieved. It is evidently provisional. In other

---

[196] Chris Rumford, ibid, p. 54.

cases, the agencies or persons responsible for borders allow a certain level of unfixity selectively, sometimes to achieve political purposes. The government usually chooses to unfix certain borders or it enhances the "illusion of the fixity" of borders.[197]

It is interest to see how some borders look forward to "fixity" while others exhibit the illusion of fixity and implicitly seek "unfixity." In both cases, the cosmopolitan borders perspective can be involved in the politics of fixity and unfixity as well. This perspective stems from many resources which allow converting the border work from nation-State borders, to bordering in everyday life in which different actors can contribute to the bordering process as a political resource.[198]

The first sort of borders is the result of appointing this task to agencies of the State or residents of the area, in order to guarantee institutionalization of the borders. For instance, the initiative of some towns in the UK to use a local currency in Brixton town, to preserve their town from the side effects of globalization by protecting the local economy with invisible borders to regulate the motion of money so that it serves the people inside the town in the most efficient way, since global currencies might be an insecure source to institute economic life. In this case, the economic borders seem fixed and achieve the function of institutional borders. Whereas the second sort of borders is an example of "geopolitical unfixity". This policy proceeds totally from national sources. It aims to construct borders that are fixed and unfixed at the same time. For example, when the EU built Frontex, which is considered a new border, it was meant to enhance the cooperation between the member States in the border security domain.[199] Frontex was a mechanism that sought to extend the bordering activity of the EU to include the required security offshore in the Mediterranean Sea and the West Coast of Africa as a very flexible border. However, Frontex, was also an opportunity to highlight the failure of its "African partners" in implementing human rights, as the detention camps in Libya revealed.[200] The point of the offshore

---

[197] Ibid. P. 56, 57.

[198] Ibid. P. 68.

[199] Vicki Squire: Europe's Migration Crisis, Borders Deaths and Human Dignity. University of Warwick. New York, Cambridge University Press, first published 2020. P. 29,30, 31.

[200] Chris Rumford, Cosmopolitan Borders. Department of Politics and International Relations, Royal Holloway, University of London, UK: Palgrave Macmillan 2014. P. 61.

borders is that they are fixed and unfixed simultaneously, besides, this relation between both fixity and unfixity might enhance "the governance of security" when the EU Frontex agency imposes restrictions and prevents the boats of immigrants from crossing the Mediterranean Sea and the West Coast of Africa from reaching their destinations in Europe. In this sense, borders would be fixed in this context against those who want to enter Europe illegally but, at the same time, they would remain unfixed with the "illusion of fixity" when the EU allowed "non- European partner countries" to contribute in the border policy to detect their failure in the perfect control or total fixity on the borders. This is how Frontex modifies the institutionalization of borders and enhances this unfixity, but in an unpredictable and unaccountable way.

Another example that shows the tension between fixity and unfixity is the UK's major airports, such as Healthrow, where their policed persons introduce themselves as welcoming to all people who arrive. At the same time, the UK border policy increases monitoring procedures in offshore borders to prevent undesirable immigrants from arriving in the UK territories. This example shows how selective borders might sometimes swing between fixity and unfixity, not because of its ambiguous function, but because this contributes to governance's interests deliberately .[201] In case irregular migration is not one of the government's interests, the State immediately combats it in four ways (exit controls, travel controls, entry controls, and residence and employment controls) to prevent irregular migration at its points of departure or to return illegal migrants if they succeed to enter the territory. To this end, the State deliberates on "enhancing border control" by the military, and intelligence for monitoring the smugglers on networks or paths, in addition to other national measures related to "labor markets" such as imposing sanctions to diminish irregular immigration.[202]

On the other hand, some borders are actually made to support national security, but they shift to being unfixed incidentally while fulfilling their function. This is all because of their strategic location, which may serve for commercial and civilian activities, which would cause an accidental unfixity

---

[201] Ibid. P. 56, 57.
[202] Alexander Betts (2011): Global Migration Governance. Edited by Alexander Betts. First edition. Oxford University Press. P. 100.

of borders. For example, the drones or UAVs which were initially used for commercial purposes such as "delivering pizza", and then became part of the military equipment. By increasing the activities and tasks that these drones can accomplish, they threaten the borders because the enthusiasts' piloted drones fly in areas that include bordering activities, such as near rural airports, This way, these drones "are not only messy" because they could be everywhere in the State, but also because they have become so affordable that they can be used by anyone who does not necessarily belong to a specific club. In addition to that, these drones can fly up to 3,500 feet, and their plans need to be approximately over 2,500 feet near the airport. According to this, drones infringe the privacy of the States and could be used as intrusive surveillance instruments, violating national security, which is the basic function of borders, as well as threatening the safety of a State's territory in case any accident happened to real planes.[203]

The fourth dimension of cosmopolitan borders is connectivity or monumentalizing borders, this means the national monuments located on common borders between two States or more. These monuments get to be a part of the borders, however, in many instances, they were not borders in the negative meaning of the term, but rather were bridges to connect globally and promote cooperation between States. There are so many examples of border monuments, like the Peace Arch that is at the "Canada-USA border, between Blaine, Washington and Surrey, British Columbia." It was erected in 1921 at 20 meters high and has two famous inscriptions on both the US and the Canadian sides. The US inscription reads "Children of a common mother", while the Canadian inscription reads "Brethren dwelling together in unity." The most significant inscription is drawn on both sides of the arch where there are two iron gates with "May these gates never be closed" written on each side of them.[204]

According to Rumford, to understand border monuments as contemporary cosmopolitan borders, we need to think of them not just as "markers of divisions", but in a more positive perspective, in which they can be sites of connections and "cultural encounter." Consequently, the cosmopolitan borders, based upon this meaning, enable persons to connect by such places

---

[203] Chris Rumford, ibid. P. 67, 68.
[204] Ibid, P. 74, 75.

as monuments and outline the essential function of borders in this context, which is simply connectivity. Perhaps the effective way to reach global connectivity is monumentalizing borders so that, eventually, they will become cosmopolitan borders. The relationship between monuments and borders is ancient, although it has changed over the years. Monuments can constitute a border and make it more significant, as has been the case of Gretna, the Star of Caledonia, among others. The welcoming function of these monuments is evidently still the most tangible dimension of connectivity.[205]

The four dimensions of cosmopolitan borders explain why borders should be reinterpreted in new ways based on a cosmopolitan perspective, in which the borders become a "cosmopolitan workshop." However, the most critical question that comes to mind here is: to what extent can cosmopolitanism serve for opening borders and on which basis can we rely to serve this purpose? According to Kant's overview, which was previously discussed at the beginning of this section, he proposed the right to hospitality under cosmopolitan law, regardless of conventional borders. Then, he established the right to hospitality as an "innate human right to freedom," which would be a legal justification of open borders. The innate right to freedom means the free-acting and controlling of all "internally what mine or yours," as well as "the right to be there where nature of chance (without one's will) has been placed", according to Kant in his "Metaphysic of Morals." Kant also mentioned that "being on land is necessary for the very existence of human beings" and, consequently, there is a corollary of the innate right of being where persons find themselves naturally after birth, but if this right has been denied that inevitably means denying their existence and hence their freedom.[206] Thus, Kant emphasized that the human right to freedom is almost the key to building the principle of hospitality for it depends on it. In this context, he concluded two aspects: the first is that the visitors cannot call on the right to freedom when they forcibly intrude others' freedom. The second one is that no one has the right to expel visitors so long as that would violate their freedom.[207] Furthermore, Kant strengthens his doctrine of cosmopolitan law, which is based on the right to freedom by affirming that

---

[205] Ibid. P. 78.
[206] Pauline Kleingeld, Kant's Cosmopolitan Law, World Citizenship for a Global Order. Washington University, St Louis. Kantian Review, Volume 2, 1998. P. 79.
[207] Ibid. P. 79.

when a person has the right to request entry, exchange, or interaction that will not infringe others' freedom, they can decide whether to accept or refuse, since this request does not diminish their freedom. Nevertheless, the real problem here could emerge when a visitor uses someone else's property, for this action infringes their property rights against their will. As a result, there is a fundamental clash between the claims of both, the "innate" right to freedom and the property right. This shows a contradiction between Kant 's doctrine of cosmopolitan law and his private law theory. However, it could be "temporary enjoyment" of those people's property. Kant's theory did not entitle the visitor to "goods, food and other things freely", although it is still considered troublesome to use someone else's property regardless of whether this enjoyment was confined to a particular time or was forever.[208]

Kant justified his theory by arguing that the State's taxes, which are imposed on citizens for aiding the poor people who do not have money, can be used for helping refugees or "co-citizens". His point relies on granting refugees or any person who needs protection the right to temporarily use someone else's property so that he obtains the required safety, if this is beneficial for his benefit. In this regard, Kant argued that if the property's owners are legally committed to "give up" some rights to "strangers" whose life or existence is threatened, these rights would be conditional and temporary. In other words, Kant contended the institutionalization or enforcement of cosmopolitan law, as he considers that cosmopolitan law suffers from a lack of implementation or enforcement, and he affirms the necessity of enforcement for the enjoyment of the rights, otherwise, cosmopolitan law would be "put at peril." He did not provide any solution for this problem, he rather denies "the transnational enforcement of international law" to avoid the extension of enforcement possibilities from international law to cosmopolitan law.[209] He exemplified his argument of the enforcement of cosmopolitan law with "Monetary greed," which is, in his opinion, the sole motivator of peace between States. That means trade and money, which are the States' interests to establish negotiations and then "international interaction", which is the essence of cosmopolitan law. However, this interaction cannot result in hospitality rights because a State would not allow to all its citizens to travel

---

[208] Ibid. P. 80.
[209] Ibid. P. 81, 82.

to another State as a result of the interaction between both States. This, in turn, violates the cosmopolitan rights of persons and does not prevent the destination State from returning the persons coming from the State with which it shares interests. Moreover, the destination State will not hesitate to expel non-commercial foreigners, so that mutual interests (commercial interaction) promote peace but do not guarantee the hospitality right, and hence, cosmopolitan rights for every person.[210]

Kleingeld adds an interesting argument to explain why cosmopolitan rights cannot have enforcement. Individuals are the subjects of international law so long as they are State citizens, so a person will be held accountable if he commits a crime according to international law, even though his behavior is not considered a crime by his State's national law. Individuals should appeal to national laws to settle their disputes and because of the States' sovereignty, which has been affirmed by the Charter of the United Nations, as well as the non-interference in their own affairs, the States always use the sovereignty as a "pretext" to not recognize the cosmopolitan rights of an individual, such as the hospitality right, as long as it is inconsistent with its interests. Consequently, although the 1951 Geneva convention assured that no one has the right to expel persons who are at serious harm for reasons of "religion, race, political view, or membership in a certain social group," the principle of States' sovereignty is still abused when the State has the final decision on accepting or refusing asylum seekers according to its sovereignty.[211] In this regard, the restriction on migration, which all States aim to include in their migration policies to curtail the opportunities of foreigners to leave their countries of origin and resettle in the destination country, hinders cosmopolitan justice despite the fact that it seems to help. These restrictions would not be cosmopolitan. For example, the principle of "Priority of Disadvantages" establishes the clearest example because Higgins wanted this principle to build an image of immigration justice.[212] Higgins also argues that there will not be "a good or right immigration policy" to be applied by all States in the same way because he assures that there is an internal difference in their dealing with different political, social, and economic circumstances.

---

[210] Ibid. P. 82.
[211] Ibid. P. 83, 84.
[212] Jose Jorge Mendoza: Does Cosmopolitan Justice Ever Require Restrictions on Migrations? Article in Public Affairs Quarterly. ResearchGate. Volume 29, Number 2. April. 2015. P. 175, 176.

This makes States to adopt their own immigration policy, which is, of course, different from another policy in another State, and this variety of immigration policies enhances the "current injustice." Rather, their function has been considered as neo-colonialism policies in our World now[213], Which is why philosophers try to find an answer to the question of: "What would immigration justice look like in our World, which is not an ideal utopian world?

Higgins claims that his principle of "Priority of Disadvantages" at least guarantees not making things worse for those persons who are already unjustly disadvantaged. With this principle, Higgins proposes an immigration policy that takes into account not causing harm as the best and fairer policy, unlike other policies, such as the prescriptive nationals that States must include in their immigration policies, or moral sovereignty of States, or even the cosmopolitanism to open borders based on "the moral equality of citizens and foreigners requires States to open their borders by eliminating all or most restrictions on immigration." This principle does not grant the State the right to favor its citizens over foreigners in the immigration policy, which is avoidable harm, and it also considers the principle of "cosmopolitan justice" by putting restrictions on migration to protect those persons "who are already unjustly disadvantaged" in their countries from predictable harm that they may face in the host countries, because the harm of many kinds of exploitation and discrimination while seeking new opportunities outweighs any benefits they could obtain there. That is if the borders were open. On the other hand, the lack of restrictions on migration will increase the inequality among the citizens in the poor States due to the ease with which people with more advantages will be able to migrate due to open borders. Besides, there is also brain drain, which is a potential problem that we could face in case there were no more restrictions on migration.[214] Therefore, restrictions on migration would help cosmopolitan justice, but from another perspective. They make the mission of achieving cosmopolitan rights of freedom impossible. This is why the best solution is to open borders, and any other problem that might emerge could be solved later in a way that does not

---

213 Maurice Stierl: Migrant Resistance in Contemporary Europe, edited by Jenny Edkins and Nick Vaughan-Williams. New York: Routledge, 2019. P. 193, 194.
214 Jose Jorge Mendoza, ibid. P. 177.

restrict migration.[215]

Conclusion:

Even though cosmopolitan law could frame the political borders in new ways to serve individual interests, the right to migrate as one of the cosmopolitan rights still has the problem of how they can be institutionalized worldwide, although our World' inequality in many ways hinders the implementation of cosmopolitan rights. However, the philosophers who support the "strong form" of cosmopolitanism seek to achieve global egalitarianism through equal distributive justice, although the inequality in the welfare between States constitutes an obstacle that makes States close their borders against undesirable persons, based on the "common argument" of the sovereignty of the States.

Surely every person who faces any kind of persecution in his country of origin, be it for religion, race, political view, or membership in a certain social group, has the right to protection and asylum in a host country, although the final decision of granting asylum is "left to the State", as shown previously. Therefore, cosmopolitan rights should coincide with the interests of the State in order to be implemented. Consequently, borders are closed even though "the citizens of the world" have the right to freedom and hence the right of hospitality if the State does not benefit from opening them.

The Connection between the Right to Leave and the Right to Stay:

International Law and the EU Law affirm the right of those persons who are persecuted, to seek asylum in other countries, and it is these countries' duty to allow those persons to seek asylum and, thus, endorse their right to get protection, which is the sole requirement to allow them to live their lives safely. However, it may be insufficient to force States to host persons and give them residences after crossing their borders, especially since the Universal Declaration of Human Rights UDHR did not establish an obligation on the States to allow persons who need protection to enter their territories. Consequently, two questions come to mind: first, to what extent does the right to leave make sense in case of non-existing guarantees to impose on the States to allow persons to enter and reside in their territories?

---

[215] For further information look at ibid. P. 181-184.

Second, is the right to asylum considered an effective and sufficient right even though the right to leave can be considered a claim more than a right, especially since the right to stay may not exist in International Law at all?

These questions will be analyzed in the third chapter but, in this section, we will see how the right to leave is connected to the right to stay by very logical considerations which are, in fact, the basic elements of the right to asylum to be a real right, so that all the States recognize and implement it genuinely in order to aid the people who might be facing persecution in their countries of origin.

The Universal Declaration of Human Rights established the right to seek asylum, as was said before, in Article 14 in its preamble, which says:

> "1. Everyone has the right to seek and to enjoy in other countries asylum from persecution.
> 2. This right may not be invoked in the case of prosecutions genuinely arising from non-political crimes or from acts contrary to the purposes and principles of the United Nations."[216]

After the UDHR's endorsement of the right to seek asylum when facing persecution, the United Nations General Assembly created the United Nations High Commissioner for Refugees (UNHCR) in 1950, which worked hard to help displaced people worldwide. About one year later, the Refugee Convention undertook the task of protecting people who are forced to leave their countries in case of internal conflict or persecution in general.

This means that all those people who are considered refugees are so according to some regulations or conditions mentioned in the UNHCR. For instance, article 14 of the UDHR found its way to be implemented in most of the asylum seekers' applications, as well as article 13, which enshrined a person's right to leave his country of origin, and article 15 on the right to nationality[217].

---

[216] United Nations Universal Declaration of Human Rights 1948, Article 14. http://www.jus.uio.no/sisu. P. 5.
[217] United Nations Human Rights Office of The High Commissioner, 70 Years Universal Declaration of Human Rights.
https://www.standup4humanrights.org/layout/files/30on30/UDHR70-30on30-article14-eng.pdf.

According to this, all the persons who faced any kind of persecution are either able to flee their country or remain there because they have been prevented from leaving by the persecuting States. In the first scenario, the people who fled their countries of origin seek asylum in a host country, thus falling under the provision of the Refugee Convention. This is based on the assumption that the Refugee Convention obliges States to protect the persons who enter their borders while escaping from persecution. In contrast, the second scenario uses a diplomatic method to deal with the persecuting States. Thus, the Convention provisions are applied to persons who fled their countries or have already entered the host country's territories.[218]Therefore, the right to asylum cannot be defined as a right in most cases, unless the person entered the host country seeking protection. Otherwise, the right to asylum differs from the right to migrate in that the right to asylum should meet both rights (the right to leave and the right to stay).

---

[218] David Miller, Christine Straehle: The Political Philosophy of Refuge: Cambridge University Press 2020. P. 46.

THIRD CHAPTER

IS THERE A RIGHT TO STAY?

Introduction:

This chapter concentrates on the nature of the right to stay in the host country, not just temporarily, but as a right to resettle there and stay maybe in the long-term as a permanent right to stay. To study this, we will analyze the relationship between international human rights law and the Refugee Convention, as well as some European treaties. This chapter will attempt to justify the right to stay morally, in case there is one or, if it is a claim based on the idea that only the State can allow people to stay within its territories. There are many approaches to the right to stay, such as what international law dictates to States in terms of having to protect migrants who are persecuted around the World, or it can also be considered a migrants' right in terms of autonomy. Yet, the sole legal protection which frames a person's right of to stay in the host country is the principle of non-refoulement. This principle was mentioned in the Refugee Convention of 1951 as a right that anybody who might be facing any kind of persecution and needs protection since their life is at stake can claim in order to stay within the territories of the host country and not to be returned to his country.

Although the Refugee Convention establishes a person's right to get asylum, it also gives States the discretion of granting asylum with the freedom of choosing which rights asylum seekers will be entitled to, such as giving them temporary visas to stay and work within its territories while maintaining the authority of withholding the right to stay. This way, States have the right to previously determine the period of the asylum seeker's residence, so they will not be able to stay permanently, but rather the State can return him to his country of origin whenever the situation improves. Therefore, the Refugee Convention establishes a genuine gap, according to Adam Omar Hosein, and

I will elaborate on this gap in detail in this chapter as well.[1]

This gap could create a problem which stems from member countries like the USA and Australia eluding obligations States in the Refugee Convention and not complying with the right to asylum by the member countries, for example, the USA, and Australia, place preconditions in addition to the serious harm condition which the Refugee Convention mentioned in order to be achieved in the asylum seeker's application as a way to elude their obligations. In these cases, the threat of serious harm is not sufficient for these countries to grant asylum, however, more people should get legal permission from the host State to be potential candidates for asylum.[2] It has been observed that International human rights treaties do not mention a specific form to determine how States should carry out their obligations of granting protection to persons under threat. Rather, they leave the method of implementation to the member States in accordance with all provisions that those treaties adopted. Consequently, asylum seekers face more difficulties to be granted this right because these people cannot provide "substantial documents" for getting asylum, so that it all depends on their testimony to prove why they should be granted refugee protection.[3]

This chapter will give a future vision of the asylum and discuss the debate between individuals and the State to reach a conclusion of that an individual's self-determination can outweigh a State's self-determination to be considered a basis of a person's claim to asylum. Last but not least, we will highlight the implementations and the major restrictions on the right to stay in the host country, or even the right to enter its territories in some cases.

The Status Quo:

Asylum policies have evolved, especially among EU member States. This evolution embodied efficient cooperation after agreeing upon the Schengen Convention, which drew the first step in organizing the whole process of asylum application in the European Union. According to this initiative, all member States that signed this Convention necessarily agreed to the Dublin

---

[1] Adam Omar Hosein. Refugee and the Right to Remain. (Chapter 6 of The Political Philosophy of Refuge by David Miller and Christine Straehle). Cambridge University Press 2020. P. 117
[2] Ibid. P. 116.
[3] Anette Faye Jacobsen: Human Rights Monitoring, A Field Mission Manual. Martinus Nijhoff Publishers 2008. Boston P. 467, 468.

Convention, which regulated the jurisdiction of asylum. However, the Dublin Convention did not enter into force until 1997, and it aimed to develop a coherent system for asylum in which any person needs to prove that he faced serious harm or was subject to a threat of serious harm to enable him to apply for the asylum, as well as to assign the jurisdiction of asylum for preventing persons from applying for asylum in many States. Both the Schengen and the Dublin Conventions have had an important role in the measures of the asylum process since 1995, when the Schengen Convention entered into force. Then, the Treaty of Maastricht explicitly assured that granting asylum is, in fact, an "intergovernmental decision", so that it is a national practice of each member State. In addition to that, it was a very important adjustment of the final form of the asylum policy in the EU, regarding the content of the visa policy (short stay visas) that the Maastricht Treaty established and was based on the Schengen acquis. After this, there was the treaty of Amsterdam which has, in addition to the Treaty of Lisbon, constituted a complete framework of an asylum system, later called the Common European Asylum System after the last development by the European Council in 1999.[4]

The most practical problem here is the inability of the Common European Asylum System (CEAS) to control and regulate the movement of migrants from their own countries, crossing seas and continents, to arrive in Europe despite its objective of establishing "legislative harmonization" between the member States. For example, the recent movements of thousands of people crossing the Mediterranean and perishing there while trying to reach Europe. Overall, the CEAS provided a refugee protection system among all member States by adopting a reception policy for all asylum seekers, receiving their applications, and granting them protection and all merits of being either refugees or subsidiary protection persons. Thus, this system has proved its efficiency of implementation, despite the failure in the national legislation on asylum systems in many European countries, such as the Greek asylum system. Migration into Europe is tied to the asylum conditions in the neighboring countries before arriving in Germany, Norway, Netherlands,

---

[4] Kay Hailbronner and Daniel Thym: EU Immigration and Asylum Law, A Commentary. Second edition 2016. C.H. BECK. Hart. Nomos. Germany. P. 5. And see
And see Elspeth Guild, Jan Niessen: Institutional and Policy Dynamics of EU Migration Law, Immigration and Asylum Law and Policy in Europe. Vol 10, Georgia Papagianni, Martinus Nijhoff Publishers 2006. Leiden, The Netherlands. P. 13, 111-113.

Denmark, and Sweden.

The way of dealing with refugee needs to be a strongly coherent asylum system. Therefore, the "open flake" which results from the national legislative leverage has complicated the situation when any member State can evade its obligations because of the absence of a national legislation based on its national rules of asylum, where the asylum seeker often cannot get a long-term residence and, in many cases, cannot integrate into society by working or having an employment opportunity. Rather the host country has the right to expel "illegal migrants" who reside or work without authorization and hold a residence in another member State, those called the third-country nationals. In this case, the person becomes an undesirable person according to the Council Recommendation of September 27, 1996, on combating the illegal employment of third-country nationals, which supports the member States in establishing a standard document for expulsion. Regardless of the illegal migrants who have residences in other member States, there are those migrants who fled from persecution and did not have other choice but to cross the sea to earn in search of asylum. These people have the minimum fundamental rights in the host country, as well as the right to benefit from the non-refoulement principle, which keeps them from being returned to their countries where they could face serious harm.[5]

Therefore, this section aims to elaborate on the multiple faces of the right of asylum and analyze the legal basis of asylum in International Human Rights Law, International Migration Law, the Refugee Convention, and the UNHCR, as well as European treaties. After that, we will address the right to stay and resettle in the host country with the aim of finding out if it is a right or just a claim grounded on the non-refoulement principle, so that the person will have a short-term residence, while the State has the right to expel him in case the threat or internal conflict in his country has come to an end, despite the unwillingness of the refugee or the subsidiary protection person to go back to his country, especially if he has integrated into the host country by resettling and working there.

---

[5] Ibid. P. 7,8. And see Lamis Elmy Abdelaaty: Discrimination and Delegation. Oxford University Press 2021. New York. P.17. and see Elspeth Guild, Jan Niessen, ibid. P. 126,127.

The Faces of the Right to Asylum:

The first face of the right to asylum is a State's right to grant asylum. This means that every State has the right to grant asylum to any individual under its control according to the principle of the sovereign State, which is widely recognized in International Law. This principle establishes that a State can either grant or deny asylum to any individual located within its territories due to its control or sovereignty over its territories, as well as the individuals within them. Hence, the right to asylum in International Law is considered a State's right and not an individual's right. Nevertheless, the Universal Declaration of Human Rights in article 14 has enshrined a person's right to asylum outside his country where he faces persecution. The Declaration on Territorial Asylum in 1967 also stated in article 1 that asylum should be granted by a State in accordance with its sovereignty to every persecuted person, and all the other States should respect that. Also, it considers that the State has the full authority to grant asylum without any restriction, so that the State can determine the suitable grounds to grant asylum or to deny it.[6] Similarly, the Convention on Territorial Asylum, which was conducted in 1954 by the Organization of American States, has adopted the State's right to grant asylum in Article (1) that says: "every State has the right, in the exercise of its sovereignty, to admit into its territory such persons as it deems advisable, without, through the exercise of this right, giving rise to a complaint by any other State."[7] Other international conventions have affirmed this right as a State's right, such as the Asian African Legal Consultative Committee in 1966, and the declaration on Territorial Asylum by the Committee of Ministers of the Council of Europe in Art.2.

However, the State having the authority to grant or to deny asylum to asylum seekers exacerbates the problem of "the growing scale of irregular migration", particularly since many States adopt certain measures to diminish the opportunities for people to get asylum by claiming the refugee status. This forces asylum seekers to choose other destinations, causing irregular movement and making the situation more complicated due to the difficulties

---

[6] Roman Boed: The States of The Right of Asylum in International Law. Articles, Duke Journal of Comparative and International Law, Vol.5:1. P. 3-5. And see Declaration in Territorial Asylum, art.1. UN Doc. A/6912 (1967).

[7] The Convention on Territorial Asylum, Mar. 28, 1954, art.1. And see the Declaration on Territorial Asylum, Nov.18,1977, art.2. Roman Boed, ibid. P. 5.

of distinguishing between asylum seekers, regular or irregular migrants, refugees and subsidiary protection persons. This becomes more complicated since all of them need protection and asylum, so that the State requires determining the status of all applicants accurately, which also causes "backlogs" of asylum applications and the inability of the States to expeditiously deal with huge numbers of applications every year.[8] Consequently, there is a genuine tension between the State's right to grant asylum by regulating the access to it, the period of stay, residences, and a person's right to seek and be granted asylum. To relieve some of the tension between both rights, the UNHCR has emphasized the importance of not preventing international migration, and hence of decreasing people's claims of getting protection and asylum, while also emphasizing how migration can improve the States' economies and benefit human development. It also establishes that promoting human rights in their countries of origin would play an essential role in decreasing the numbers of migrants. Thus, States should not prohibit migration insofar as implementing their obligation to promote security and human rights in the countries of migrants, this prohibition by States will not reduce irregular migration because the latter is almost based on the lack of implementing human rights.[9]

In this sense, promoting security could effectively diminish the most common cause of migration, which is a challenging task, although it is also necessary to raise the living conditions in poor countries, as well as achieve the required security in countries that have internal conflicts and civil wars. That puts the onus on the "developed countries", particularly the powerful ones, as they need to work with the UN and support "peacekeeping and peacebuilding" in those vulnerable countries.[10]

Even though the State has such a right due to its sovereignty, what would happen if the States were compelled to the humanitarian obligation of granting asylum since the right to asylum, at its core, is a right to get protection against torture or persecution from an ethical perspective?[11] In

---

[8] Jeff Crisp and Damtew Dessalegne: New Issues in Refugee Research, Refugee Protection and Migration Management: The Challenge for UNHCR. Working Paper No. 64. UNHCR, CP 2500, 1211 Geneva 2, Switzerland. Evaluation and Policy Analysis Unit 2002. P. 2.
[9] Ibid. P. 4.
[10] Ibid. P. 5,6.
[11] Maurice Stierl: Migrant Resistance in Contemporary Europe, edited by Jenny Edkins and Nick Vaughan-Williams. New York: Routledge, 2019. P. 145.

that case, States should share the burden to provide protection, regardless of the pretext of the sovereignty, which would not be affected if asylum seekers gained the protection and safety that they are looking for in the host State. Moreover, the right to asylum should be respected. First of all, because it stems from one of the fundamental human rights, which is the right to life. As long as this right is threatened by persecution and is at risk, the person has at least the right to stay alive and to live in a secure and safe place outside his country if these circumstances are not possible in their own country. These person's country must take the appropriate measures to protect him in these dangerous situations, although most of the times this is not likely to be possible due to the armed conflict in its territories, or even due to its being a potential part of the internal conflict itself against the person in other cases.

The second face of the right to asylum is a person's right to seek asylum when facing persecution or when his fundamental rights have somehow been denied in his country. As a consequence, the only solution that he can think of is to go to another country rather than stay there at risk of serious harm and waiting for death. This is the reason why many international instruments stipulate a person's right to seek asylum elsewhere to get the protection he needs. The right to seek asylum was stipulated in the Universal Declaration of Human Rights 1948 in Art. 13(2), which has been previously outlined in the second chapter of this research. It says: "Everyone has the right to leave any country including his own, and to return to his country."[12] Apparently, article 13 intended to give the person the freedom of movement, not only inside the borders of his country, but also abroad so that they would not be constrained. Further, it enshrined the right to leave one's own country, making it an obligation of the States to respect and support it as a right belonging to the Modern Customary International Law. At the same time, it did not announce the right to leave as a recognized right, so that it is not the duty of the States to admit that person in any country after leaving his own. Consequently, it is just a right without any duties or commitments from the States for it to be a firmly binding right.[13] The right to leave has also been reaffirmed in other international instruments like the International Covenant on Civil and Political Rights when it asserted in article 12 (2) that: "everyone

---

[12] Roman Boed, ibid. P. 6. And see the Universal Declaration of Human Rights, art.13 (2). https://www.un.org/en/about-us/universal-declaration-of-human-rights.

[13] David Miller and Christine Straehle, ibid. P. 45.

shall be free to leave any country, including his own."[14]

Also, the United Nations Commission on Human Rights and the Sub-Commission on Prevention of Discrimination and Protection of Minorities have recognized the right to leave. Similarly, "the regional instruments" have respected the right to leave in Protocol No.4 to the European Convention for the Protection of Human Rights and Fundamental Freedoms. In addition to the Draft Charter on Human and People's Rights in the Arab World in 1987, the American Covenant on Human Rights enshrined the right to leave in article 22 (2) that reads: every person has the right to leave any country freely, including his own.[15]

The third face of the right to asylum is the person's right to be granted asylum. Article 14 of the Universal Declaration of Human Rights granted the right to seek asylum in another country to the person fleeing persecution if this claim was not based on prosecution or an objective, for this would be inconsistent with the purposes or principles of the United Nations that say:

1. Everyone has the right to seek and to enjoy asylum from persecution in other countries.
2. This right may not be invoked in the case of prosecutions genuinely arising from non-political crimes or from acts contrary to the purposes and principles of the United Nations.[16]

Thus, the UDHR has declared a person's right to seek and enjoy asylum in any country where he could find protection and be free of any threat of persecution. However, there are no guarantees because article 14 does not explicitly oblige "other countries" to allow asylum seekers to enter their borders and resettle there without any difficulties, and it has not imposed them to facilitate the exit of asylum seekers from their countries of origin either. It is just an underspecified right like many other rights included in the UDHR.[17]Article 14 merely intended to mention a provision for asylum, which is an existing right of the States to grant it. So, it did not create anything new for the right of asylum. This article was very accurate in the draft before

---

[14] International Covenant on Civil and Political Rights, art.12 (2).
[15] Roman Boed, ibid. P. 7. And see American Convention on Human Rights, Nov. 22, 1969.
[16] Universal Declaration of Human Rights, art. 14.
[17] David Miller and Christine Straehle, ibid. P. 45.

being modified. It specified the right to seek and to be granted asylum in other countries, and it obliged the States to grant asylum in the case of persecution. However, it faced criticism later for substituting "to enjoy" for the words "to be granted", to avoid the obligation of the States to grant asylum.[18]

The Refugee Convention in 1951 laid out some responsibilities for the States to comply with the refugee status when it affirmed the right to seek and enjoy asylum for the persons who have already entered the borders of the host State to guarantee their rights to have protection from persecution and live within its territories. Therefore, the Convention encompasses the State's duty to provide protection to the refugees who are located in its lands and is not entitled to implement a system for admitting or rejecting asylum seekers. In other words, it does not intervene in the State's decision if the State decides not to admit an asylum seeker or in other cases, when the State chooses to conduct negotiations with the persecuting State to resolve some issues regarding refugees. Moreover, the Convention obliges the host States to grant the rights of refugees to all refugees, whether they exist within their territories lawfully or unlawfully, and the refugees, in turn, should comply with the national laws in the host countries and respect the public order there as well. Certainly, the Convention did not impose an obligation on the States to open their borders for the persecuted persons seeking asylum nor did it guarantee asylum seekers' stay in the host country after successfully entering its borders. Thus, it leaves the decision to the host State about whether or not admitting the refugee or to expelling him if he unlawfully entered its territories, taking into account not returning him to his country of origin, where he could face persecution.[19] If the persons who are not qualified refugees according to the definition of refugee status in the 1951 Convention failed to get protection in the host country, they have the opportunity to be granted asylum as subsidiary protection, which is established by International Human Rights Law based on specific circumstances. Some of them are: persons who are not persecuted or have a well-founded fear of persecution but could be at risk of being subjected to serious harm as a result of a violation of human rights or internal conflict or civil war, in case they are expelled and returned to their

---

[18] Roman Boed, ibid. P.9, 10.
[19] David Miller and Christine Straehle, ibid. P. 46- 48.

country.[20] Even though this is a way to seek asylum, it does not promote to be claimed before leaving the person's country and entering the borders of the receiving country. Thus, any person who seeks asylum elsewhere can be granted asylum after entering the borders of the destination country and providing an application according to its legal system. Nevertheless, that does not mean that he has the right to get asylum in law, and the State does not have any other choice but to grant him asylum. The situation depends on fulfilling certain provisions to qualify for subsidiary protection if he was not considered as a refugee. That will be accomplished if both requirements are fulfilled: the person was already in the receiving country, and there is no reason to prohibit him from granting asylum, such as committing crimes or posing a threat to the national community, or any other reason that constitutes an obstacle and makes granting asylum an impossible option. In other words, the right to asylum is still unrecognized in International Law since States do not have the duty to grant asylum to individuals who left their countries seeking protection, as international and regional instruments did not establish it as an enforceable right since the Refugee Convention 1951 and its Protocol 1967 did not include a person's right to be granted asylum. Further, the UNHCR has assured in its Handbook on Procedures and Criteria for Determining Refugee Status under the 1951 Convention and the 1967 Protocol Relating to the Status of Refugees in 1979 that: "the granting of asylum is not dealt with in the 1951 Convention or the 1967 Protocol".[21] The refugee may have a positive right not to be expelled of the host country territories given the principle of non-refoulement. Hence, he is protected from expulsion but does not have the right to stay and resettle in the country. The refugee in this context has a temporary residence that could be removed whenever circumstances in his country improve, or if his stay in the host country territories poses a threat for other persons within. Thereby, the refugee residence is somehow constrained by conditions, and it merely provides protection from persecution regardless of the refugee's desire to stay in the host country or to live his life in the way he sees fit.[22]

---

[20] Maria-Teresa Gil- Bazo: New Issues in Refugee Research, Refugee status, subsidiary protection, and the right to be granted asylum under EC law. Research Paper No.136. Refugee Studies Centre, Oxford University UK. UNHCR Policy development and Evaluation Service, November 2006.P. 10.
[21] Roman Boed, ibid. P. 9-11.
[22] David Miller and Christine Straehle, ibid. P. 48,49.

Regarding regional instruments, there is an ambiguity in the enforceability of a person's right to be granted asylum when article 13 of the Directive 2011/95/EU of the European Parliament and the Council of the European Union says that: "Member States shall grant refugee status to a third-country national or Stateless person who qualifies as a refugee in accordance with Chapters II and III". This article has not necessarily provided a person's right to get asylum vis-a-vis the State, but rather the State is still free to admit or refuse him because the term "refugee status" is determined by the definition of the Refugee Convention of 1951 and how much the third-country person or the stateless person fulfills its requirements. Then, the States are entitled to decide not to grant refugee status to a person in case there are reasonable grounds for being him a danger to the national security or public order in the host State, or if the person has been convicted of a crime which constitutes a danger to the community of the State according to the paragraph 4 of article 14 of the Directive. Moreover, article 18 of the same Directive has not firmly determined the right of a person to be granted asylum, instead, it gives the third-country national or a stateless person the right to be granted subsidiary protection if they are eligible for it in accordance with Chapter II and V. Thus, the discretionary obligation of member States reveals the failure of transposing the right to be granted asylum into the domestic legal orders of the States.[23]

Also, the International Human Rights Law has not conferred a right to enter and resettle for a permanent term for non-nationals. At the same time, the United Nations Human Rights Committee enshrined the right to return to one's country in article 12(4), regardless of his nationality. This has broader implications as it did not confine this right to nationals, but is available to individuals who are living in that country and have residences although it is not their country of origin.[24] Therefore, international instruments did not enable to explicitly legitimate and recognize the right to enter asylum permanently for other individuals who are not nationals. They deliberately left this right unrecognized, serving the State's interests, and maybe, to establish reciprocity between States in the future regarding the right to enter.

---

[23] Maria-Teresa Gil- Bazo: New Issues in Refugee Research, Refugee status, subsidiary protection, and the right to be granted asylum under EC law, ibid. P. 8,9.
[24] Ibid. P. 12.

This dualism leaves the right to be granted asylum in an arguable place, when the right to enter is determined by some clauses and can be denied to some individuals. In this regard, human rights in general, face a challenge of "inter-State reciprocity", which means that we should go back to States to protect human rights and then to the refugee's right to be granted asylum in the host country. The host State' willingness is almost the crucial factor for granting refugees their basic rights, such as work and housing, and the host State could increase the pressure on them, especially since refugees would be looking forward to working to obtain a better life and find safe accommodations to resettle within the territories of the host country where they find the safety and security.[25]

The Legal Basis of the Right to Asylum:

Migration was of vital interest to people in 1948 when the UDHR provided some potential resources regarding migration, such as the right to seek and enjoy asylum in Art.14, besides Art. 15, where the right to a nationality and the right to change nationality have been stated and recognized for everyone. A major migratory movement emerged in 2015 and surpassed 250 million people. Over 5 million of them were driven by internal conflicts and arrived to Europe by death boats, challenging all perils to reach European territory, where they intend to live safely after been granted asylum.[26] More than 46,000 persons have perished in the Mediterranean Sea while trying to cross it since 2000, and about 4000 migrants died in 2015 alone.[27]

There is definitely a huge problem in our contemporary World, since despite enshrining the right to asylum in many international instruments, migration as a right in Human Rights Law, is still contingent on the States' sovereignty. Human Rights Law should be more enforceable and impose duties on the States to grant protection to asylum seekers by providing visas at first and enabling refugees to enter their territories and stay there as long as they want. Furthermore, all the States should consider the human rights of refugees over their sovereignty because those rights naturally precede the sovereignty of the

---

[25] David Miller and Christine Straehle, ibid. P.11,13

[26] Vicki Squire: Europe's Migration Crisis, Borders Deaths and Human Dignity. University of Warwick. New York, Cambridge University Press, first published 2020. P. 109, 110.

[27] Gordon Brown (ed.), The Universal Declaration of Human Rights in the 21st Century: A Living Document in a Changing World. Cambridge, UK: Open Book Publishers, 2016. http://dx.doi.org/10.11647/OBP.0091. P. 48,49.

State, and should therefore be prioritized over it.[28] Thus, a person's right to stay in the State which granted him asylum has some legal clarifications in International Human Rights Law and the Universal Declaration of Human Rights, as well as the Refugee Convention and European Treaties. Therefore, we can understand the nature of this right by studying the relationship between all the mentioned international instruments, which will be illustrated in the following section.

Asylum in International Human Rights Law and the Universal Declaration of Human Rights:

The most contradictory issue in International Human Rights Law lies in the relation between international human rights or "universalism of human rights," which stem from the global citizenship concept, and the self-determination right of a State to protect its national security. However, since international human rights do not limit migration in general, but rather they strive to manage it, particularly "conflictual migration," migration due to internal conflicts around the World furthers this mission of human rights law in preventing conflicts from arising and dealing with them whenever they arise, to control the migratory movement implying the idea that human rights do not only limit the States 'attempts to hinder migration, but it could also work to control migration without preventing it altogether.[29]

The International Human Rights Law has an effective and enforceable role in implementing human rights by imposing obligations on the "responsible actors" in the States in order to come up with "creative actions" to deal with any change in social and political space, in a proactive and active manner. Thereby, International Human Rights Law reframes the response to migration in a much better way than the national law does, although it is still lacking the effectiveness that the national law has. International Law can manage "transnational issues" as migration in a more comprehensive way. For instance, International Law can receive claims of persons directly through international courts concerning human rights, thus enhancing migration management. In this context, International Law proves that

---

[28] Marie Claire Foblets, Luc Leboeuf (eds): Humanitarian Admission to Europe, The Law between Promises and Constraints. 1 Edition, Nomos. Germany 2020. P. 50,51.
[29] Markus Kotzur / David Moya / Ulku'Sezgi Sözen / Andrea Romano (eds): The External Dimension of EU Migration and Asylum Policies, Border Management, Human Rights and Development Policies in the Mediterranean Area. 1st Edition. Nomos Verlagsgesellschaft, Baden-Baden, Germany 2020. P. 15,16.

sovereignty may not be completely impenetrable to international migration management, so that national sovereignty may not always win against an individual's freedom as a human right, as long as the State has signed international conventions that safeguard them. Otherwise, the principle of sovereignty mentioned in the UN Charter is interpreted differently, especially regarding the idea that sovereignty does not necessarily mean that the State's borders must be closed to serve it, but rather persons' freedom should make them open relying on human rights.[30]

However, human rights sometimes do not prevail over the State's sovereignty. For example, the protection of refugees, according to the second paragraph of article 32 of the Refugee Convention of 1951, does not come before the national security of the State. Consequently, this kind of tension between the State's sovereignty and human rights, and the fact that security interests are prioritized over human rights creates conflicts that require dealing justifiably, which is the function of International Human Rights Law.[31] Primarily, the efficiency of protecting universal human rights depends on the States grounded on its sovereignty. Moreover, the State has the right to grant asylum to those who are in its jurisdiction. Also, human rights cannot force States to grant "more than asylum", such as permanent residence or citizenship to foreigners. In this context, States are just committed to not returning those persons to their countries of origin according to the principle of non-refoulement in International Law. Thus, the problem is that States have the tool of sovereignty to utilize when implementing their obligations regarding human rights and, in fact, human rights are firmly guaranteed, but witness a kind of gradual applicability which depends on the authority of the State and how many persons are proximate to this authority as well.[32]

According to International Human Rights Law, States that have signed human rights treaties should be responsible for providing protection to their own citizens and all the residents in their territories. This provision includes States in which many infringements on human rights have been observed with internal conflicts and civil wars outbreaking in Syria, Iraq, and Libya, as well as States that respect and apply human rights protection, such as

---

[30] Ibid. P. 17,18.
[31] Ibid. P. 19.
[32] Marie Claire Foblets, Luc Leboeuf (eds): Humanitarian Admission to Europe, ibid. P. 51.

Germany, Denmark, and Sweden. Consequently, that raises the question of whether States that are foreign to the human rights violations should be responsible for these violations that are happening in other States due to civil war, for instance, or if they are exclusively responsible for protecting their citizens and residents in their jurisdiction. That follows intervention in internal affairs of the State where human rights are violated. In some cases, a humanitarian intervention can be justifiable, because the Security Council has the authority to decide any measures it sees fit, besides having the responsibility to protect (R2P) in Chapter 7 of the UN Charter and maintain peace and security.[33] Thus, the protection of international human rights clashes with the sovereignty of States, especially if the States are unable or unwilling to provide the required protection for their citizens[34]. Nevertheless, International Human Rights Law does not have sufficient guarantees for effectively implementing the right to stay in the host country as a universal human right as it is at the discretion of the State to decide who will be protected and what kind of residence they will have. Even though the Universal Declaration of Human Rights enshrines the right to leave, this right was recognized without considering the right to enter and resettle in asylum within the host country' territories. This led to an increasing awareness of international immigration and the need for recognizing it as a human right, although neither the UDHR nor the International Human Rights Law stipulated a person's right to stay wherever he finds asylum. This is particularly relevant for the refugees who left their countries seeking security, without any kind of recognition being likely to happen. Instead, Human Rights Law developed the principle of non-refoulement as a way to restrict a State's and to extend the range of refugees who could benefit from this by including every one of the refugees who would be subject to "a serious risk of torture or inhuman treatment" if the State returned him to his country of origin. This way, Human Right Law guarantees the protection of fundamental rights to new categories of migrants who are not considered refugees according to the traditional meaning of the term[35]. This principle could be applied as an extraterritorial jurisdiction principle, whereas the refoulement

---

[33] Ibid. P. 55.
[34] Ibid. P. 55,56.
[35] Anne T. Gallagher (2013): Migration, Human Rights, and Development: A Global Anthology. International Debate Education Association. New York, NY 10010. P. 135, 136.

(expulsion), according to the European Court of Human Rights (ECtHR), is "principally territorial," and the contracting State can also utilize its jurisdiction to include cases outside its territory, which manifests in "a collective expulsion."[36] Therefore, the claim to asylum, regardless of whether the person is a refugee or just enjoys asylum by subsidiary protection, relies on the fact that International Human Rights Law, as well as the Universal Declaration of Human Rights, were unable to provide effective guarantees to sufficiently protect the human rights of persons who are subjected to persecution in their countries of origin. Moreover, those persons who are seeking asylum outside their countries would never be granted the same rights that citizens of the host country have, especially the permanent residence and nationality, which give the person a right to stay without being constrained by time and under the threat of refoulement in case persecution or internal conflict in his country is solved. This may be due to the unlimited sovereignty of the State, which could be the biggest obstacle in implementing the core of human rights conventions grounded on the need of international cooperation between the States serving the provisions of the International Migration Law regarding human rights. In contrast, States consider that this kind of protection negatively affects their national security and public order, finding it inconsistent with their sovereignty. Nevertheless, whatever the limitations human rights impose on the States' sovereignty, they always fail in curtailing the States' enjoyment of their sovereign right to freely determine the persons who deserve the residence and terminate their residence to be, limiting the non-refoulement principle and thus depriving persons of their human rights of being granted protection.[37]

Although the Universal Declaration of Human Rights has enshrined in Art 14 the right to seek and enjoy asylum, it cannot undermine the States' sovereignty in terms of their authority to decide who enters their territories. It cannot impose duties on the States to facilitate persecuted persons leaving their countries of origin and being able to get asylum somewhere safe.[38]

The reason for this could be to avoid overcrowding, especially that the States were demanded to safeguard human rights to all individuals grounded on the

---

[36] Marie Claire Foblets, Luc Leboeuf (eds): Humanitarian Admission to Europe, ibid. P. 70, 71.

[37] Ibid. P. 72.

[38] David Miller and Christine Straehle, ibid. 45.

approach that the transnational sources of human rights' implementation are indeed more beneficial and effective than the domestic ones. Moreover, many states consider that not all issues can be dealt with in the same way, especially when it comes to a person's need for legal protection, which can be based on another framework, such as International Humanitarian Law that aims to limit persecution and the negative effects of armed conflicts around the World. Perhaps this could be the solution in this case, or perhaps some cases could be established, not on human rights, but on criminal law when the case binds to a crime committed by the persecuting side in the country of origin.[39]

Asylum in the Refugee Convention of 1951 and United Nations High Commissioner for Refugees:

The Refugee Convention, which was signed in Geneva and which constitutes with its Protocol 1967 the essential pillar of the International Refugee Law, states in Art 33 the right to asylum by prohibiting the expulsion or refoulement of persons who are actually residing outside their countries of origin after fleeing persecution. It confined its provisions to asylum seekers and, this way, it established the right to enter territories where they could apply for asylum. However, it did not discuss the situations of those who still live in their countries since they could not leave and seek asylum elsewhere. This gap in the convention has constituted a plight of recognizing the right to asylum as an absolute right and enforceable by law without any clauses. The Convention has placed duties on the member States concerning the persons who are in fact asylum seekers within its territories to provide protection by granting them residences to keep them safe from persecution. Regarding the States' sovereignty and its right to decide who enters their national borders, the duty imposed by the Convention to grant asylum only applies to the persons who have succeeded in passing the borders and have started living in its lands. Furthermore, the Convention left it to the States to conduct any negotiations serve issues relating to refugees' distribution between member States, or to make agreements with persecuting countries to release persecuted persons in some cases, if any of the member States want

---

[39] Marie Claire Foblets, Luc Leboeuf (eds): Humanitarian Admission to Europe, The Law between Promises and Constraints. 1 Edition, Nomos. Germany 2020. P. 73.

to admit them and grant them asylum.[40]

However, the member State is still not obliged to facilitate the exit of persecuted persons from their countries to claim asylum in the host country, especially since the Convention explicitly announced that the right to asylum would be enforceable for persons who have already left their persecuting countries and applied for asylum in the host country. Thus, the big obstacle lies in the procedures of accessing asylum and having the legal protection that all EU member States promise to provide. That, in turn, pushes persons to leave their countries and irregularly enter the European territories after passing the sea by death boats just to be able to apply for asylum.[41]

The Convention assumed that the refugees would only reside in the host country temporarily, so it did not discuss a long-term residence in its provisions. The reason for this may be to avoid the negative consequences of a permanent residence of migrants in their countries of origin, which could lead to brain drain and would conclude potential problems in the countries of origin that occur when they are unable to rebuild once the internal conflict has been resolved.[42]

However, the definition of refugee in the first article of the Convention was very restrictive when it included the reasons for persecution "race, religion, nationality, membership of a social group or political opinion", and excluded other reasons which could significantly motivate the mass influx of migrants every year. Some of these reasons are armed conflicts, civil wars, or even climate change and its consequences or environmental disasters. As a response, Art 33 of the Convention was more comprehensive and enshrined that: "No Contracting State shall expel or return ("refouler") a refugee in any manner whatsoever to the frontiers of territories where his life or freedom would be threatened on account of his race, religion, nationality, membership of a particular social group or political opinion". This article has established the right of the refugee not to be expelled, as long as the threat is ongoing in his country of origin. This also applies only to the refugees who entered the host country, regardless of the way in which they passed its borders. Thus,

---

[40] David Miller and Christine Straehle, ibid. 46. And see Markus Kotzur / David Moya / Ulkü Sezgi Sözen / Andrea Romano (eds): The External Dimension of EU Migration and Asylum Policies, Border Management, Human Rights and Development Policies in the Mediterranean Area, ibid. P. 26.

[41] Marie Claire Foblets, Luc Leboeuf (eds): Humanitarian Admission to Europe, ibid. P. 92.

[42] Markus Kotzur / David Moya / Ulkü Sezgi Sözen / Andrea Romano, ibid. P. 29.

illegal entry is the only way to arrive at the destination country because of the difficulties in getting humanitarian visas, despite the serious threat of fundamental human rights violations.

Art 33 has guaranteed human rights on a legal basis and without being a person in danger.[43] However, the principle of non-refoulement is still not enough "too thin" in terms of its function, which includes only granting temporary residences to refugees and not being expelled and returned to origin countries. Those persons should be able to resettle in the host country freely without clauses or complications. The general approach should concentrate on the mere right to migrate, while considering the ability of each country to receive a certain number of migrants.[44]

The Refugee Convention, in principle, limited the status of persecution or the fear of persecution to certain circumstances and did not mention armed conflict as one of them. Nevertheless, it granted the right to subsidiary protection to persons suffering from armed conflict in their countries in order to give them an opportunity to live in safe conditions in the host country. Art 33 of the Convention affirmed that the right to stay "temporarily" in the host country should be tied to the situation of armed conflict in the country of origin in order to be able to benefit from the right to migrate and resettle in a country where the person enjoys is safe. However, this right depends on the extent of attachment between the person and the host country, so that the more serious the threat, the stronger the attachment will be to the host country, which would strengthen the right to stay that the Convention has protected in the case of armed conflict.[45]

Undoubtedly, the non-refoulement principle in the Convention does not effectively force States to admit asylum seekers and allow them to enter without the States agreeing altogether. When the State accepted asylum seekers, it still has the right to expel them whenever it considers their presence affects public order or national security, even though the Refugee Convention establishes that all member States should protect refugees regardless of their unlawful method of entry. However, according to the

---

[43] Ibid. P. 30.
[44] David Miller and Christine Straehle, ibid. 48, 49.
[45] Markus Kotzur / David Moya / Ulkü Sezgi Sözen / Andrea Romano (eds): The External Dimension of EU Migration and Asylum Policies, Border Management, Human Rights and Development Policies in the Mediterranean Area, ibid. P. 32, 33.

Convention States can use their authority in refusing asylum seekers or expel refugees if they have been convicted of serious crimes in the host community due to the real danger that those persons cause to others. In this case, the expulsion of refugees and returning them to their country could be allowed if the State has no other choices. Especially since one of the States' obligations to their citizens is to protect their lives from any danger that could threaten national security and public order.[46]

The Convention was not completely biased toward the right to asylum for asylum seekers against the States' authority and their right to self-determination. It explicitly asserted that States should prioritize their common goods and serve their citizens over the right to asylum for non-citizens and displaced persons. The Convention has framed the good treatment of refugees and, at the same time, opened the possibility for States to refuse them and return them to their countries of origin in certain situations, trying not to burden the States when they admit massive numbers of asylum seekers that are more than they can deal with, for that would have negative consequences, such as increasing the unemployment rate and poverty among their citizens.[47] However, the Refugee Convention is still applicable until 2021, despite some member States' attempts to evade their commitments toward refugees.

The Convention was keen on providing protection to all refugees who fall under its definition of refugee, regardless of the permit of residence that the host State can grant an asylum seeker who entered its territory, based only on his claim to be a refugee. Besides, it assures in Art 31 that States should not punish those asylum seekers who entered the host territories illegally. Nevertheless, some of the member States do not have certain provisions in their national legislations to implement their commitment in Art 31 of the Convention, so that an impartial and objective application of the "executive discretion" will be the reference for full compliance with the Convention in this situation.[48]

---

[46] David Miller and Christine Straehle, ibid. 54, 55.
[47] Ibid. P. 58.
[48] Guy S. Goodwin-Gill, Article 31 of the 1951 Convention relating to the Status of Refugees: Non-

Some governments of member States seem to unwelcome refugees or to reduce their number within their territories. They have such policies to control immigration by studying the claim of asylum seekers and the whole process of their applications to determine "genuine asylum seekers" from those who are just "bogus asylum seekers."[49] Furthermore, all the norms and international agreements related to refugee affairs are also developed by the governments under the surveillance of the UNHCR, that seeks to resolve the essential problems in the refugee crisis. The UNHCR assures that all norms and principles of the "global refugee regime" are well implemented by the States, in accordance with the primary task of the UNHCR that the Refugee Convention has defined explicitly.[50] Those norms and principles to protect refugees suppose that the enormous numbers of refugees often flee their countries due to certain human rights violations and political persecution, besides other kinds of persecutions. As a consequence, the mandate of the UNHCR aims to oversee displaced persons grounded on armed conflict or are victims of some kind of discrimination since most refugees seek asylum after facing persecution. Therefore, the 1951 Convention mainly focused on the resettlement and asylum of persecuted persons or those people who would be at risk if they returned to their countries, which is why they were granted temporary protection. The Convention has determined the States' commitments toward refugees and appointed the UNHCR as the main responsible organization for monitoring the States' implementation of the provisions of the Convention and all the norms that frame the global refugee regime to provide sufficient protection for all refugees worldwide.[51]

Overall, the Refugee Convention has assumed that refugees are highly in need of international protection because they left their countries where normal legal protection is a right, and the governments should try to ensure them for all citizens. The refugees should also have international protection outside their countries, such as the right to employment and integration into the host country. Consequently, the principle of non-refoulement, which was

---

penalization, Detention and Protection. A paper prepared by the Department of International Protection for the UNHCR Global Consultations. University of Oxford. October 2001. P. 32.

[49] Teresa Hayter (2004): Open Borders, The Case Against Immigration Controls. Second Edition, Pluto Press. London. P. 65.

[50] Alexander Betts (2011): Global Migration Governance. Edited by Alexander Betts. First edition. Oxford University Press. P. 189.

[51] Ibid. P. 91, 92.

stipulated in the Convention, was grossly a questionable right for all refugees have the right not to be returned to their countries if the risk of being persecuted is still present. The Convention almost seems to widen the refugee definition to be more consistent with the human rights principles in an attempt to respond to a new regime of protection which aims to include those persons who have not had any kind of international protection after the loss of their national governments' protection.[52] Although the principle of non-refoulement provides temporary protection to refugees in the same territory, neighboring States should preferably host refugees who fled States with which they have common borders. Lebanon, as a neighboring country to Syria, demanded the UNHCR in May 2015 not to register any Syrian person who had entered its borders after that date and enacted new burdensome regulations and measures against Syrian refugees, which resulted in a large number of Syrians staying in Lebanon without legal permission.[53] When other States do not have an equivalent number of refugees, they do not deal with the burden of responsibility. This uneven distribution of refugees constitutes "the international collective responsibility" to achieve the best implementation of the non-refoulement principle by implying international cooperation, which is known as "burden sharing." Nevertheless, this policy failed in the Syrian crisis where the increasing numbers of asylum seekers crossing the Mediterranean to get asylum in the EU member States have put pressure on the redistribution of receiving asylum applications between the States. Thereby, the UNHCR attempts to achieve international solidarity and burden sharing were grossly complicated, particularly because some of the northern States tried to evade their responsibilities and send them to other States by ensuring their incapacity to bear with additional burdens.[54]

Apparently, the UNHCR has a crucial role in this context, for it can execute its activities in tandem with the limits that the influential States set on the policy of hosting refugees. Therefore, the global refugee regime and how

---

[52] Jane McAdam. New Issues in Refugee Research, The Refugee Convention as a rights blueprint for persons in need of international protection. Research Paper No. 125. Faculty of Law, University of Sydney, Australia. Policy Development and Evaluation Service UNHCR. July 2006. P. 7, 8.

[53] Anne Marie Baylouny: When Blame Backfires: Syrian Refugees and the Citizen Grievances in Jordan and Lebanon. Cornell University Press. First published. Ithaca, New York, 2020, p. 116.

[54] Alexander Betts (2011): Global Migration Governance, ibid. P. 193-195. And see also Ernst Hirsch Ballin, Emina Ćerimović, Huub Dijstelbloem, Mathieu Segers: European Variations as a Key to Cooperation. The Netherland Scientific Council for Government Policy (WRR). Published by Springer Nature Switzerland, 18 September 2020. P. 141

effective it can be, depends on the contributions of the States, and not only on the organization itself. States can provide initiatives to assume activities to help refugees and in doing so support the UNHCR mission of expanding the range of the hosting States and establishing cooperation between the northern States, which are required to donate for refugees and the southern States that are already hosting them.[55] The UNHCR has faced real pressure because of the asylum crisis since 1990 with all its challenges, especially since the global refugee numbers have increased in a very problematic way at the time that all States in the global north and south have started to set restrictions on asylum in general. Some States adopted the policy of closing borders against asylum seekers and returning refugees to their countries, denying the basic rights that the Refugee Convention stipulated in 1951. Thus, the right to asylum has become constrained by the States. For instance, southern States have isolated the refugees in their territories in camps far from the national community, and they depend on international assistance without doing any national endeavors to improve the refugees' situation and integrate them into the community. However, the UNHCR must find solutions to the asylum crisis and provide protection to refugees, which will not be possible without cooperation among the States. Therefore, the UNHCR had an initiative in 2000 to converge the States' interests and the necessity of resolving the refugee plight by granting them international protection. Unfortunately, this process was not totally beneficial to the global refugee regime.[56]

On the other hand, the Executive Committee of the Programme of the UNHCR (ExCom) has had the most significant executive functions, such as decision-making in the field of the global refugee regime. It enhanced the interaction between industrialized countries, which are the strongest donators for refugees given the fact that the program of the UNHCR basically depends on such contributions to carry out its function, and the developing countries, which are hosting the largest numbers of refugees.[57] Since the program of the UNHCR hugely depends on the contributions of members present to support international protection of refugees worldwide, many donating States play an effective role in the UNHCR related to their "perceived interests".

---

[55] Alexander Betts, ibid. P. 196.
[56] Ibid. P. 197, 198.
[57] Ibid. P. 200.

For instance, the USA has a "global hegemon" of the refugee regime entirely due to its power and a large percentage of contributions to the UNHCR budget. Despite this kind of demonstration by northern States on the UNHCR' work and their unserious efforts to make the required cooperation for the global refugee regime, those countries genuinely cooperate with the UNHCR in terms of the resettlement of refugees to fulfill international protection and the burden share.[58] Thereby, the UNHCR considers resettlement as "a durable solution" for enhancing international solidarity and sharing the responsibility towards refugees. Even more so in the countries hosting refugee and the countries that are coping with the asylum concept and the vast numbers of refugees, regardless of the negative consequences of resettlement such as "brain drain". Besides, it is still unclear whether resettlement is the sole solution for the refugee plight, or if "remote funding", for example, could be well applicable while these persons stay in their countries of origin.[59]

However, the UNHCR has many challenges. The most important one is the ability to use the interests of the States to motivate them to carry out their commitments to refugee protection, without being engaged in the political domain, only to be extremely politicized and lose its core aims. Therefore, the future effectiveness of the global refugee regime strongly depends on the success of the UNHCR in achieving its objectives by focusing on international cooperation with the States and fulfilling the burden sharing among them to solve the global refugee problems and grant refugees the required protection.[60]

The UNHCR has given the authority of refugees' status determination to the national governments, so it is their legal responsibility to admit or reject asylum seekers after studying their applications. Meanwhile, the Refugee Convention and its instruments regarding its refugee definition are considered the criterion to make the final decision in which the State protects the asylum seeker from expulsion, as long as they meet the requirements of the refugee status based on its definition. In contrast, some countries leave it to the UNHCR to decide on their behalf relating to the refugee status

---

[58] Ibid. P. 203.
[59] Ibid. P. 204, 205.
[60] Ibid. P. 207.

determination. Certainly, the refugee status determination could be conducted separately by the full authority of the State, or jointly, by the State and the UNHCR, so that the responsibility would be distributed or depend only on the UNHCR.[61]

Persons who have fled from civil wars may less opportunity of getting asylum than those who have faced persecution or face serious harm for being persecuted. That could be true due to some flawed assumptions by most of the host countries that the asylum seekers who come from civil wars would transmit their terroristic ideas and threaten the national security in the host countries.[62]

The UNHCR is still involved in the determination of the refugee status under the Refugee Convention instruments and its protocol in 1967, perusing to grant asylum seekers international protection by temporary residences in the host countries even though some of them have left their countries because of civil wars where the violation of any fundamental human rights was likely to happen.

The problematic issue in the asylum concept in our World lies in the inability of countries to implement an efficient and expeditious asylum system to determine the refugee status. The current system has shown its shortcomings in the backlogs of asylum applications, delay problems, and the weakness of skipping all rejected claimants. In addition to that, the UNHCR cannot highly influence the State's power regarding its migration measures and its policies toward migrants. Many States have restrictive measures to limit irregular migration, such as imposing sanctions and detaining asylum seekers whose entry to their territories is illegal. Consequently, a real tension would consequently emerge between the right of States to regulate settlement, the arrival arrangement and to admit or reject applications, and the right of the persons to seek and enjoy asylum and the protection that they need.[63] The UNHCR works hard to resolve such tension, or at least it deals with it in a meticulous way. It encourages developing and developed countries to

---

[61] Lamis Elmy Abdelaaty, Discrimination and Delegation. Oxford University Press. New York, 2021. P. 44.
[62] Ibid. P. 57, 58.
[63] Jeff Crisp, Damtew Dessalegne (2002): New Issues in Refugee Research, Refugee Protection and Migration Management: The challenge for UNHCR. Working paper No.64. August 2002. UNHCR Evaluation and Policy Analysis Unit. Geneva. P. 2. 3.

promote human rights in the whole World and to refrain from supporting persecuting regimes in the countries of origin of asylum seekers. This would facilitate the mission of the UN to maintain peace and safety worldwide.[64]

It is important that the refugee problem is resolved in their countries of origin, because "Exile" is not a permanent solution. Besides, this kind of upholding human rights is not considered an intervention and does not really constitute a threat to the national sovereignty of the persecuting countries. Rather, it promotes safety as a means to find effective solutions internally. For instance, western countries must refrain from trading arms and selling them to countries with civil wars and armed conflicts. In other words, the advocacy of human rights and protecting them from any violence across borders have, in fact, become "a legitimate concern" of the whole World.[65]

Asylum in European treaties:

The asylum term in the European Union was not a new form of protection, but it has developed gradually from the sanctuary that prevailed in the Roman era, in which every person in need of protection got a new life in a safe place. Over the years, asylum has been framed in a new shape. It is no more a "State's right" where the State has the right to grant a person asylum against persecution under such conditions that asylum seekers should have to have to be able to claim asylum in the European Union. It has become everyone's right to seek, to apply, and to enjoy asylum. That has been affirmed in certain instruments of different European treaties which have established the asylum system in the EU Law that is characterized by pursuing "Freedom, Security and justice" in the European Union. The aim is to be without borders by legitimizing the freedom of movement between member States, while remaining compliant with all the commitments stipulated in the Refugee Convention and all human rights agreements. This implies solidarity and burden sharing among EU member States to respond to the need of protection to asylum seekers.[66]

---

[64] Ibid. P. 5, 6.
[65] Gilbert H. Gornig, Hans-Detlef Horn (2017): Migration, Asyl, Flüchtlinge und Fremdenrecht. Deutschland und seine Nachbarn in Europa vor neuen Herausforderungen. Staats- und völkerrechtliche Abhandlungen der Studiengruppe für Politik und Völkerrecht, Volume 31. Dunker& Humblot. Berlin. Germany. P. 113.
[66] Bacaian, Livia Elena (2011): The protection of refugees and their right to seek asylum in the European

To analyze nature of asylum in the European Union, whether it is a State's right or an individual right, I will initially elaborate on some of the most important European treaties which have affirmed that each European State must receive asylum applications from asylum seekers to grant them international protection.

The most important step in the asylum law in Europe was functioning treaties. The first of them is the Treaty of Functioning of the European Union in 1957. The Consolidated Treaty on the Functioning of the European Union (TFEU) delved into the right to asylum in the European asylum law, which enshrined it along with the non-refoulement principle in Art. 78.1 that says: "The Union shall develop a common policy on asylum, subsidiary protection and temporary protection to offer appropriate status to any third-country national requiring international protection and ensuring compliance with the principle of non-refoulement. This policy must be in accordance with the Geneva Convention of July 28, 1951, and the Protocol of January31, 1967 relating to the status of refugees and other relevant treaties.[67] The treaty considered this right as one of the main objectives in the EU, when it ensured that free movement would be possible not only between member States, but also across borders so that asylum seekers would be able to enter European territories as stated in Art. 3 (2), which says: "The Union shall offer its citizens an area of freedom, security and justice without internal frontiers, in which the free movement of persons is ensured in conjunction with appropriate measures with respect to external border controls, asylum, immigration, and the prevention and combating of crime."[68]

In this regard, this article is also entitled to the European Parliament and the Council of the EU, assuming all the procedures for implementing the Common European Asylum System are compatible with the ordinary legislative procedure, because of the capacity of the Council of the EU to create new rules and consistent measures to fill in the big gaps in the basic

---

Union Mémoire présenté pour l'obtention du Master en études européennes par Livia Elena Bacaian rédigé sous la direction de Nicolas Wisard Jurée: Master in European Studies, Geneva. INSTITUT EUROPÉEN DE L'UNIVERSITÉ DE GENÈVE. P. 22, 23.
[67] Consolidated Versions of The Treaty on European Union and The Treaty on the Functioning of The European Union. Official Journal of The European Union (C 326). Volume 55. 26 October 2012. P. 16,17.
[68] Ibid. P. 22. And see, Consolidated Versions of The Treaty on European Union and The Treaty on the Functioning of The European Union. Official Journal of The European Union (C 326). Volume 55. 26 October 2012. P. 17.

rules of protection of aliens in the European Community Law (EC). This assumption is based on the old ideas that the EC law has concerning residence rights which relied on the economic activities of migrants and their incomes to be able to get a residence in the member States.[69] Nevertheless, the Charter of the Fundamental Rights of the European Union included in articles 18, 19 the right to asylum that should be guaranteed and compatible with the Geneva Convention and its Protocol, as well as the Treaty on European Union and the Treaty on the Functioning of the European Union. In addition to the non-refoulement principle in which the Charter asserted that "collective expulsions are prohibited" and returning, expelling, or extraditing persons to their countries where they would be subjected to the death penalty, torture, or any other inhuman or degrading treatment or punishment, is prohibited as well.[70] This Charter is still considered as a reference for the human rights which have become fundamental principles in the EC Law and hence, are legally binding. Furthermore, after the European Commission's Agreement of Publishing the Charter, this Agreement ensured that any legislative proposal or any drafts of an instrument should be compatible with the Charter to be adopted later by the Commission. Therefore, since the right to asylum was mentioned in the Charter and the EC Law, then it must be obligated.[71]

The right to asylum and residence in the host State shifted from being a State's right to "a harmonized" right in the European Union. The Schengen agreement in 1985 was the first attempt to control the borders and regulate the entry into European territories legally, which drew the initial project of eliminating all the internal borders and maintaining the external borders to secure the area of freedom from all aliens. The agreement has framed the rules and measures of the asylum applications' process, which ensures the responsibility of every member State to examine all asylum applications according to chapter 7 and to comply with the Geneva Convention of 1951, as well as all the UNHCR recommendations. Thus, every member State should process asylum applications to admit or reject the claim. So that the

---

[69] Elspeth Guild, Paul Minderhoud (eds). Security of Residence and Expulsion, Protection of Aliens in Europe. 2000. Kluwer Law international / The Hague/ London/ Boston. P. 21.
[70] Official Journal of the European Union, Art. 18, 19. ibid. P.399.
[71] Maria- Teresa Gil-Bazo. New Issues in Refugee Research, Refugee status, subsidiary protection, and the right to be granted asylum under EC Law. Research Paper No. 136. Refugee Studies Centre. Oxford University. United Kingdom. November 2006. P. 6.

State is not obliged to give the asylum seeker a residence and to permit him to stay within its territory. The Schengen agreement has also granted the right to family reunification to the refugee's family members once the asylum seeker is admitted as such and given a residence in the host country. The Agreement also prohibits the asylum seeker from applying in more than one State for asylum. Nevertheless, member States are still not ready to examine thousands of applications for asylum expeditiously, nor to grant asylum seekers the accommodations that they need.[72]

The Dublin Convention added more regulations to the asylum system in the EU by imposing a new provision relating to the asylum application, which should be examined by the member State that the asylum seeker has entered first, or where a member of his family has refugee status, or even where the applicant still has a valid visa or residence.[73] It is important to highlight that the core of the Schengen and Dublin Conventions was responding to all asylum applicants by ensuring that the application will be examined by a member State, guaranteeing that the application will be studied by a competent State to reach a decision. Also, that State shall be responsible for the process until a final verdict is reached, in accordance with the State's national legislation as well as the international commitment of the State to its international obligations relating to immigration and asylum matters. Therefore, both conventions have drawn the basic features of the new asylum system in the European Union.[74]

The instruments of the Dublin Convention in 1990, in addition to the Amsterdam treaty in 1999, created a common asylum system in the EU in terms of migration and the asylum principle.[75] At the time it was somewhat sufficient, but migration in the nineties and the migrant's influxes pushed States to increase their control on the national borders, the Dublin Convention adopted the objectives of the EU migration policy, and furthermore, the increasing number of migrants revealed the importance of

---

[72] Markus Kotzur / David Moya / Ulkü Sezgi Sözen / Andrea Romano (eds): The External Dimension of EU Migration and Asylum Policies, Border Management, Human Rights and Development Policies in the Mediterranean Area, ibid. P. 38. And see also, Bacaian, Livia Elena (2011). The protection of refugees and their right to seek asylum in the European Union, ibid. P. 23, 24.
[73] Dublin Convention, Art. (7), (5) 15 June 1990, O.J. C254, 1997, pp.1-12.
[74] Bacaian, Livia Elena: The protection of refugees and their right to seek asylum in the European Union. P. 24, 25.
[75] Maurice Stierl: Migrant Resistance in Contemporary Europe, edited by Jenny Edkins and Nick Vaughan-Williams. New York: Routledge, 2019. P. 23, 24.

conducting cooperation with third national countries and the refugees' countries of origin as a means of promoting security. Even more so given the huge amount of irregular migration to Europe in the last couple of years. As a response, the EU has developed an obvious competence regarding freedom, security, and justice, which is a collection of home affairs and justice policies" (AFSJ) to work under the instruments of the Maastricht Treaty for limiting irregular migration to Europe and encouraging the return of irregular migrants to their counties or to the country that they left to access Europe based on readmission agreements. Hence, the asylum policy in European territories nowadays aims to reduce the number of migrants, particularly, those who have entered third countries and have a chance to get the residence and the protection that they need there, without being under compelling circumstances to seek asylum in the European Union.[76]

The EU, through the Tampere Programme conclusions, has adopted new procedures to oversee migration by drawing the leading causes of migration to apply the readmission policy, as well as to implement "the comprehensive approach" which has been adopted by the Hague Programme lately. This approach considers all the internal and external perspectives of migration and asylum, as well as the (AFSJ) objectives to create the Common European Asylum System (CEAS), in which all the member States share the same measures concerning asylum and migration including the process of receiving the applicants and the solidarity and responsibility of burden-sharing among all member States. Furthermore, the Stockholm Programme in 2009 also affirmed the need of implementing participation in burden-sharing in all migration and asylum issues.[77]

Similarly, article 63. 1 of the Treaty Establishing the European Community (TEC) has firmly stated that: 'The Council shall adopt measures on asylum, in accordance with the Geneva Convention of July 28, 1951, and the Protocol of January 31, 1967, relating to the status of refugees and other relevant treaties.' Thus, the Council's measures include the reception process, determining qualification standards of third countries nationals to be recognized as refugees, and the measure on giving temporary protection to displaced persons who left third countries and cannot return to their

---

[76] Markus Kotzur / David Moya / Ulkü Sezgi Sözen / Andrea Romano (eds), ibid. P. 40, 41.
[77] Ibid. P. 42.

countries of origin, as well as all the procedures of granting or withdrawing the status of refugee. Besides its role in promoting the burden-sharing efforts and bearing the consequences of hosting asylum seekers among all member States, the council defines illegal migration and residence, the rights, and conditions under which third countries nationals who have legal residence in a member State can reside legally in another member State.[78]

Moreover, the European Council has explicitly provided recommendations on the security of long-term residence for nationals of certain member States and excluded third countries nationals from this privilege, which is considered discrimination because of some considerations concerning nationality and reciprocity. But rather, it could be possibly more impartial if the grounds for granting migrants a residence depended on equality and the deepening of the relationship between the migrant and the country of residence.[79] Community law is not the criterion for the right to asylum because it mainly concentrates on the movement across borders, and it has no relation with the obstacles for implementing the right to asylum, such as the expulsion of foreigners from any of member State regardless of their nationality. In this case, they could be nationals of another member State or even nationals of third countries. Then, the big issue that community law has to challenge is balancing the right to eliminate the obstacles for implementing the right of free movement in the union without discrimination, and the State's right to expel a foreigner.[80]

Although the argument concerning the term asylum considers the right to be granted asylum a right of an individual who is seeking protection by the State, the States were indifferent, since the right to asylum includes the right to enter, the right to stay and the right not to be expelled forcibly.[81] Therefore, it needed to be recognized as a person's fundamental right through International and European treaties, so States must oblige to respect this right and facilitate its execution. Thus, the implementation of the right to asylum is safeguarded by fulfilling the States' commitments although, States do have

---

[78] Elspeth Guild, Paul Minderhoud (eds): Security of Residence and Expulsion, Protection of Aliens in Europe, ibid. P. 22.

[79] Ibid. P. 22.

[80] Ibid. P. 60.

[81] Maria- Teresa Gil-Bazo. New Issues in Refugee Research, Refugee status, subsidiary protection, and the right to be granted asylum under EC Law, ibid. P. 8.

the right to expel and exclude persons from their territories.

In addition to that, States have total discretion to determine the period of the refugees' residence, and they can, according to their governmental, administrative and judicial authorities, revoke, end, or even refuse to renew the residence of a refugee, which has been stipulated as exclusion provisions in Art. 14 (4), (5) of the EC Council Directive 2004/83/EC on Minimum Standards for the Qualification and Status of Third Country Nationals or stateless Persons as Refugees or as Persons who, otherwise, need international protection and the content of protection.[82]

On the other hand, the European treaties which predated the Directive, such as the Maastricht Treaty and the London Resolutions, did not address the right to resettle and stay in the asylum after being granted protection by the host country. They just provided supplements to the criteria of the Geneva Convention about defining the status of refugees to exclude all unreal asylum applications which do not fall under the refugee definition of the Geneva Convention. Moreover, the Maastricht Treaty has asserted that the asylum policy must be based on cooperating in justice and home affairs. This is why the European Council will take over the task of coordinating the asylum systems of the member States to find a common and harmonious asylum system in the European Union. The Council adopted the London Resolutions to achieve a common asylum system. The Council Resolution of November 30, 1992, on Manifestly Unfounded Application for Asylum, it established that the essence of the asylum seeker's claim is not the fear of persecution in the country of origin or a deliberate deception. Another Resolution includes some conditions to return or expel an asylum seeker to a third country where he can live in safety under protection, because his life should not be threatened in the third country, otherwise, the principle of non-refoulement would be applicable in this situation. Furthermore, the Council recommended States, while examining the applications for asylum, to make sure that there is indeed a serious risk of persecution in the country of origin of the asylum seeker according to the London Resolutions. These Resolutions include some conclusions drafted by the ministers of

---

[82] EC Council Directive 2004/83/EC of 29 April 2004 on Minimum Standards for the Qualification and Status of Third Country Nationals or Stateless Persons as Refugees or as Persons who otherwise need International Protection and the Content of the Protection granted (OJ L 304/18 of 30.9.2004).

immigration affairs in the member States, which defined that there are some main elements to determine whether a country is safe or not.[83] However, member States should not refuse applications automatically if the applicant's country of origin is considered a safe country. In this situation, the State must examine the application to determine whether there is a genuine reason for the applicant to be considered as persecuted or at risk of being persecuted.[84] In contrast, the Treaty of Amsterdam in 1997 asserted the need of making the asylum concept applicable, especially since it considered that this concept has the potential to turn the European Union into an area of "freedom, security, justice". The treaty has also adopted new measures relating to the visa, immigration, and free movement of persons in asylum. The Council of Europe was invited to take new measures to increase the security of national citizens in the European Union and to regulate free movement and immigration while maintaining solidarity and burden-sharing of responsibilities among member States. Consequently, the Council and the Commission have suggested the Vienna Action Plan in which they have determined the minimum standards to grant refugee status or withdraw it, on the one hand, and have also reduced the procedures of receiving and examining an asylum seeker's application on the other. The Vienna Action Plan also included some criteria to distinguish the status of nationals of third countries as refugees from persons under subsidiary protection.[85] The Council of the EU and the Commission in the Vienna Action Plan have affirmed that within two years they will adopt an "instrument on the lawful status of legal migrants" to protect the nationals of third countries and to limit illegal migration in the area. The Amsterdam Treaty has been included into the Treaty Establishing the European Community (TEC) and the Treaty on European Union (TEU) structures to be part of Community Law in the European Union. In other words, the Amsterdam Treaty created a competence in the field of visas, asylum and immigration, as well as policies concerning the free movement of persons in the European Community. Further, it has made this "common interest" the first pillar, and Art. 73k of the Amsterdam Treaty, as well as Art. 63 of the EC Treaty Establishing the

---

[83] Bacaian, Livia Elena: The protection of refugees and their right to seek asylum in the European Union. P. 25. 26.

[84] Ibid. P. 26.

[85] Ibid. P. 26.27.

European Community encouraged the Council, within five years after the Amsterdam treaty entered into force, to adopt new measures relating to asylum and subsidiary protection to displaced persons. There was a particular emphasis on third-country nationals and the immigration policy that deals with monitoring illegal migration, residences, and returning the illegal migrants to their countries of origin. This is known now as the "Title IV of the EC Treaty".[86]

The EC Treaty has somewhat changed the conditions of expelling nationals of member States by reducing the reasons which enable a member State to expel or exclude a community national or his family members from its territory. These conditions extend the protection, which was only for economic nationals, to include the economically inactive persons who could be third-country nationals.[87] After the previous article of the Amsterdam Treaty, the Council enacted a directive 2003/ 86/ EC concerning the reunification of refugees' families based on the reasons that prompted them to leave their homes and separate from their families. In addition, many directives have also followed the article to elaborate on the means of implementing cooperation regarding the right of asylum and have also confirmed the member States including the right to asylum into the European Union. This required the Tampere European Council to take another step towards the development of the Common European Asylum that should be grounded on a partnership between the countries of asylum seekers and the Common European Asylum System. Thus, the Tampere Program and then the Hauge Program had the same approach of promoting the third countries to establish an area of freedom, security, and justice (AFSJ), especially after the tension between irregular migration and European security increased, which linked migration with terrorism and organized crime according to the Justice and Home Affairs of the Maastricht treaty. Subsequently, the Treaty of Lisbon in 2007 focused on the EU achieving certain objectives as part of the asylum.

The Treaty of Lisbon proceeded from the need to harmonize the asylum process in the area and create the Common European Asylum System that

---

[86] Elspeth Guild, Paul Minderhoud (eds): Security of Residence and Expulsion, Protection of Aliens in Europe, ibid. P. 22.
[87] Ibid. P. 59.

the treaty has determined the first steps towards establishing this system in Art 63(2) in the chapter Policies on Border Checks, Asylum and Immigration of the Treaty of Lisbon.[88] According to Art 63 (1): "The European Union shall develop a common policy on asylum, subsidiary protection, and temporary protection with a view to offer appropriate status to any third-country national requiring international protection and ensuring compliance with the principle of non-refoulement. This Policy must be in accordance with the Geneva Convention of July 28, 1951, and the protocol of January 31, 1967, relating to the status of refugees, and other relevant treaties."[89]

For that objective, the Parliament and the Council should work together according to the ordinary legislative procedure to adopt new measures aimed at establishing the Common European Asylum System by endorsing a uniform status of asylum for asylum seekers of third countries, that should be valid in the whole union, which means harmonizing the procedures of asylum to be perfectly recognized in all European Union, besides, creating a uniform status of subsidiary protection for third-country nationals who do not meet the criteria for an asylum status and need international protection. It is also important to adopt standard conditions for receiving asylum or subsidiary protection applicants to determine the competent member State, in addition to applying a common system for granting and withdrawing a uniform asylum and subsidiary protection status. These measures are aimed at instituting cooperation with third countries in order to manage the influx of persons who come to Europe to get asylum, subsidiary protection, or temporary protection. In this sense, the Lisbon Treaty has provided criteria to distinguish the three terms of protection: first, the asylum seeker who meets the criteria of the refugee definition according to the Geneva Convention and so became a refugee, the asylum seeker who needs international protection but is not qualified as a refugee so he gets subsidiary protection, and third, temporary protection is for persons who fled their countries of origin or residence "in the event of a massive inflow" and cannot

---

[88] Markus Kotzur / David Moya / Ulkü Sezgi Sözen / Andrea Romano (eds). The External Dimension of EU Migration and Asylum Policies, Border Management, Human Rights and Development Policies in the Mediterranean Area, ibid. 41. And see Bacaian, Livia Elena: The protection of refugees and their right to seek asylum in the European Union, Ibid. P. 30, 31.

[89] Treaty of Lisbon amending the Treaty on European Union and the Treaty Establishing the European Community, signed at Lisbon, 13 December 2007. Official Journal of the European Union. (2007/ C306/ 60).

return.[90]

Conclusions:

The right to asylum highly lacks recognition in International Human Rights Law as one of the fundamental rights of any individual regardless of his nationality, origin, or even region. The right to be granted asylum should be preserved by International and European instruments, although it has no guarantees to be applied forcibly in both, the country of origin if the person is unable to leave because he is being persecuted and prevented from leaving, and the host country that does not cooperate with the country of origin to facilitate movement until the person arrives to the host State. Unfortunately, the Geneva Convention did not highlight this point. It just focused on the right to asylum and imposed the States their commitments of granting international protection only to those persons who have already left their countries of origin and entered the host State. Consequently, the right to asylum cannot be an effective genuine right without fulfilling this condition, which could transform its nature to being just a right and it could even be a claim to get protection in a country after crossing its borders, although the State would not be forced to admit the asylum seeker nor to grant him international protection. All States have discretion in the final decision after examining the application under the provisions of the Geneva Convention and its Protocol.

Furthermore, the right to asylum has practical difficulties although the Universal Declaration of Human Rights explicitly stipulated the right to seek and enjoy asylum in the host country according to Art. 14, but it did not oblige States to host asylum seekers nor to grant them the same rights that citizens have, such as unlimited-period residences. The declaration did not include provisions relating to any duties on the States to facilitate the movement of persecuted persons from their countries of origin. Similarly, International Human Rights Law has not done any endeavors regarding this. It has just developed the criteria of the principle of non-refoulement, thus extending the international protection that Geneva Convention established by including a new category of persons who need to be protected because if

---

[90] Bacaian, Livia Elena: The protection of refugees and their right to seek asylum in the European Union. P. 32.

the host State repatriated them, for they would be at "serious risk of torture or inhuman treatment". Nevertheless, International Human Rights law has not offered guarantees to make the right to asylum binding in the international community. This deprives it from one of the basic features of a right. Accordingly, the right to asylum does not imply just the right to enter the host country, but it also requires guarantees to enjoy asylum by staying in the host country without limiting the residence, especially since the person who applies for asylum does not have fundamental rights in his country of origin, which is why he seeks protection in another country, regardless of any other considerations. The person should be free to opt for either voluntary repatriation, if he desires to go back to his country of origin, or living in the sanctuary with new aspirations for the coming future. When a person requires asylum in the host country, he must waive the ability to plan for the long-term. In other words, refugees or persons of subsidiary protection have no horizon in asylum, except for enjoying international protection temporarily.[91]

On the other hand, the State's duties, according to international instruments, are limited to permitting a person to enter its territory as well as examining his application for asylum. This does not make the right to asylum binding. European treaties have not expanded their approach to the right to asylum, which is mostly not safeguarded in international instruments. Non-binding international or regional instruments have taken a step toward prohibiting competent States rejecting asylum seekers. The following section will discuss the States' right to exclude migrants when States are obliged to execute their commitments of granting international protection for persecuted persons who claim asylum within their territories. This leads to the following question: shall the right to asylum (to access asylum and stay there) be prioritized over the right of States to exclude asylum seekers?

The Right to Access to Asylum and Resettlement:

The right to asylum is still contingent on the State's sovereignty, as the State has the discretion of admitting or rejecting asylum seekers, thus excluding them or deporting them from its territories. On the other hand, States should act according to the refugee plight to find solutions and provide international

---

[91] David Miller, Christine Straehle. The Political Philosophy of Refuge: Cambridge University Press 2010. P. 34.

protection to asylum seekers and displaced persons. A researcher has asserted the need to differentiate between "observation and witnessing", from a critical perspective, for we should not just observe the "Mediterranean migration crisis" but, instead, we must encourage "response-ability", which means that States must act with full responsibility and solidarity in burden-sharing toward the refugee plight.[92] However, there is an evident tension between the self-determination of the State and its international commitments to the European Union, or even to the international community if it is not a member State of the Union, which creates a sovereignty 'crisis.[93] In this context, this section will focus on the other features of the right to asylum, which manifest in the right to enter and stay in the host country. Consequently, it will analyze the principle of non-refoulement to find an answer to the following question: to what extent does the non-refoulement principle protect asylum seekers from the State' excluding right according to the State's right of self-determination against a person's right to asylum and international protection there?

The Right of Resettlement and the Principle of Non-Refoulement:

Initially, the Refugee Convention did not explicitly impose obligations on the State to allow persons to enter its territory, for Art. 31 and 33 established provisions regarding the persons who have already entered the State's territory. However, the Convention enshrined duties on the member States to admit asylum seekers with respect in their territories, but it did not force them to necessarily admit asylum seekers as refugees or persons of subsidiary protection. The States have the right to reject their applications and exclude them from their territories if they threaten national security and public order in the host State. If those entered the host countries lawfully and do not threaten the States' national security and public order, then the States shall not expel them according to Art. 32 (1). The Convention has ensured that illegal entry of refugees should not affect the final decision of granting the refugee status if they come directly from "a territory where their life or freedom was threatened". Art. 31 (2).[94] Although the Convention has

---

[92] Vicki Squire: Europe's Migration Crisis, Borders Deaths and Human Dignity. The University of Warwick. New York, Cambridge University Press, first published 2020. P. 199, 120.

[93] Ibid. P. 24, 25.

[94] Convention and Protocol Relating to The Status of Refugees. Art.31, Art. 32.

stipulated the principle of non-refoulement in Art. 33, it excluded refugees who are considered a danger to the security of the host country or who have been convicted of a certain crime, which would imply they pose a threat to the community. This article mentions two exceptions for implementing the non-refoulement principle. The first one allows the member State to "refoule" a refuge based on reasons that make him a real danger to the security of the State. This means that a State should not expel a refugee from its territory due to the fact that he might pose a threat to another State. Reasonable reasons require a specific assessment of the threat by the State. Consequently, a possible threat to national security is not considered a sufficiently reasonable ground for excluding refugees, otherwise, the State can abuse this exception to expel refugees like, for instance, if the number of asylum seekers is too big, for it could be considered a threat to national security. The Convention also prohibits them from refouling persons who do not pose a genuine threat.[95] Likewise, the Executive Committee of the High Commissioner's Program has affirmed the necessity of the principle of non-refoulement although it has been violated in many cases. It places an international obligation on the States to abide by this principle in all situations, including mass influx.[96] The second exception entitles the member State to expel a refugee who has committed a serious crime, and has been convicted by a final judgment, this refugee has become a serious threat to the national community of the host State. In this case, it should be pointed out that not all crimes pose a threat to the community because of the legal nature of the non-refoulement principle, which protects most of the refugees' vital interests, and such exceptions must be carefully utilized. [97]

When analyzing national security morally, it tends to be a "contingent and self-limiting rationale", because it can be used in immigration and free movement negatively. This only works if the immigrants constitute a serious threat to the national security of the host country. It can also limit immigration and justify refouling refugees because of a real danger that they

[95] Anette Faye Jacobsen: Human Rights Monitoring, A Field Mission Manual. Martinus Nijhoff Publishers. Boston. 2008. P. 452.
[96] Hailbronner, Kay (2000): Immigration and Asylum Law and Policy of the European Union. Kluwer Law International. The Hague/ London/ Boston. P. 353, 354.
[97] Anette Faye Jacobsen. Ibid. P. 452, 453.

cause to the host community.[98]

Certainly, refugees in a certain State could overwhelm it. Maybe because of their huge numbers and by causing chaos, which damages public order and justifies the State controlling migration and excluding refugees. Despite the legitimacy of this reason to be used by the host State for refouling refugees, the Convention did not mention it expressly in the exceptions of the non-refoulement principle, rather it intended to prohibit the host State from expelling refugees by prioritizing protecting their lives over the State's ability to manage mass numbers of them. Nevertheless, threatening the host State's community can justify limiting rights under the ECHR according to community standards which are different between States. This justifies the exclusion of third-country nationals, as well as other persons granted subsidiary protection based on "public order" grounds.[99]

The host State's security is the sole primary ground that can limit the right to asylum. The Directive of the European Council on Minimum Standards for the Qualification and Status of Third Country Nationals and Stateless Persons as Refugees or Persons Need International Protection in 2001 determined two categories of international protection: the first is the persons who meet the definition of refugee according to Geneva criteria, and the second one, in which the Council granted lawyers the right to interpret the Geneva convention and to include persons who cannot obtain the refugee status and need protection. Instead, they can be granted subsidiary protection, which is addressed in the principle of non-refoulement and extends the concept of protection to encompass a new category. This is an obligation on the States following the Geneva convention or another international human rights treaty, and it is considered an important development in the International Human Rights Law.[100] Art. 63 (2) of the ECT exhorts to protect refugees and displaced persons by adopting measures to give displaced persons from third countries the status of subsidiary protection since they cannot return to their countries of origin, thus including them in the implementation of the non-refoulement principle and implied to

---

[98] Carens, Joseph H.: The ethics of immigration. 1. issued as an Oxford Univ. Press paperback. New York: Oxford University Press; Oxford Univerisity Press (Oxford political theory). 2013// 2015. P. 276.

[99] Maria- Teresa Gil-Bazo. New Issues in Refugee Research, Refugee status, subsidiary protection, and the right to be granted asylum under EC Law. P. 19.

[100] Maria- Teresa Gil-Bazo, ibid. P. 13, 14.

the exception of the principle as well.[101] The International Covenant on Civil and Political Rights stipulated the non-refoulement principle in Art. 12 (1), which says: "Everyone lawfully within the territory of a State shall, within that territory, have the right to liberty of movement and freedom to choose his residence." This includes both, nationals and non-nationals, in the right to free movement and residence anywhere within the host State's territory, although only nationals have the exclusive right to enter a territory, and foreigners shall not have such right without a preliminary permit of the host State, and despite the fact they have the right to reside if they have already entered.

Additionally, Art.12 (3) ensures the right to reside and not to be excluded to all persons, without any restrictions on the implementation of those rights, except the limitations enacted by law grounded on the protection of national security, public order, public health, morals, or the rights and freedoms of others in the host State. The right of freedom to reside should be consistent with the other rights established in the Covenant. Therefore, the right to asylum, according to the Covenant, is an arguably right because of the dependence on the prohibition of exclusion, on the one hand, and the temporary nature of the right to reside, on the other. This is relevant because European member States usually grant refugees three years of residence and persons of subsidiary protection one year, which can be extended in case the circumstances in their countries do not improve.[102] Articles (6) and (7) of the Covenant have implicitly enshrined the principle of non-refoulement by asserting the right to life, which is protected by law for every human being against any reason, such as the death penalty after committing a serious crime in his country of origin, or even when the person's life is threatened by genocide. According to article 6, no one shall be deprived of his life, although this does not abolish "capital punishment" in any member State partaking in this Covenant. In relation to that, article 7 grants the person a right to live freely without being subjected to "torture or to cruel inhuman or degrading treatment or punishment".[103] Since it includes a prohibition against torture

---

[101] Hailbronner, Kay (2000): Immigration and Asylum Law and Policy of the European Union. Ibid. P. 370.

[102] Ibid. P. 12.

[103] The International Covenant on Civil and Political Rights. Adopted and opened for signature, ratification and accession by General Assembly resolution 2200A (XXI) of 16 December 1966. Entry into force 23 March 1976, in accordance with Article 49. Art. 6, 7.

and inhuman or degrading treatment or punishment, member States must not refoule persons to their country of origin, where they would be subjected to torture or inhuman treatment. In addition to this prohibition in article 7, refoulement as a forcible return of asylum seekers is unlawful in any case.[104]

Article 3 of the European Convention on Human Rights has approached refouling similarly, stipulating it as "an absolute prohibition", regardless of the reason, or what the person might have done: "No one shall be subjected to torture or inhuman or degrading treatment or punishment."[105] This way, article 3 was crucial in concluding the most positive implementation of the non-refoulement principle when it ignored the risk that the refugee might pose to the national security of the host State, and focused on the person's need of international protection. However, after the events of the 11th of September in the USA, the European Court was forced to ease the absolute prohibition in article 3, and to find a balance between the need for protection and the interest of the State of maintaining its national security.

The Convention Against Torture has also expressly enshrined the prohibition of expelling, returning, or extraditing any person to another State where he would be at risk of being subjected to torture.[106] But what should be highlighted is the ambiguous meaning of the term torture, for there are no standards determined to affirm whether there is, in fact, torture in a country. Rather, article 3 resorted to prohibiting returning a person to his country if there is "a pattern of gross, flagrant or mass violations of human rights", So, if a country violates its citizens' human rights, it could also torture the persons returned, expelled, or extradited to it.[107]

On the other hand, the Directive encompassed provisions relating to exclusion and the principle of non-refoulement in articles 14 (4), (5) of Chapter IV (Refugee Status). It authorized the member States, according to the Geneva Convention, to revoke or refuse to renew the status of a refugee if he has been convicted by a final judgment of a serious crime and

---

[104]Ernst Hirsch Ballin, Emina Ćerimović, Huub Dijstelbloem, Mathieu Segers: European Variations as a Key to Cooperation. The Netherland Scientific Council for Government Policy (WRR). Published by Springer Nature Switzerland, 18 September 2020. P. 131.

[105] the European Convention for the Protection of Human Rights and Fundamental Freedoms. supra note 28. Art. 3.

[106] Ibid. P. 21.

[107] Bacaian, Livia Elena: The protection of refugees and their right to seek asylum in the European Union, ibid. P. 38.

endangered the host community. It also entitles the member State's discretion to refuse granting the refugee status based on the crime that the person has committed. Nevertheless, the non-refoulement principle is firmly preserved in article 21, which ascertains the obligation of member States to respect the non-refoulement principle according to paragraph 2 of it. Therefore, the Directive of the European Council has attempted to balance the obligation of member States regarding the principle of non-refoulement and their authority to refoule a refugee based on reasonable reasons, as we have already mentioned, only in these cases can member States "revoke, end, or refuse to renew or grant a residence permit to the refugee, regardless of whether or not he is formally recognized.[108]

A member State may refoule a refugee at any time. Even if he has been granted refugee status, or the decision has not been made yet, or if he has been convicted by a final judgment of a serious crime, which is typically considered similar to the exception to the non-refoulement principle that was included in Art. 33 (2) of the Geneva Convention.[109] Arguably, the exceptions to the principle of non-refoulement should not exclude persons from subsidiary protection, considering that the reason for which a person would be refouled and returned to his country, shall not be prioritized over the risks of the death penalty or torture that the person could face in his country. Thus, third-country and Stateless persons may be granted subsidiary protection and residence permit by the host State, as long as the danger remains in their countries. Despite the previous consideration, all member States agreed to the obligation of the exclusion of persons under subsidiary protection mandatorily, depending on security concerns. For example, Sweden still supports the optional decision of excluding persons for the previous reasons, in addition to the need of member States implementing exceptions to exclusions to comply with non-refoulement and prohibit excluding persons for whatever reason.[110] Notwithstanding, the Jurisprudence of the European Court of Human Rights has affirmed that the exception of the non-refoulement principle, which has been stipulated in Art.33 (2) of the Geneva

---

[108] Maria-Teresa Gil-Bazo, ibid. P. 22, 23. And see, The Council Directive 2004/ 83/ EC of 29 April 2004. On minimum standards for the qualification and status of third country nationals or Stateless persons as refugees or as persons who otherwise need international protection and the content of the protection granted. Chapter VII Content of International Protection. Art. 21 (Protection from refoulement).
[109] Ibid. P. 15.
[110] Ibid. P. 16.

Convention, is not utilized if there is a risk of inhuman or degrading treatment, so that those persons should not be expelled even if they constitute a threat to the public order or national security of the host State.[111] Moreover, the jurisprudence of the European Court of Human Rights ECHR has adopted an absolute character of the non-refoulement principle, which differentiates between the danger of political persecution and the danger of inhuman or degrading treatment. Accordingly, it expanded the right to protection, regardless of the limits of the non-refoulement principle in the Geneva Convention. Therefore, the limitations on the principle of non-refoulement, which are related to national security or public order in the host State according to Art. 33 of the Geneva Convention, are no longer considered the determining criteria and the new interpretation of danger, as discussed above, becomes the primary criteria included in International Refugee Law.[112]

Regarding the persons who have an opportunity to resettle in the host State, they are either refugees or persons who have been granted subsidiary protection. Their residence is contingent on three basic clauses: The first clause is that they did not commit international crimes or serious crimes in the host community. The second one is that person should not be considered a danger to the public order, security, and public health in the host State. In this case the host State has the discretion to assess the danger. The third clause requires taking into account "the background of the migratory history" of the person who needs international protection. This clause includes the migrants who had previously gotten an alert released in the Schengen Information System, in addition to those who entered the European territories irregularly (except for the third country nationals and displaced persons who come from Turkey), but shared the information with the UNHCR to regulate their movement to Europe, according to the Declaration with Turkey.[113]

---

[111] Hailbronner, Kay (2000): Immigration and Asylum Law and Policy of the European Union. Ibid. P. 494, 495.
[112] Hailbronner, Kay (2000). Ibid. P. 496.
[113] Markus Kotzur / David Moya / Ulku Sezgi Sözen / Andrea Romano (eds): The External Dimension of EU Migration and Asylum Policies, Border Management, Human Rights and Development Policies in the Mediterranean Area. 1st Edition. Nomos Verlagsgesellschaft, Baden-Baden, Germany 2020. P. 108, 109. And see, Elspeth Guild, Jan Niessen (eds): Immigration and Asylum Law and Policy in Europe.

However, International Law has firmly imposed certain obligations on States regarding refugee resettlement. The Asylum System in the EU is framed to enable access to Europe to those who need international protection, once they arrived at the borders of member States. This requires a balance between the State's interests of controlling the number of asylum seekers that a member State receives and the solidarity or burden-sharing of responsibilities among all member States.[114] Especially considering that the European Council (in Resolution 14) in 1967 ensured that no one shall be subjected to refusal of admission at the frontier, rejection, … or any other measure which would have the result of compelling him to return to, or remain in, a territory where he would be in danger of persecution".[115] Accordingly, the asylum seeker has a right to remedies against refusal at borders, as enshrined in Art. 13 of the Regulation 562/ 2006/ EC on the Community Code governing the movement of persons at the borders (Schengen Borders Code) which gives the asylum seekers who have been prevented from entering a country an opportunity to be allowed to enter and remain in a member State.[116]

There are only three conditions in which the State can expel a third-country national who seeks to enter and remain within the State's territory: first, if he is convicted of offenses, including at least three years of custodial sentence. In this case, the person must be expelled. Secondly, if he committed a serious crime or there are reasonable grounds that ensure his involvement in a terrorist organization or his support thereof. In this category, the State usually decides to expel the person. While in the third category, when a person violates Immigration Law by, for example drug offenses, the State has the discretionary authority to expel the person. Otherwise, the third-country nationals have the right not to be expelled.[117]However, in case an asylum seeker has been refused and prohibited from entering, he would be informed in writing of all the underlying causes for the decision by the border officials

---

Digital Borders and Real Rights, Effective Remedies for Third-Country Nationals in the Schengen System. Vol 15, Evelien Brouwer. Martinus Nijhoff Publishers 2008. Leiden, Boston. P. 393- 397.
And see also, Ernst Hirsch Ballin, Emina Ćerimović, Huub Dijstelbloem, Mathieu Segers: European Variations as a Key to Cooperation. The Netherland Scientific Council for Government Policy (WRR). Published by Springer Nature Switzerland, 18 September 2020. P. 131.
[114] Ibid. P. 110, 112.
[115] Resolution 14 (1967) on Asylum to Persons in Danger of Persecution, Art.2. Collection of International Instruments, supra note, 17, P. 307.
[116] Elspeth Guild, Jan Niessen (eds): Immigration and Asylum Law and Policy in Europe. Digital Borders and Real Rights, ibid. P. 288, 289.
[117] Ibid. P. 392.

according to the Schengen Borders Code. Regarding the data protection principle of transparency, it is supported by the EC Immigration and Asylum Law, and it requires measures to inform the person of his data being stored by a member State of the Schengen Information System SIS.[118]

Once asylum seekers enter the host State, they move to the next stage in which all persons should pledge to apply for international protection. Then, the host State examines the person's application and decides to grant him either a refugee status or subsidiary protection, according to its international obligations and the international provisions relating to both statuses and depending on which category suits him best. Once this happens, the person accesses resettlement within the territory and starts to integrate into the community and shall have the same treatment as aliens in general in the host State. Thus, he has a right to employ, work, reside, etc., during the three years residence. After this period, the refugee may have the same rights as national according to the State's discretion in "the absence of reciprocity".[119] Thereby, the refugee or person of subsidiary protection has the rights provisioned in the Geneva convention, in addition to those in International Human Rights Law and in all human rights treaties, such as the ICCPR, which granted asylum seekers more beneficial rights than the rights mentioned in the Convention. In this regard, the Convention has not given the right of international protection to rejected asylum seekers. In contrast, human rights treaties have extended rights to include not only the persons with a refugee status, but also the asylum seekers who did not meet the conditions of the Refugee Convention and cannot return to their countries.[120]

In addition, Art. 3 of the Geneva Convention did not give asylum seekers the right to non-discrimination. It recognized this right only to refugees, while Art. 26 of the ICCPR expressly stipulates the right of freedom from discrimination to all persons, which expands this right to protect asylum seekers as well from any kind of discrimination due to race, color, sex, language, religion, political or another opinion, national or social origin,

---

[118] Ibid. P. 518.
[119] Convention and Protocol Relating to The Status of Refugees. Art. 7 (Exemption from Reciprocity), ibid. P. 17, 18.
[120] Anette Faye Jacobsen: Human Rights Monitoring, ibid. P. 458.

property, birth or another status.[121]

Let us recall that the non-refoulement principle does not prohibit States from returning asylum seekers to another country where they will not be at risk. Also, this principle has another interpretation relating to its extension: even if the host State has returned the asylum seeker to another State where he will not face any kind of risk, but the latter repatriated him to his country of origin, both States will be considered responsible for infringing their obligations in respecting the non-refoulement principle. Therefore, the State should rely on the ground of the asylum seeker's application, in addition to ascertaining if certain conditions according to the human rights instruments are applied in the country to determine whether the country is safe and, consequently, if the asylum seeker would be at risk once he returned to it. This guarantees the asylum seeker of being readmitted and allowed to access asylum and apply for international protection in accordance with multilateral agreements. These agreements also determine which member State is competent in examining the asylum seeker's application.[122]

The UNHCR defined a criteria to ascertain a country that can be considered safe. Any State that organizes a list of safe countries should adopt transparency in making such qualifications. The States should also bear in mind the status of asylum seekers and the changeable circumstances in their country. In this case, the asylum seeker can confirm or rebut the general safety considerations in his country, according to his circumstances.[123]

The Residences of Asylum Seekers and the Right to Stay:

Regardless of the implementation of the non-refoulement principle, to what extent do asylum seekers have the right to stay in the host State even if the grounds of their claim have totally disappeared? This a relevant question since the basis of the claim, which is the danger these persons faced, is not expected to be short-term, and there is no potential end to that danger. Thus, the claim of asylum seekers to get a permanent residence is considered the only way to end the danger, albeit granting it to persons who require protection would be

---

[121] International Covenant on Civil and Political Rights. United Nations Human Rights Office of The High Commissioner. Article 26.
[122] Anette Faye Jacobsen. Ibid. P. 470.
[123] Ibid. P. 471, 472.

morally unacceptable, in addition to being risky and expensive.[124]

Going back to the motivating instance of the Syrian asylum seekers in Germany, there are other rights that can explicitly be a part of the right to asylum, even if the discourse of the right to asylum has been morally approached to analyze asylum seekers right to stay without adequate conditions in the host State. Should asylum seekers claim their right to stay? Especially since there are other types of refugees, such as Lampedusa groups from Sub-Saharan Africa who left Libya because of an armed conflict and arrived in Italy, where they claimed asylum in Germany despite having been provided residences by the Italian government when they entered its territory.[125] Their case challenged the Dublin provisions relating to immigrants moving when they raised a demand that "we are here to stay" in Hamburg, struggling to obtain sufficient health care and social rights such as access to education and jobs in addition to political rights. Because of their previous Italian residences, these migrants faced more complications in accessing social rights in Germany, where they protested to stay but could not even get accommodations like other refugees. Instead, they faced indefinite rejection because of their specific situation of "exclusion from social rights."[126]

Both cases are different according to the basis of the claim, which is the nature of the danger they faced. Whether it is a long or short-term danger in their country of origin. The Syrian asylum seekers suffered from long-term danger, which is why they were granted refugee status in the host country, whereas the Lampedusa faced uncertain danger because it was supposed to disappear once they were granted residences in Italy. But is that considered sufficient to settle the case? or should all asylum seekers have the right to stay in the receiving country regardless of the basis of their claim?

Initially, in any State, there are a lot of extraordinary claims (if we do not want to call them rights) that citizens and all permanent residents have against the State, such as "the entitlement to vote, to access public benefits". Similarly,

---

[124] David Miller, Christine Straehle (2020): The Political Philosophy of Refuge: Cambridge University Press. P. 214.

[125] Vicki Squire: Europe's Migration Crisis, Borders Deaths and Human Dignity. University of Warwick. New York, Cambridge University Press, first published 2020. P. 164.

[126] Sieglinde Rosenberger, Verena Stern, Nina Merhaut (eds): Protest Movements in Asylum and Deportation. Switzerland: Springer Open, 2018. P. 194, 195.

asylum seekers have "a claim against the host State which is the entitlement to remain." Because of the strong relationship between the State and its citizens, as well as permanent persons who are very well integrated into the society in which they live and share interactions with it, asylum seekers also should establish such relations with the host State and be involved in the "social membership" of that society to claim the right to stay there.[127] This is consistent with Carens' argument concerning social membership, which is considered as a means of granting a person the claim to stay in the country for an indefinite period without fear of being removed at any time. In this case, the basis of the claim is the relationship between the person and other people in the State, such as members of a family, a club, or a social group, which creates entitlement and does not establish the need of protection. Thus, asylum seekers must integrate into society in many aspects such as language, lifestyle, family, among others. This way, they have affiliation and social bonds with the host society, and that requires a long resettling period for the person in the host State, according to Carens. Consequently, if the person becomes "a long-term member" based on the significant amount of time that he lived there, as well as the fact that he cannot return to his country, then he would have a plausible claim to stay in the State.[128]However, this moral approach to justify an asylum seeker's claim to stay would not work before the international community where there is no place for such moral considerations. Furthermore, the State's authority does not aim to serve the persons' willing to live under its governing according to its rules, thus, they would not enjoy this claim without serious endeavors of the State to "enhance the person's autonomy" giving him an opportunity to establish a new autonomous life according to its laws and rules which are still regulating other matters as property, engaging in policy, marriage, etc.[129] Therefore, the most extended period of resettlement for refugees is of three to five years, initially, and then it can be extended to grant them a permanent residence after having spent there at least five years, which would require a comprehensive examining of the status of refugee, his integration into society, language skills, subsistence, and other factors that affect the decision of granting the refugee a permanent residence. Refugees and their

---

[127] David Miller, Christine Straehle (2020), ibid. P.125.
[128] Ibid. P. 125, 126.
[129] Ibid. P. 128, 129.

resettlement differ from other beneficiaries' resettlement because the "beneficiaries of other humanitarian admission schemes" do not need more than "a durable solution" in which they have been granted temporary protection with a short permit residence, based on the assumption that the conflict in their countries will end in a specific and short term. Thus, they are granted a permit of one year of residence, and they can extend it every year until the conflict ends, which is when they will be able to return to their countries without being at risk of danger.[130] In contrast, asylum seekers do not have the right to stay if they have not been granted the refugee status according to the Geneva Convention. In that case, they would have a residence as persons eligible for subsidiary protection until the danger in their countries ends. Once this happens, they would not have grounds to claim a right to stay permanently in the host State. On the contrary, the refugees can get a permanent residence after spending five years in the host state, which depends on some conditions such as being very well integrated into the host society and independent in financial subsistence.[131] This is similar to Carens' argument on a long-term of residence that enables the person to constitute an affiliation with the host State in order to be entitled to claim a permanent residence. In the case of the Lampedusa, how Germany dealt with them because of their previous Italian residences is simply the best scenario that could happen in terms of attempting to find solutions for Refugees, because of the host State (Germany) has received a big number of refugees around the world so far. In contrast, some countries in the EU use "deterrence of unwanted migrants" in such cases.[132] In the case of subsidiary protection, which has been intensively granted to large numbers of applicants from Syria in 2016 until now, the period of residence is still too restricted, as well as the total discretionary authority of the State concerning the reunification depending on "humanitarian grounds." Furthermore, the question of when did the applicant arrive in Germany, and how did he enter its territories? is still the criteria for determining the status of protection that the asylum seeker will be granted, being the refugee status the most beneficial one according to

---

[130] Marie Claire Foblets, Luc Leboeuf (eds): Humanitarian Admission to Europe, The Law between Promises and Constraints. 1 Edition, Nomos. Germany 2020. P. 218, 219.

[131] Carol M. Swain (2018): Debating Immigration. Second edition, Cambridge University Press. New York, USA. P. 369.

[132] Maurice Stierl: Migrant Resistance in Contemporary Europe, edited by Jenny Edkins and Nick Vaughan-Williams. New York: Routledge, 2019. P. 139.

the Refugee Convention, for then the person can have the right to stay permanently in the host State, as mentioned earlier. Ideally, the need for protection should determine and qualify the protection status that the person should have, and not other considerations such as the time of arrival.[133]

The most relevant point is the problem of the different interpretations regarding the obligation of international responsibility of all the States thar are signatories of the Refugee Convention and other human rights conventions (the northern and southern States). The Northern countries usually evade their responsibility towards refugees, especially those who did not arrive at their borders directly. Moreover, some deny their responsibility by preventing asylum seekers from arriving at their external borders by monitoring the high seas before arriving at their national frontiers. There are other countries that are not members of the EU, such as the USA and Canada, that waived their sovereignty over some territories to evade their responsibilities.[134]

Conclusion:

The problem in the implementation of the non-refoulement principle can be summarized in returning asylum seekers and refugees to their countries whenever States consider that they constitute a danger to their national security or even to their communities. Sometimes they exaggerate the considerations to revoke residences based on personal statuses aiming to predict potential safety in the country of origin. However, this principle must be an efficient guarantee for all asylum seekers, including the refugees and persons of subsidiary protection. Currently it is still an elusive tool that States use to pretend that they respect their international obligations of granting international protection to asylum seekers, when in fact they comply with such obligations selectively. States usually intend to return refugees and asylum seekers without following the recent reports of the UNHCR, which are released to respond to the new circumstances relating to whether a country is a safe area or not before expelling or returning asylum seekers to their countries where they may be at serious risk of torture or persecution

---

[133] Marie Claire Foblets, Luc Leboeuf (eds), ibid. P. 223-225.
[134] Elspeth Guild, Jean Monnet: Current Challenges for International Refugee Law with a Focus on EU Policies and EU Co-Operation with the UNHCR. Directorate- General for External Policies, briefing paper, EXPO/B/DROI/2012/15. PE 433.711. December 2013. P. 10.

and of cruelly perishing there. States still prefer their national interests over the individuals' interests, which is the result of the States' right to self-determination. Thus, the non-refoulement principle cannot entirely safeguard the right to asylum or the right to stay specifically. It just protects some categories of asylum seekers temporarily, so that, if they do not integrate into society and do not find jobs and are still under the government's protection and financial aid, there are no guarantees of having a right to stay in the host State.

Additionally, States have the discretion of cancelling the refugee status based on the grounds for cessation or revocation, which have been established in the Refugee Convention. This will depend on relevant considerations of the case, such as the length of the refugee's stay in the country, his social situation, whether he has integrated into the community or not, as well as his criminal record. All these circumstances need to be taken into account by the host State before the cancellation. The State's decision should lawfully rely on the mentioned factors. Nevertheless, one cannot expect the best exercise of this discretion because it can be conducted based on false documents. Even though examining all the circumstances of the refugee status is mandatory according to national legislations of most countries and the procedural rights to fulfill the duty of fairness, some countries, such as Germany, decide most cancellations without hearings. Nevertheless, the cancellation decision should respect all guarantees under Art 1(F) of the Refugee Convention in all cases.[135]

Besides this lack of coordination concerning the refoulement decisions, there is insufficient attention by the EU member States to the recommendations of the UNHCR relating to the asylum concept: 'accelerated procedures for granting asylum' and its primary objective of protection, at the time the European States and some of their migration policies frustrate that objective. [136] Moreover, some countries do not admit "their fair sharing of refugees" and, because they do not have a right to deprive refugees of entering, deporting them could be a suitable way to compel them to fulfill their responsibilities. That means that not all the countries curry out their

[135] Sibylle Kapferer: Legal and Protection Policy Research Series, Cancellation of Refugee Status. Department of International Protection. Protection Policy and Legal Advice Section PPLA/2003/02. United High Commissioner for Refugees CP 2500,1211 Geneva2. Switzerland, March 2003. P. 29-34.
[136] Elspeth Guild, Jean Monnet, ibid. P. 4,5.

obligations voluntarily. Some of them view refugees as a burden that can negatively affect various aspects of the host country, which is why countries always come up with different measures to evade their responsibilities.[137]

To summarize, countries will seize any opportunity to cancel refugees' residences as long as they do not violate the non-refoulement principle in its "traditional meaning", but under their discretion of lawful cancellation they can remove refugees to a safe third country, or their countries of origin in case they have become safe. Therefore, to avoid this prospective outcome for refugees and subsidiary protection persons, there must be a claim for asylum seekers, refugees, and persons eligible for subsidiary protection against the host State to stay within its territories without being forced to return to their countries afterward. Such a claim is still unavailable to those people who do not have an affiliation with the host State. States should take into account the period of stay for a refugee and to what extent he effectively integrated into the new society, as well as his prospectively ambitious desire to live a new autonomous life there.

A Future Vision of the Right to Stay (ought to be free movement):

The Length of Residence and the Basis of the Claim:

The Council Directive on the Status of Third-country Nationals who are long-term residents 2003/109/ EC was an essential initiative to address the basic norms concerning the length of residences in the European Union according to the European Migration Law for refugee status, subsidiary protection, and other qualifications of humanitarian protection. The second chapter focused on the "long-term resident status", which determines the obligations of member States to grant long-term residences to third-country nationals if they "resided legally and continuously within its territory for five years immediately prior to the submission of the relevant application". The consecutive period means that the resident should not exceed six months outside the territory and ten months within the five years. Simultaneously, the Directive has set out some conditions for the status acquisition to reach equal treatment with nationals, such as providing evidence of their stable

---

[137] David Miller, Christine Straehle (2020): The Political Philosophy of Refuge: Cambridge University Press. P. 119, 120.

subsistence without recourse to the social assistance system of a member State. In addition, the Directive has emphasized the potential unlimited or permanent residences that member States may grant to third-country nationals, which could be more favorable than the residences stipulated in the Directive. Therefore, a member State can issue a permanent validity of residence to applicants based on its discretion, and that does not "confer the right of residence in all member States". However, granting these residences should be in accordance with the norms in the council regulations (EC) No 1030/2002.[138]

According to the Directive, long-term residents have the right to equal treatment in relation to nationals. This is an accomplishment, especially concerning the free movement among the member States without any restrictions by the discretionary authority of the member State in which the resident has been granted long-term residence. Further, in Art. 14 (1,2), the long-term residents also acquire the right of long-term residence in another member State to exercise economic activities, employment, pursue studies or vocational training, etc. As a corollary, the Directive has totally ignored the status of refugees as well as the persons of subsidiary protection and ensured that it does not apply to them according to Art. 3, where it expressly excluded third-country nationals who resettle in a member State under the status of temporary protection, or are still awaiting the decision on such status, in addition to the persons who are eligible for subsidiary protection and refugees or persons who applied for refugee status. In that way, the Directive has instituted a gap regarding the "ambiguous position" of the refugee residences permits, especially since the EC has not reframed a certain status of refugees' residences. This questions the meaning of third-country nationals, and whether this term applies to refugees after spending five years of legal residence after which they will be implicitly included in the Directive. As a result, the status of the family members of refugees is also arguable regarding whether they will be included by the Directive and so eligible to get long-term residences as long as they do not have social assistance from the

---

[138] Council Directive 2003/109/EC of 25 November 2003 concerning the status of third-country nationals who are long-term residents. Art. 4, 5, 6. 8. 12. 13. And see Handbook on European law relating to asylum, borders and immigration. Luxembourg: Publications Office of the European Union. 2013. P. 51.

member State, and do not fall under any type of protection status.[139]

However, the Directive covers all categories of third-country nationals who are legally residing in a member State and are not explicitly mentioned in Art.3. Thus, it implies to those who have regularized their status. In other words, the person has the right to reside long-term from the regularization date in the member State onwards. This right has an accruing nature, and States have objected to this clause if the person has lost any documents, which are essential for lodging his application. Does this lack of documents affect the legality of his residence during the five years? because of the contrary interpretation of a lawful residence term, this term should be defined as "a standard community" to achieve uniformity based on its impacts on every member State and not only within the member State in which the person has applied for a long-term residence. However, this right would imply to the family members of third country national if they met all the clauses of the criteria and hence, they obtained the long-term residence.[140]

All in all, there was no affirmation of the refugee and subsidiary protection persons' right to stay permanently in the host State. Rather, the Directive has articulated certain provisions relating to the right of third-country nationals to acquire long-term status, but that would not happen easily, especially since refugees and other categories who fall under international protection cannot invoke this way if they are still under that protection with all its merits. They should waive the protection and become "worker immigrants" so that they could have another kind of residence to stay for long-term in the State, and then be able to obtain permanent residence. Otherwise, they would stay for five years or one year for subsidiary protection persons, regardless of their hope of belonging to the new State which has become their country and where they totally recognize all their duties towards it. They should be entitled to have rights as nationals, such as the right to stay and the right to be involved in the political system, to vote, etc.

From the political perspective, the nation-State undoubtedly is "a vulnerable form of political organization". For instance, the European nation-State has been recently affected by both "the internal regionalism and the sub-

---

[139] Peers, Steve, und Nicola Rogers. EU Immigration and Asylum Law. Martinus Nijhoff, 2006. P. 629, 630.
[140] Ibid. P. 631.

nationalism," that weaken the trust of many European States of the "center sovereignty."[141] Supranational power, globalization and its effects on all life aspects, as well as telecommunications are particularly considered a risk to the nation-State. They all have attempted to eliminate the nation State organization over the years, although the nation-State is still the current political system, and all the European practices aim to serve its objectives of freedom, security, and justice and to protect its interests. Even though transnational power has not been able to abolish the nation-State, it could influence the political participation of immigrants to make it more prospective both, in their country of origin and in their country of residence. Furthermore, the Maastricht Treaty has reinforced the nation-State in the policy of the European Union and has reaffirmed the Common Asylum System concerning the immigration policy at the European Union Level.[142]

Regarding the immigrants' integration as a basic component for the right of long-term residence, some political opinions tend to consider integration possible even without real political participation or enjoying other similar rights because immigrants lack the "prerequisites" and are then considered incompetent to participate in the "democratic process" altogether.[143]

One should keep in mind that immigrants' suffering in their countries, where they were deprived of the necessary prerequisites, was not their free choice. They were somehow persecuted, and their fundamental human rights have been cruelly violated. Therefore, it would be inhuman to deal with them as if it had been their choice, which is why their "new country" should trust them by granting them a new opportunity to enjoy all human rights without discrimination and be able to exercise "national rights" such as the right to stay permanently in the country as long as they want.

The general considerations and public attitudes towards immigrants and their participation in the new society as part of an integration process have changed recently because of the strong influence of new priorities in the political and socio-economic fields, in addition to the refugee crisis. Nevertheless, this evolution in immigration issues was somewhat limited by

---

[141] Rainer Bauböck (ed) (2006): Migration and Citizenship. Legal Status, Rights and Political Participation. Amsterdam University Press, Amsterdam. P. 90.
[142] Ibid. P. 91.
[143] Rainer Bauböck (ed) (2006): Migration and Citizenship. Ibid. P. 95.

the rule of "ius sanguinis", the right of blood which is a general principle of nationality law by which citizenship in a State is acquired only by either the nationality or ethnicity of the parents, which is why some host countries still account immigrants as temporary guests, not granting them permanent residences. In contrast, other countries use a combination of "ius sanguinis" (the right of blood) and "jus soli" (which is the right of soil) to grant nationality or citizenship, thus, they do not recognize the immigrants' right to stay permanently in their territories. In this context, immigrants would not have this right unless they accessed the labor market. Consequently, there are three political models for treating immigrants: first, countries such as Germany, Denmark, Austria, Greece, and Italy respond to resolve the refugee crisis accidentally, where they grant refugees residences that are consistent with their migration policy, and suitable for refugees, based on a near return of refugees to their countries of origin sooner or later. According to this model, accepting immigrants could cause potential social tension because of including new members in the nation-State who are basically in "a legally uncertainty situation". This could deepen the lack of identification in the social order of the host countries as well as the xenophobic reaction to immigrants.[144] However, articles 13 and 14 of the UDHR consider the right to immigrate a fundamental right and so, immigrants should have all these rights because an equal treatment between immigrants and citizens who live in the same territory is the only way to discover whether the fundamental rights are recognized or not. Thus, they should enjoy the right to immigrate and stay and all civil and political rights in the host country. However, the EU law does not recognize that immigrants have the same rights as European citizens.[145] On the contrary, they put on the refugees' shoulders a duty to leave if the circumstances in their country improve, so that they would not have a claim to stay in the host stay for a longer period after the reason of their fleeing their home is resolved.

This assumption stems from the Refugee Convention in Art. (1) which defines the refugee situation and envisages it in certain circumstances that are

---

[144] Maciej Duszczyk, Marta Pachocka, Dominika Pszczolkowska (eds): Relation between Immigration and Integration Policies in Europe, Challenges, Opportunities and Perspectives in Selected EU Member States. First published, Routledge. London and New York. 2020. P. 30, 31.

[145] Alessandra Silveira, Mariana Canotilho, Pedro Madeira Froufe (eds) (2013): Citizenship and Solidarity in the European Union, from the Charter of Fundamental Rights to the Crisis, the State of the Art. Peter Lang. Brussels. P. 420, 421.

necessary to grant the refugee status. In case these circumstances have "ceased to exist" for whatever reason, then the refugee must return to his country of origin to contribute and help his compatriots in this national obligation. This duty could be seen as a refugee's duty of gratitude toward his host State, based on the idea of asylum as a kind of hospitality. Therefore, if the refugee "outstays" his invitation in the host State, he should act according to his welfare to consider the state's responsibility for him as a refugee fulfilled and done.[146]

The second model is the assimilationist, which depends on the loyalty to the nation-State. According to this model, all immigrants are considered members of the host society by naturalization. For example, France does not grant the immigrants distinctive rights, but rather they become French citizens where there are no political differences between them and the authentic citizens because the host State considers the immigrants' objective of enjoying citizenship based on the principle of equality in political participation. Thereby, it facilitates assimilation by imposing some obligatory instruments to enhance the incorporation of immigrants into the host society through language, education, etc.

The third model is based on the right to soil to grant citizenship at birth according to "a pluralist idea of democracy," by which the immigrants of various backgrounds can participate in political life grounded on cultural diversity which is essential to the composition of the host society. Accordingly, the host State supports these "target groups" by integration policies such as the UK integration policy that depends on a "pragmatic management of relations between ethnicities."[147]

In this regard, States have the total discretion in determining the integration policy with their national laws, obtaining EU incentives so that their integration policies are specialized in third-country nationals who reside legally in the host State and according to the Agenda for Integration of the Third-Country Nationals which was adopted by the European Commission in 2011: "the legal migration and integration are inseparable and should mutually reinforce one another". In 2016 an action plan to support European

---

[146] David Miller, Christine Straehle: The Political Philosophy of Refuge: Cambridge University Press. 2020. P. 144-148.
[147] Ibid. P. 31, 32.

States in their integration policies and financial assistance for third-country nationals was developed. Although the acts of law regulate all the aspects of immigration and asylum, such as entry, residence, stay, and work, which implicitly include acts concerned with eliminating all discrimination, racism, and xenophobia while promoting cohesion in the host society, there is no legislation that recognizes the right of asylum seekers to stay without conditions of integration, work, or even naturalization. Thus, refugees have to work on alternative means to have a right to stay in the host country other than humanitarian protection, such as accessing the national labor market and obtaining a work residence.[148] However, Canada has not received large numbers of Syrian refugees for it considers the refugee crisis a big challenge for achieving real integration into the Canadian' society. Social cohesion is difficult because the Syrian refugees come from an extremely mismatched country so they would be faced with social, cultural, and even religious differences. In this context, the integration process should be grounded on both social bonds and social bridges. The first one helps newcomers as the first step to overcome their trauma when they build relations with the other Arabs or even Syrians, and social bonds guarantee a short term to adapt the Syrian refugees, although social bonds are insufficient for developing a feeling of belonging. The second step promotes their adaptation by learning the official national language and creating friendships and relations with the native Canadians in order to be a part of practical life. In this sense, social bridges mean adapting in the long-term and developing social relations with the government, securing an efficient integration. All in all, both steps should be part of the integration process.[149]

Reciprocity as a Basis of the Claim:

The legal basis of the right to stay could be based on another ground in the future, and not only on the humanitarian need for protection. For instance, reciprocity between States may be employed to enable immigrants who come from country (A) to enjoy the right to enter and stay in country (B) because the citizens of country (B) have the right to reside and stay within the territory

---

[148] Maciej Duszczyk, Marta Pachocka, Dominika Pszczolkowska (eds): Relation between Immigration and Integration Policies in Europe, Challenges, Opportunities and Perspectives in Selected EU Member States. First published, Routledge. London and New York. 2020. P. 36-40.

[149] Edward Shizha, Rosemary Kimani-Dupuis, Priscilla Broni (eds): Living Beyond the Borders. Essays on Global Immigrants and Refugees. Peter Lang. New York, 2018, p. 94-96.

of country (A), regardless of the assimilation ability of both countries, especially in the case of civil wars, armed conflict, and persecution situations.

Some writers addressed the argument of "the social features of citizens" as a ground for free residence in another State based on "mutual relationships and interactions". According to this argument, there are many reasons why there should be such obligations in the political society in which the citizens are active persons towards other civilians based on their social features.

This participation of all citizens is based on "a mutually beneficial scheme of cooperation", in addition to their fundamental interests which are affected by the State's power, so that citizens are forced to follow all of the State's law. Furthermore, citizens in a political society are equal without exception, and they are all subject to a "dense network of laws" that governs them.[150] Then, a political society could be established on normative objectives of a "mutual beneficial scheme" if the State allows its citizens to achieve their "joint projects," which should be regularized and expected by the State. Likewise, Richard Dagger has articulated the reciprocity of the "fair play" principle, which means that all participants in the social mutual scheme are bound by "special obligations" to each other, so that they should prefer each other's needs over others'.[151] Notwithstanding, there are some significant problems in the reciprocity argument, according to Abizadeh:

First, reciprocity cannot include all persons because not all persons can efficiently participate in a social cooperation scheme. For example, it could not be applied to infirm or unproductive persons. Nevertheless, society has special obligations regarding those extremely disadvantaged persons who cannot contribute to the mutual benefits. The second problem relates to the first argument in that the problem is envisaged in the provision of mutual benefits by cooperating with others, for these mutual benefits are considered a moral duty more than being a precondition of that duty. Thus, the special obligations require fulfilling 'pre-existing' duties, and if they have not been adequately fulfilled, the special obligations to the disadvantaged persons in society will not be established.

---

[150] Fine, Sarah; Ypi, Lea (eds) (2016): Migration in political theory. The ethics of movement and membership. First edition. Oxford: Oxford University Press. P. 109.
[151] Ibid. P. 109.

The third problem is the special obligations towards co-participants of the social scheme cooperation, which can justify the additional obligations towards co-participants but cannot justify prioritizing special obligations towards them over non-participants, because doing so would be at the expense of general or moral duties towards non- participants. Therefore, cooperation in the social scheme justifies only the additional obligations to co-participants. A mutually beneficial scheme could serve the State's interest, like when a State facilitates the immigration process for some persons and restricts it for others. Reciprocity, grounded on mutual benefits, appeals to the State's interests, it could not be provided to special obligations because arising such additional special obligations to persons in need should not 'be discharged at the expense' of evading moral duties to 'disadvantaged non-participants'.[152]

Dagger has provided a pragmatic method to endorse the social cooperation scheme as a ground to justify the reciprocity argument as a sufficient requirement to recognize a person's right of free movement and to reside in another country with which his country of origin cooperates in a certain beneficial social scheme. Although the social cooperation serves the interests of the State more than appealing to the special obligations, reciprocity could be a successful first step for recognizing the right of free movement because it would be an initiative for achieving special obligations among fellow citizens regarding the citizenship status. This could also help the most disadvantaged people in society.

According to Abizadah, Dagger's argument would be more successful if it included not just the citizens in the State's territory, but all the residents who live there to allow everyone to contribute to the social and economic activities of a 'modern State' making them adequate participants in a mutually beneficial scheme.[153] According to Dagger's dimension of the modern State which claims jurisdiction over all residents and not just the citizens in its territory, this means that the modern State should encompass both, the territorial and civic boundaries. In other words, it organizes 'the social relations and activities territorially' to include all territorial residents to constitute social features rather than civic features as a foundation for special

---

[152] Ibid. P. 110.
[153] Ibid. P. 110, 111.

obligations among them. These special obligations may justify immigration restrictions by limiting free movement to both citizens and residents as beneficiaries of the obligations based on social features.[154]

Thus, reciprocity is still not the prospective global solution for the refugee plight because it can only be implemented in a beneficial social scheme and would not be utilized controversially between all States, especially since it would not be based on justice. Rather, this would increase the borders restrictions to foreigners who do not benefit from the special obligations among compatriots. Furthermore, reciprocity, grounded on social features cannot mitigate the inequality, persecution, civil wars, and other factors causing immigration and refugee crises globally for it does not include non-participants (neither residents nor citizens) in the mutually beneficial scheme. Consequently, it does not apply to third country nationals who are not residents of the European Union, so they cannot freely reside within its territories.[155]

In this regard, long-term residences currently compromise the refugee plight in the European Union in which they have the right to stay in the host countries without danger of being returned to their countries. Nevertheless, this is a controversial issue for it is still the sole guarantee to resettle in the host country, otherwise, refugees have no explicit right to stay for the host country has the total discretion to refuse their claim. Thus, the right to stay for all asylum seekers is still in its infancy because it lacks many features, such as the forcibility to oblige the States to comply with it. It could be a claim since it is not a recognized right for persecuted persons to live freely in another country for an indefinite period, which is why the claim to stay should be established on a coherent legal basis to be recognized and set aside from the residence that is given to refugees or persons of subsidiary protection.[156]

Member States rely on Community Law, which gives them the discretion and authority that should be in accordance with the European Asylum Law to offer the required protection of the fundamental human rights enshrined in

---

[154] Ibid. P. 111.
[155] Elspeth Guild, Jan Niessen (eds): Immigration and Asylum Law and Policy in Europe. European Asylum Law and International Law. Hemme Battjes. Vol 8, Koninklijke Brill NV, Netherlands, 2006. P. 603, 604.
[156] Ibid. P. 603, 604.

the EU Charter of Fundamental Rights. The right to asylum has been recognized in Art. (18) and despite being an unclear instrument, the Charter is still the reference in the interpretations of the legal status of the applicant for asylum and its provisions. However, these interpretations do not mention restrictions of the right to asylum in International Law instruments with which all member States comply. The right to asylum has been not extended in the Charter and other European Treaties because they do not provide assured guarantees to stay in the host State. Instead, they stipulate the right to asylum for third-country nationals and arguably reinforce their right not to be expelled from the host State as long as they are still in need of protection.[157]

The present status of the right to stay is uncertain and depends on many factors. One of the most important ones is the "safety norm," which determines the status of the applicant's country of origin regarding whether it worsens or improves. Depending on this the right to stay will be determined by the extent of his integration into the host society, transforming the grounds from humanitarian protection to social and economic grounds. Moreover, limiting the decision-making process could not be a positive incentive for future International Asylum Law besides the European Asylum Law. This negatively affects the status of applicants and precludes third-country nationals' free movement. In other words, restrictions hinder political obligations from being accomplished effectively. Thus, the decision-makers composed of the Commission and the European Council, as well as the European Parliament, need a substantial evolution and prospective step to reinforce the right to asylum and its forcibility, including the right to stay. It is important to not leave to States the decision to determine the asylum applicant' term of residence, and they should also adopt new measures to improve the present European Asylum System Law.[158] The decision-makers used to prioritize protecting the national system over their responsibility towards asylum seekers. As a consequence, they may refuse applicants depending on their discretion regarding whether they consider the applicant "sufficiently vulnerable" to deserve or not.[159] Some countries, such as

---

[157] Ibid. P. 605, 606.
[158] Ibid. P. 610- 615.
[159] Laura Affolter: Asylum Matters on the Front Line of Administrative Decision-Making. Palgrave Socio-Legal Studies. University of Bern, Springer Nature Switzerland, 2021. P. 161.

Switzerland, have a restricting-migration policy where the government tries to fulfill its commitments to International Law and the Geneva Convention on the one hand, and to filter the "undeserving" out of protection on the other.[160] Therefore, the right to asylum should be enforceable by law regardless of some arguments, such as national security, which are utilized by States to restrict foreigners from having the civil and political rights that citizens enjoy as a means of protecting the national system.

The Moral Obligation as a Basis of the Claim:

Aside from the present absence of the right to stay in legal instruments, the international community should have duties towards refugees from the moral perspective. This should include States as well as individuals because morality attributes to individuals at the first step, those who recognize a moral obligation towards refugees by helping them and responding to other global crises. Thus, morality is personal, and it can also be extended globally to the political and economic aspects.[161]

Charity enables individuals to act or not act according to their personal morality, However, more is needed to resolve the problem of refugees, which requires responding to major needs worldwide. Serena has illustrated the UNHCR's underfunding as an example to elaborate on "the enormous needs of refugees" that, although the UN body attempts to sort all the refugees' needs, it still has a financial problem, evidences the vastness of the plight. Moral obligations will contribute to resolving the refugee problem, which is why all individuals and governments should fulfill their moral obligations towards refugees, for this would imply achieving "the minimum conditions of human dignity." This dignity requires much more than charity or any other individual interest to help refugees, hence the need of morality.[162]

However, to what extent do we have moral obligations towards refugees? Moral obligations in general refer to people's duty of doing things just because they are right, regardless of whether they want to do them or not. Moral obligations can take many forms such as to be legal obligations and contractual obligations, which are a legitimate sort of obligations because of

---

[160] Ibid. P. 163.
[161] Serena Parekh: No Refugee: Ethics and the Global Refugee Crisis. Oxford University Press. 2020. P. 52.
[162] Ibid. P. 53, 54.

their forcibility. This means that, if people broke the law, they would be punished. To do this, legal obligations have "external mechanisms of enforcement", whereas other kinds of moral obligations do not have this external mechanism that forces people to fulfill them. In this case, people should have a moral reason to fulfill their obligations, like our obligations towards our family or towards helping people, albeit no law would punish us if we did not do so. It is an unwritten rule to help each other, regardless of what we might gain from it or the consequence that not doing it might entail.[163]

This leads us to the question of whether asylum seekers can establish their claim to stay in the host State based on the moral obligation to help people. Some agree that people do things based on their moral obligations so they undoubtedly exist in our World, at least from a philosophical perspective. But to what extent can those obligations be extended to refugees? Immanuel Kant considered morality as human reasons that make us act morally, not seeking some greater outcome, but rather just because we are all human beings, and we should not treat each other as commodities. We must live ethically because it is a virtue and not because of what we might obtain from doing so. Kant rejects the idea of utilitarianism. However, for some people moral actions depend on the outcome or how that action might be beneficial for them, but moral actions should benefit the whole world and not just certain individuals. [164]

Kant considers that doing the right things is not a means of getting a good outcome. What determines whether an action is right or wrong is rationality. Thus, doing that right thing is a "categorical imperative" that implies an unconditional moral obligation and is not dependent on the individual's inclination or objective. Moral obligations towards refugees, according to Kantian ethics, stem from the "non-arbitrary resources" that make people act in a certain way regardless of the enforcement. In other words, there are some good reasons to make people act morally, either by maximizing a value such as general welfare, or according to a reason that justifies the chosen action as the right thing. In both situations the "moral demands" are a serious claim

---

[163] Ibid. P. 54, 55.
[164] Ibid. P. 56. 57.

regardless of its enforcement.[165] The moral obligations towards refugees should proceed from appealing to human rights, which are virtues that do not discriminate people for any reason like nationality, color, religion, etc. All individuals are morally equal and have the same rights based on the claim of human dignity. If a person has the right to asylum in another country, he can justifiably demand to stay in that country and enjoy all the citizens' rights there, for all persons should have an "equal moral status". This justifies their demands for having certain rights and in case the demands have fail to be met, their right has been denied as well.

Human rights should be the basis of moral claims that have to be protected by political norms and that should be the yardstick of how we treat each other in the same country or in other countries. Human rights could make our moral obligations clearer because, if there is any violation of human rights in any country, it would constitute a moral obligation for the other countries to protect them or to help. The International Community is responsible for protecting those persecuted persons whose human rights are violated by their country of origin, which did not protect the human rights of its citizens but, instead, infringed them just because they have another political opinion.[166]

Western countries have fact moral obligations, and these might also come from the "moral sentiments which direct our attention to the suffering of others and make us want to remedy them", which is considered a "political force".[167] Such obligations extend to helping and protecting refugees, based on the concept of protecting human dignity, regardless of who they are. Any violation of human rights is an immoral act and requires an imperative response to protect them, grounded on moral obligations. Consequently, the most important question here is whether moral obligations can be a basis for the right to stay in a host country.

First, moral obligations encompass two categories: the host State has moral obligations towards both asylum seekers who entered the host country and the refugees who live in camps in its territory to get a residence. They have legitimate claims on the host State for protection, which could be temporary

---

[165] Ibid. P. 60.

[166] Ibid. P. 68- 73.

[167] Maurice Stierl: Migrant Resistance in Contemporary Europe, edited by Jenny Edkins and Nick Vaughan-Williams. New York: Routledge, 2019. P. 138.

or permanent, depending on the refugee's position in the 'International system'. There is an argument that considers that every person should participate or have a citizenship in the international system, which must protect their human rights worldwide, thus all States have a collective responsibility to repair the damage. However, this argument can only be fulfilled partially because we need a natural cosmopolitan system in our World to be able to fulfill its obligations. Thereby, States cannot be forced to accept more refugees and give them permanent residences.[168] Instead, States have moral obligations towards refugees when they admit certain number of asylum seekers and grant them temporary residences, but States do not live up to their commitment of allowing refugees to stay in their territories for an indefinite period based on their moral obligations to protect the human rights of refugees. States thought that when they granted residences to refugees located in their territories they fulfilled their moral obligations without considering their right to stay permanently as part of these obligations.[169] This solution does not resolve the problem, but contributes to it by depriving the refugees the simple civil right that all EU citizens have, which is the right to stay and resettle in the country. Further, the States can indeed revoke their residences, making them irregular migrants and giving the State the right to expel them from its territories by law.[170]

In addition to this durable solution for refugees, some States have explicitly announced that they do not have the ability or the willingness to receive refugees or give them the right to reside temporarily in their territories. In some cases, these countries that do not welcome asylum seekers prevent them from residing there by deterrence policies to not seek asylum and consider them illegal immigrants to obviate their obligation of applying the principle of non-refoulement. Countries can also appeal to national security and public order threats to justify their decisions to exclude asylum seekers.[171] For instance, the "long summer of migration" to Europe was in 2015 after the civil war in Syria, and the following numbers of refugees since that year

---

[168] Serena Parekh: No Refugee: Ethics and the Global Refugee Crisis. Oxford University Press. 2020. P. 83, 84.

[169] Ibid. P. 128.

[170] Alessandra Silveira, Mariana Canotilho, Pedro Madeira Froufe (eds) (2013): Citizenship and Solidarity in the European Union, from the Charter of Fundamental Rights to the Crisis, the State of the Art. Peter Lang. Brussels. P. 328, 329.

[171] Serena Parekh: No Refugee: Ethics and the Global Refugee Crisis. Oxford University Press. 2020. P. 128.

indicate the significance of the refugee problem and the failure of the European migration policy. The deterrence policy that the UK government has utilized by imposing punishments on the number of refugees who entered the UK, as well as repeated detention actions against asylum seekers there gave place to an initiative to recognize the refugees' right to work and to stop their inhuman detention.[172] The International Community should implement efficient measures to find practical solutions for the refugee plight, especially considering that the number of refugees, according to prospective predictions, will increase in the coming years due to the deteriorating status in most areas of the world affected by civil wars, internal conflicts, climate change and the environmental crises. The deterrence policies that some States apply will not limit the influx of refugees. Instead, they will exacerbate the refugee crisis and overburden the economy of the States that admit refugees and try to help them, even if this help is a temporary solution, to somewhat mitigate the extent of the crisis.

The Global Compact in 2018 emphasized the need of resettlement and the need to share the international responsibility among States toward refugees. All States agree that their responsibility should be shared and grounded on the aim of remedying the refugee situation. However, there needs to be an allocation mechanism to determine the responsibility of each State. The lack of it results in two types of States: the first type is when States have an immigration policy that welcomes refugees by burden-sharing, seeking to achieve international solidarity. The second type is States evading their responsibility of protection by adopting an externalization policy with the aim of reducing the numbers of immigrants with either a 'non-entry policy' to avoid the legal responsibility towards refugees or the policy of transferring the responsibility to other States.[173] According to these categories, the situation requires a regulation that includes a common resettlement policy which has been fulfilled by the Establishment of the European Asylum Support Office (EASO) that came into force in 2010 and ensured the

---

[172] Vanessa Agnew, Kader Konuk, Jan O. Newman (eds): Refugee Routes, Telling, Looking, Protesting, Redressing. Vol,1. Transcript Verlag, Bielefeld. 2020. P. 258, 259. And see Maciej Duszczyk, Marta Pachocka, Dominika Pszczolkowska (eds): Relation between Immigration and Integration Policies in Europe, Challenges, Opportunities and Perspectives in Selected EU Member States. First published, Routledge. London and New York. (2020) P. 62, 63.

[173] Marie Claire Foblets, Luc Leboeuf (eds): Humanitarian Admission to Europe, The Law between Promises and Constraints. 1 Edition, Nomos. Germany 2020. P. 311, 312.

importance of supporting resettlement by providing international protection to refugees in third countries and "showing solidarity with the host States".[174] Further, it stipulated that the resettlement policy should be preserved by sharing responsibility among the member States. In this regard, the National Programme of Asylum Migration and Integration Fund (AMIF) has pursued to implement the same policy and has promoted recommendations for cooperating with third countries. The scheme in 2015 asserted the objective of granting rights to persons who need international protection.[175] As a corollary, the resettlement policy that the EU adopted according to the previous scheme has played a negative role by externalizing the responsibility to the third countries by appealing to the idea of safe countries and the international protection that refugees should be granted there. Many European countries utilize the supposed cooperation with third countries to limit irregular immigration by preventing asylum seekers from crossing the borders to enter European territories. Consequently, many countries used to resort to the irregular immigration concept as a pretext to justify their preventive migration policy and elude their responsibility of protecting persons who need international protection.

In this context, the immigration crisis requires effective European solutions to find a balance between two basic dimensions: the European Union's objectives of achieving freedom, security, and justice by protecting the external borders of its member States on the one hand, and to regulate the legitimate immigration in a more effective way to respond to the needs of third-country nationals who seek to reach European territories to be granted international protection based on respecting their fundamental human rights. One way of doing this is by respecting their right to stay without being threatened to return to their countries of origin or third countries that they have already left.[176] This requires a new treaty to legitimate the right of third-country nationals to stay in the European host State, while maintaining the provisions of the Amsterdam Treaty, which have previously addressed the

---

[174] Ibid. P. 313, 314.
[175] Handbook on European law relating to asylum, borders, and immigration (2013). Luxembourg: Publications Office of the European Union. P. 51.
[176] Julia Iliopoulos-Strangas, Michael Potacs, Elena Simina Tanasescu, Jacques Ziller (eds): Migration-Migration-Migrations. Neue Herausforderungen für die Staatssouveränität und für den sozialen Rechtsstaat- New challenges for Europe, for State Sovereignty and for the Rule of Law and the Welfare State- Nouveaux défis pour l'Europe, la souveraineté de l'Etat et l'Etat de droit social. Germany: Nomos Verlagsgesellschaft (11). 2017. P. 233.

first step of the "gradual communitarization" of the policy of immigration and asylum in the European Union. This step is based on the non-discrimination of the rights of third country nationals, especially the social rights and what the Nice Charter of Fundamental Rights eluded when it used the term of "person" and not of "EU citizen". According to this Charter, the demands of non-discrimination of the social rights of third-country nationals are fulfilled in the amendment of Regulation 1408/71. This amendment states that third-country nationals have the same social rights that the European citizens have if they entered the host State from another member State. However, this excludes the right of free circulation, which means that third country nationals cannot move to another member State for employment objectives.[177] Thus, third-country nationals are still treated as "second-class residents". This raises the following question: to what extent should member States respect asylum seekers' right to stay even though these States do not confer the same social rights for third-country nationals (who legally resettled within the territory of the host State) that EU citizens have?

The Self-Determination of States and the Self-Determination of Individuals:

Persecuted persons should seek asylum only in the State where they are allowed to establish such a claim, because most States adopt the 'remote control' technique to keep asylum seekers far from their borders to evade their responsibility towards them. Thus, those States resort to preventing asylum seekers from reaching their borders and, regardless of the legality of this action, or in addition to that, this opens up a moral debate of whether this policy is good from a humanitarian perspective or not, grounded on the fact that persons do not choose where to be born and have no choice in being persecuted or a free citizen.[178] That is what the philosopher John Rawls has called a 'veil of ignorance', when a person does not previously know what rules or asylum policy he would have because he cannot opt the social order of the State in which he is born.[179] Some other philosophers, like Michael

---

[177] Maurizio Ferrera: The Boundaries of Welfare: European Integration and the New Spatial of Social Protection, New Boundaries, New Structuring? On the Future of Social Protection in the European Union. Oxford University Press Scholarship Online: February 2006. P. 11, 12.

[178] David Scott FitzGerald (2019): Refuge Beyond Reach: How Rich Democracies Repel Asylum Seekers. Oxford Scholarship Online: March 2019. Oxford University Press. P. 253, 254.

[179] Carol M. Swain (2018): Debating Immigration. Second edition, Cambridge University Press. New York, USA. P. 296.

Walzer, argue that we may have grosser responsibility towards refugees that are in the same 'physical space' as us. Therefore, the remote-control technique, by which States prevent asylum seekers from reaching their borders, would be worse than ignoring those who are somewhat distant from the physical space of the host States. However, it could not be considered an equitable action to prefer some persons over those who cannot easily reach the borders of the host State.[180] Therefore, the most controversial point in the refugee plight manifests in the overlapping between the sovereignty of the State and its self-determination to admit asylum seekers who want to resettle in its territory and the term of residences for refugees and persons of subsidiary protection, another controversy is the exclusion or refusal of asylum seekers on the grounds of national security or public order on the one hand, and the self-determination of individuals based on their right to seek asylum in another country in accordance with the provisions of the Refugee Convention and human rights treaties on the other. To what extent does the right of self-determination of individuals work as a legal basis for the right of all asylum seekers to stay indefinitely without a negative decision of the State's discretion to admit them in its territory or not?

Adam Omar Hosein considers that States indeed have 'non-trivial reasons' to refuse asylum seekers or to not letting them stay indefinitely in their territories. Although some philosophers deem refugees to be economically beneficial for the host country, others consider that this is not so. Moreover, those who deny the right to stay could be exaggerating the disadvantages of granting such a right.[181]

Hosein affirmed that the non-refoulement principle mentioned by the Refugee Convention is still insufficient because it did not include any meaning of entitlement to stay. All that the non-refoulement has guaranteed is the right to reside for a temporary term as a durable solution to protect persecuted persons from returning to their country of origin, where they are being threatened. Thus, this principle does not prevent the host country from returning asylum seekers to other countries where they would not be threatened. Moreover, States have the right to withhold asylum or to not

---

[180] David Scott FitzGerald, ibid. P. 254, 255. And see, Carol M. Swain (2018): Debating Immigration, ibid. P. 293, 294.ns
[181] David Miller, Christine Straehle: The Political Philosophy of Refuge: Cambridge University Press. 2020. P. 115.

grant protection to asylum seekers just because they have entered their territories without legal permission or 'authorization'. If the State decides to grant protection to an asylum seeker according to the Refugee Convention, it would be free to provide the political and social rights it finds suitable to his situation. Thus, States can grant refugees the right to work, but not to stay permanently or to bring their families to stay for an indefinite period. The asylum status should include a 'package of rights'. If the State deports asylum seekers back to another country where they should be safe, does that count as a real violation of their human rights? and then, do they have the right to stay there or would it also be a temporary solution?

Hosein proposes two ways of States fulfilling their obligations towards refugees without infringing their human rights: the first is the humanitarian obligation to admit asylum seekers that need protection, it is the same when they are admitted in another country where they would be helped, while the second way is grounded on a political obligation, refugees have a claim to get protection from a legitimate government, which could be fulfilled in any safe country.[182] According to both approaches, deporting asylum seekers to another safe country does not violate their fundamental human rights. However, by doing this States do not fulfill their international commitments consistent with the burden-sharing of responsibility toward refugees. In other cases, States deliberately deport asylum seekers to third countries before adjudicating their claims to reduce their number and to evade contributing to processing the applications of asylum seekers. Instead of granting them refugee status or subsidiary protection they send asylum seekers back to third countries where they can make a claim regardless of the country's capacity of receiving asylum seekers. Nevertheless, some of the deporting countries are much more capable of receiving asylum seekers considering the low numbers of claims that these States have received compared to other States.[183] But according to the Refugee Convention, a State is not forced to admit asylum seekers and grant them protection if they enter its territory without authorization, except for those who come directly from their countries of origin where they were persecuted.[184] Based on this, how can asylum seekers claim to stay in the host country regardless of whether it is the destination

---

[182] Ibid. P. 118.
[183] Ibid. P. 118, 119.
[184] Ibid. P. 120.

country or a third country to which he has been returned?

There are many approaches on which the right to stay could be established. As we have already discussed, the affiliation approach could be a basis for the right to stay, but the self-determination of individuals would be more important for justifying the refugees and persons of subsidiary protection's right to stay for an indefinite period in the host country. This is based on the assumption that any foreigner who comes to a country for an objective will comply with its governing rules, laws, taxes, contracts, etc., so the State should reinforce the individuals' autonomy by exercising his authority to fulfill his plans and develop his life. Asylum seekers who left everything in their country to find a more peaceful and safer place, where they look forward to making new plans for themselves and helping their families in the host country or the country of origin if they are still there, and surely asylum seekers, who would be qualified after processing their claims to be under a refugee status or subsidiary protection, will be subject to the host State's authority since they entered its territories. Consequently, as long as the host State controls to some extent their lives, they shall be awaiting the State to fulfill its obligation of ensuring and promoting their autonomy.[185] To this end, the amount of time an individual has been living in the country becomes relevant. The person who has resided in the host country for a long time and has started a new life there can claim to stay in the country, which should fulfill its obligation to enable him to have some degree of autonomy. In other words, "the longer a person lives in the host country, the stronger the obligation of the country will be to enhance his autonomy to enjoy his right to self-determination".[186]

Thereby, the self-determination of the individual would not be excessively costly to the host country as the Samaritan approach considered, which failed to justify a person's claim to stay, as it is not necessarily tied to strengthen a person's roots in the host society. This is contrary to the affiliation approach in which the detention is considered a negative measure that interrupts the social relations of that person in the host society.[187] In contrast, detention could be employed according to the autonomy approach to prove that a

---

[185] Ibid. P. 128.
[186] David Miller, Christine Straehle, ibid. P. 129,130.
[187] Carol M. Swain (2018): Debating Immigration. Second edition, Cambridge University Press. New York. P. 293.

person has lost his control over his life, which will deepen the responsibility of the host country towards him and then it can serve the autonomy of that person as a basis of his claim to stay. [188]

According to the autonomy approach, the host State should take into account 'prospectively' the length of a person's stay in its territory, based on how long that the person wants to remain in the host State because the longer a person plans to stay, the stronger the claim to stay and to secure his life there is. Thus, the asylum seeker whose application has been adjudicated during a short period, such as a month or three months, is going to have a stronger claim to stay than the asylum seeker whose status has not been determined yet. The reason for this is that the former is in a position that allows him to plan for a new stable life there, while the latter cannot plan such a life because his status is not determined so he cannot plan for future. Also, the host State should look at the person's length of stay 'retrospectively'. The State should revise and bear in mind how long the person has been in its territory, since asylum seekers should have spent a long time in the host State to allow the State to exercise some degree of control over his life, which would allow him to claim the right to stay as an obligation of the State to secure his life.[189]

However, this approach is not adopted by the States because most of them still use the rationale that those persecuted persons will return to their countries and their presence in the territories of the host States would be temporary while the situation in their countries improves. Returning refugees is still considered the preferred solution to their plight. On the other hand, returning them voluntarily or forcibly could not resolve this plight because they usually face cruel circumstances like impoverishment, persecution, violation of their human rights, etc., which translates into 'repeated displacement'.[190]

That is like moving in a vicious circle of displacement. According to David Miller, refugees should have the right to self-determination by autonomy which requires having choices to choose from, so that one can opt for the most suitable solution for them.[191] Notwithstanding, the State' right of self-

---

[188] David Miller, Christine Straehle, ibid. P. 131.
[189] Ibid. P. 130, 131.
[190] Ibid. P. 154.
[191] Ibid. P. 173.

determination which stems from the principle of sovereignty in International Law allows them to exercise an excessive control over their territories. This, in turn, is considered inconsistent with the individuals' right of self-determination because any person's autonomy would be infringed if he is coercively deprived of the ability to choose. In the case of immigration, the State has the right to control its national borders and the discretion to admit or refuse asylum seekers who have entered its territory. This sovereignty is a moral right of all the States, but that does not eliminate the moral criticism of the State exercising its right to control the admission to its territory, for instance. In this regard, the argument of open borders would be a criticism of the State's sovereignty power of when it excludes peaceful immigrants.[192]

In tandem with this argument, the concept of sovereignty has changed after World War 1 and over the years to refer to State's right to regulate their national borders through passports and visas. This right does not mean that States should not have borders at all, they have special control on immigration along their borders consistent with the States' right of self - determination because, according to Wellman's view, if States do not have the right to admit or refuse association with foreigners, then they lose the essence of their self-determination.[193] Along these lines, Hobbes' idea of sovereignty is based primarily on the absolute obligations that all citizens have to compulsorily obey the State's political authority in everything, even though some of the government's decisions may be wrong. In Hobbes's words: "making War and peace, as he shall think best", meaning that the sovereign power has the right to choose war or peace.[194] He also thinks that the power of the State must not be limited by any self-enforced limits because only the unlimited power of sovereignty can achieve peace and the State's interests and, consequently, the citizens', because only this power can determine "the means of peace and defense" and whatsoever it considers necessary to maintain the State's security.[195] This perspective clashes with the human

---

[192] Carens, Joseph H. The ethics of immigration. 1. issued as an Oxford Univ. Press paperback. New York: Oxford University Press; Oxford Univerisity Press (Oxford political theory). (2013 // 2015) P. 270.

[193] Wellman, Christopher Heath; Cole, Phillip (2011): Debating the ethics of immigration. Is there a right to exclude? / Christopher Heath Wellman and Phillip Cole. New York, Oxford: Oxford University Press. P. 246.

[194] Thomas Hobbes: Leviathan, English/ Deutsch. Reclams Universal Bibliothek Nr. 18595. Germany (2013) P. 358. 372.

[195] Ibid. P. 366.

rights argument and the need of moral limits of the State's power.[196] The Universal Declaration of Human Rights was the first attempt to bind States by international obligations regarding human rights and their internal affairs. Thereby, the human rights of every human being are respected by the State's official commitments. This can also be considered a first accomplishment of limiting the State's sovereignty and establishing human rights over sovereignty.

For States, sovereignty as a national power actually focuses on protecting national interests, which is why when a State deliberately reinforces immigration restrictions, it aims to reduce the number of asylum seekers who want to reside in its territory with this policy, based on rational reasons relating to the assimilation of numerous refugees and the financial assistance they would require, for this would imply a predictable economic collapse. Even more so since most of them do not efficiently access the labor market in the host State because they find it easier to get money without working, or by doing illegal work without paying taxes to get more money and maintain the financial assistance from the government. In any case, the disadvantages outweigh the benefits. If we turn back to the Syrian refugee crisis, we will find that quite a few asylum seekers were active participants in terrorist groups and factions and have committed war crimes against innocent people, including women and children in Syria and Iraq. These people would constitute an absolute threat to the community of the host State by continuing with their terrorist actions which, in turn, would affect national security. For instance, what the USA did after the 9/11 attacks was a justifiable natural reaction when its government adopted the "clear-eyed immigration policy" to protect national security against Islamic immigrants and their radical backgrounds.[197] Since many innocent Americans were victims of terrorist immigrants, these immigrants posed a serious threat to the American community, leading to an anti-terrorist policy that was applied by the Trump administration despite the efforts of liberalists to stop the "extensive infringements of immigrant' rights". These efforts failed because the anti-terrorist approach was firmly reasonable for most citizens.[198]

---

[196] Carens, Joseph H. The ethics of immigration. Ibid. P. 271.
[197] Carol M. Swain (2018): Debating Immigration. Second edition, Cambridge University Press. New York, USA. P. 189
[198] Ibid. P. 279.

Some defenders of the freedom of movement insist on "the absolute priority" of the interests of individuals over the State's interests. Whenever this freedom becomes a serious threat to the "existence of a nation-State", only then can States carefully limit an individual's right to freely immigrate and stay in their territories.[199] States have the legitimate right of sovereignty to protect their citizens. In the previous cases, they can refuse or exclude asylum seekers on the grounds of national security or public order. But if the destination State chooses not to admit persecuted persons and return them to their country on the assumption that there is no real threat, these people will be greatly affected by this right.[200] Although this kind of discretionary control over immigration is essential for exercising sovereignty, this control of not allowing asylum seekers in their territory is not applicable to the European Union member States. Nevertheless, the real problem is when the State does not recognize the asylum seekers' right to stay and returns them forcibly to their country. The resulting harm of returning them to their country of origin or to a safe third country will be much more significant than the costs of allowing those who have spent a long-term within its territories to stay indefinitely. The immigrants who have been in the host country for long have established relations and roots with its citizens and they cannot simply abandon their stable new life to return to their countries where they will suffer from poverty, unemployment, bad general security, reintegration, discrimination of the government to prioritize the citizens who stayed, among other things. Thus, according to the Samaritan approach that believes in the duty of protecting persons without "undue cost to ourselves"[201], asylum seekers and refugees' interests, outweigh the host State's interests and the 'non-trivial' costs for granting them the right to stay. These costs are going to be low compared to the damage that will be inflicted on those persons if they returned coercively to their country. [202] This is why the non-refoulement principle has preferred the interests of individuals over the interests of State, even though it has the right to exercise its sovereignty. However, in these situations, States cannot utilize sovereignty as a pretext to return the persecuted persons to their home country when they are facing a

---

[199] Wellman, Christopher Heath; Cole, Phillip. Ibid. P. 247.
[200] David Miller, Christine Straehle. The Political Philosophy of Refuge, ibid. P. 124.
[201] Carol M. Swain (2018): Debating Immigration, ibid. P. 293.
[202] David Miller, Christine Straehle. The Political Philosophy of Refuge, ibid. P. 125-126

serious threat. Let's not forget that the State will always prioritize its sovereignty over asylum seekers and refugees who claim an entitlement to stay in its territory. In this sense, the non-refoulement principle is still too weak because it does not protect asylum seekers, refugees, and persons of subsidiary protection from being returned to their counties when there is no longer a serious threat in their countries and they have already qualified as safe countries. Then, these persons cannot claim a right to stay on the grounds by which they were admitted. They can only pursue the right to stay in the country by their local integration, proving that they are independent financially and don't have any financial assistance provided by the government. Thy need to have jobs and be very well integrated in the society by being economically, socially, religiously involved in clubs, churches, etc. If this is not so, States will choose the 'preferred solution' to the refugee plight by either repatriation or temporary resettlement in safe third countries.[203]

The Samaritan approach cannot justify the right to stay for asylum seekers, refugees, and persons of subsidiary protections because such right would constitute a burden of obligations to the host State, in addition to the 'non-trivial' costs that the host State is forced to pay. Autonomy and an individual's right of self-determination could be the most convincing approach to be adopted because the right to stay indefinitely after enjoying asylum is still unrecognized by the international community. In this context, the UNHCR and other agencies concerned with refugee affairs, along with Non-Governmental Organizations NGOs of Human Rights must take a step forward towards a new treaty that legitimizing the right to stay by combining the individual's autonomy and the Samaritan approaches to make a coherent justification to recognize this right universally. In order to do this, this treaty would have to limit the States' sovereignty by preferring the interests of individuals over the State's interests. Similarly to how the fundamental human rights enshrined in the UDHR restricted the States' sovereignty and made them comply with all the provisions established by the Declaration by considering them international obligations that need to be fulfilled. The right to stay requires enforceability, and that can only be achieved by a practical initiative that makes it an international obligation for all States.

---

[203] Ibid. P. 158-160.

Conclusion:

The purpose of this section was to envision whether the right to stay is going to be a potential right for asylum seekers in the host State or if it will remain just a claim for them. I illustrated many bases for this claim to be intrinsically established. First, we saw that the moral obligation stems from the necessity of protecting the human dignity that all persons should have regardless of any considerations. this moral obligation appeals to the virtue of human beings according to our natural human rights, although this argument is insufficient to recognize the claim to stay because Western States consider they fulfill their moral obligations towards refugees by just receiving certain numbers of asylum seekers and granting them temporary residences, without considering the right to stay as one of these moral obligations. In this sense, the right to stay is still going to remain a moral obligation, but it does not have any external mechanism to force States to forcibly recognize it. In the near future, this will only happen if the decision-makers in the European Union, as well as in the whole International Community seek to achieve a legal obligation towards asylum seekers so that they can stay in the host country for an indefinite period without any fear of being returned to their countries of origin, regardless of the 'safety norm' that may qualify their countries as safe. The right to stay should be based on their right of self-determination, which is the most vital approach to justify such a claim, along with a long-term residence if asylum seekers meet the conditions for this kind of residences to alleviate the costs the right to stay imply for States. When the refugees and the beneficiaries of other kinds of protection access effectively the labor market in the host State, and this would not be easily fulfilled, the State needs measures to mitigate the burden on itself. In order to do this, it must differentiate between the persons who really need protection and the persons who come for economic aims because a significant number of asylum seekers have other implicit inclinations than just protection. In the former situation, States are obliged to grant protection to the persecuted persons, as well as right to stay. In the latter situation, States have the right to refuse economic immigrants, for instance, and to deny their right to stay. Therefore, there should be distinctive classifications for different grades of financial assistance to be followed by the government. In other words, the host State should give less money as a financial assistance to refugees who are young and capable of working to promote being an active resident by working immediately after finishing a language level, which is considered sufficient to some extent for a job. Additionally, the State should threaten them with deportation if they worked illegally without informing the government in an attempt to evade taxes. This could be a suitable means of distinguishing immigrants without including other categories in the already problematic plight of refugees and their claim to stay. In my opinion, real integration and financial independence are going adequate guarantees for the host State to allow asylum seekers the right to stay without this translating into high costs for the government. Thus, the right to stay must be contingent on some conditions to be prospectively fulfilled, even though this right should in principle be enforceable by law without conditions.

Restrictions on the Implementation of the Right to Stay:

The State's obligations toward asylum seekers do not necessarily include admitting them. The Refugee Convention left room for the discretion of host States. Likewise, since the right to stay is not an absolute and mandatory right, the self-determination of individuals can strengthen the claim to stay if the person has the willingness to do so after establishing a new stable life in the host State. However, some obstacles can still diminish the possibility of staying. Especially since the UDHR referred to the principle of proportionality as a criterion for limiting rights in the recent Human Rights Law, under which the rights of persons could be limited to secure the rights and freedom of others. Thus, human rights could be justifiably limited for "the sake of others", meaning general welfare, public order, and morality. Also, the UDHR has implicitly mentioned national social security of the State in Art. 22.[204] According to this, States intend to limit the rights of individuals by permissible derogations in emergencies, such as the USA's policy in the "War on Terror". The UDHR has not accurately defined the emergency derogations of rights but the ICCPR has determined that some rights should not be constrained in national and international emergencies, such as the right of non-discrimination which is enshrined in International Law as an obligation. Thereby, States cannot evade their obligation in the name of

---

[204] Gordon Brown (ed.), The Universal Declaration of Human Rights in the 21st Century: A Living Document in a Changing World. A report by the Global Citizenship Commission. Cambridge, UK: Open Book Publishers, 2016. P. 58.

international or national emergencies.[205]

The right to asylum is not protected against emergency derogations, which is why it can be restricted by the State in some instances.

Irregular Immigration:

In principle, States should protect the human rights of immigrants if their presence is authorized in the host States. Thus, the right to immigrate would be entirely preserved according to four considerations: "Member States must act together to protect the human rights of migrants and expand pathways for safe, orderly and regular migration while safeguarding their borders, laws and the interests of their societies."[206]

Moreover, some States resort to withholding asylum altogether based on their right to not admit persons following the Refugee Convention, sending them back to third countries for being allowed to refuse those who entered their territory illegally. In some cases, asylum seekers come from third countries and do not come directly from their countries of origin. States focus on the 'prevention' of irregular immigration by attempting to control their external borders to prevent illegal migrants from resettling even through most of them are asylum seekers, instead of protecting them and respecting their human rights. These policies aim to stop unauthorized immigration and reduce the number of asylum seekers so many States have "won many battles against unauthorized migration". In this regard, the USA government has implemented several measures to prevent "illegal immigrants" from passing its national borders, nevertheless, the number of migrants are seemingly increasing, which shows that these measures have failed in keeping them from entering the borders.[207] This sensible issue has been referred to by the European Commission, which asserted that 'restrictive policies' to control irregular immigration would be justified if they were compatible with the protection of the human rights of the illegal immigrants that were enshrined in International Law. Then, the human rights of asylum seekers should not

---

[205] Ibid. 59, 60.
[206] United Nations General Assembly. Making migration work for all, report of the Secretary-General. Seventy- second session, Agenda items 14 and 117. A/72/ 643. 12 December 2017. P. 3.
[207] Alexander Betts (2011): Global Migration Governance. Edited by Alexander Betts. First edition. Oxford University Press. P. 101. And see Carol M. Swain (2018): Debating Immigration. Second edition, Cambridge University Press. New York, USA. P. 289, 290.

be neglected according to Art. 33 of the Refugee Convention, which prohibits returning refugees under the principle of non-refoulement. In addition, Art. 31 addressed the status of refugees who entered the host State unlawfully. It stipulated that the member States should not impose any sanctions or penalties on refugees for their illegal entry or presence in their territories if they came directly from the country where their life or freedom was being threatened. If their entry or presence was unauthorized, they must "present themselves without delay to the authorities and show good cause for their illegal entry or presence."[208] Likewise, Art. 3 of the European Convention of Human Rights has prohibited member States from returning refugees to "torture or inhuman, or degrading treatment or punishment." The Convention has tacitly included illegal immigrants to be protected against torture for as long as their origin countries are not safe. Hence, they theoretically have the right to enjoy asylum as a first step to stay in the member State, but what actually happens is entirely different because most European States still resort to their discretion to either allow or refuse asylum applications. They intend to indirectly prevent refugees from entering by punishing the traffickers and others who facilitate their entry to European territories.[209]

Undoubtedly, European States judge this kind of immigration according to its legitimacy and consider all asylum seekers who entered their territories without legal permission simply illegal immigrants. As a result, they evade their obligations to protect asylum seekers while taking into account their fundamental human rights as guaranteed by the ECHR which States that they should be prioritized over any other considerations. This reluctance is evidenced by their claim to "examine closely the conditions faced by status-less migrants within their territory".[210] Thus, European States combat irregular immigration rather than granting legal humanitarian visas to persecuted persons to protect them once they reach European territory. Nevertheless, States still have the final decision regarding admitting asylum seekers or not, and this authority is explicitly recognized by the International

---

[208]Peers, Steve, und Nicola Rogers. EU-Immigration and Asylum Law. Martinus Nijhoff, 2006. P. 900. And see also, the Refugee Convention, article 31. (1).
[209] Ibid. P. 901.
[210] Ibid. P. 904.

Human Rights Law.[211]

Albeit illegal immigrants who entered and stayed in a State without authorization or legal documents may be tolerated by the host State, this decision does not change their "unlawful presence", it just postpones temporarily their expulsion.[212] In case the asylum seeker has been refused, he will be subjected to deportation, or repatriation, which means "voluntary departure" to a third country if his country is still unsafe. Once there, he gets financial help to start a new life, besides a reservation on a commercial flight booked by the State that refused him.[213] However, European States nowadays face an "open social conflict" that has led to an increasing and continuous massive influx of asylum seekers. The way they deal with this is by taking more restrictive measures to control this kind of immigration in an attempt to achieve a balance between opening the borders to asylum seekers who need protection and closing them for those who have other objectives and could threaten the national security in the host State.[214]

The UNHCR in the Directive 2008/115/CE announced that asylum seekers whose claim for asylum has been refused should not be returned to their countries of origin. The non-refoulement principle in tandem with the prohibition of torture should be applied in this case instead of deportation, according to Art. 3 of the ECHR. This article reaffirms the necessity of prioritizing the risks and serious harms that asylum seekers could face if they returned to their country of origin or even to a third country over deportation, which was based on "inadmissible or unfounded applications," that make them illegal immigrants. However, the number of negative decisions concerning deportation in Switzerland, for instance, has not decreased much.[215] States have deliberately left room for reducing the number of asylum seekers' applications grounded on irregular and illegal immigrants, so that they can rapidly refuse them and send them back to third countries. There is still a gap that needs to be filled in by adopting specific

---

211 Ibid. P. 902.

212 Markus Kotzur / David Moya / Ulkü Sezgi Sözen / Andrea Romano (eds): The External Dimension of EU Migration and Asylum Policies, Border Management, Human Rights and Development Policies in the Mediterranean Area. 1st Edition. Nomos Verlagsgesellschaft, Baden-Baden, Germany 2020. P. 70.

213 Sieglinde Rosenberger, Verena Stern, Nina Merhaut (eds) (2018): Protest Movements in Asylum and Deportation. Switzerland: Springer Open. P. 77.

214 Ibid. P. 65.

215 Ibid. P. 75.

"uniform standards" that oblige States to fulfill their commitments to admit asylum seekers regardless of any other considerations like the way they entered their territories (illegal immigrants without legal permission) or any other ground used by States to admit or refuse asylum seekers at will.

The jurisprudence of the European Court of Human Rights has interpreted the protection that Art. 3 of the ECHR enshrined against "torture or inhuman, or degrading treatment or punishment" as absolute protection. Then, member States should grant protection to all asylum seekers including those who constitute a serious threat to national security or the public order of the host State. Even though the Court has clarified that Art.3 does not imply a right to reside in the host State, it ensures "absolute protection against expulsion or extradition."[216] Consequently, there have been many criticisms regarding this "extensive interpretation" along with the German Federal Administrative Court's objection to it for this would lead to an ambiguous commitment to admit all asylum seekers who could be victims of different kinds of torture and dangers. This would blur the line to distinguish asylum seekers who fled from persecution and internal conflict from other persons who were subject to inhuman treatment or punishment. Thus, the provisions of the Refugee Convention, which limit protection in case it is inconsistent with the State's national security or public order, will be entirely neglected according to this extensive application. In response, the Court has stipulated in Art. 8 of the ECHR that member States should find a balance between public and private interests and, in case of contradicting both, they must prefer public interests and then resort to deportation or expulsion.[217]

In this context, the States can certainly argue that asylum seekers are illegal immigrants who threaten their national security or public order to reject a significant number of applications for asylum. Hence, they would not even have an opportunity to claim a right to stay. Some countries, like Australia, adopt the 'excision concept' as an 'elusive solution' for the refugee crisis. The Australian government considers many Australian islands as "excised offshore places" to prevent asylum seekers who arrive to these islands from entering and applying for asylum in Australia. This policy considers the

---

[216] Kay Hailbronner: Immigration and Asylum Law and Policy of the European Union. Kluwer Law International. The Hague, Netherlands. 2000. P. 494.
[217] Ibid. P. 495-497

"maritime asylum seekers" who arrive to certain islands as being outside the territory in which Migration Law and the Refugee Convention should be applied. Although those islands are still part of Australia's sovereignty, the government alleges that they are excised from the 'migration zone' and, hence, they would not be subject to the non-refoulement principle which prohibits returning refugees.[218] Thus, even if Australia appears obliged to the Refugee Convention, it utilizes an "elusive solution" in the Pacific by intercepting asylum seekers in international waters to refuse them before arriving in the territorial waters of Australia in which the Refugee Convention is allegedly applied. This solution deeply infringes the "spirit of the Refugee Convention" and objects to legality itself.[219] In case the illegal immigrants succeed in arriving to "mainland" Australia, there are two different ways of dealing with them: the first is as illegal maritime immigrants who can apply for asylum only if they have been granted permission from the Australian Immigration Minister, and the second is in case that illegal immigrants arrive by air. Once they land, they will be detained and their application for asylum will be examined. If they have been refused, they have the right to appeal the decision.

As we can see, the Migration Laws of some countries are particularly complex even though they signed the Convention and expressed that their national legislations would be compatible with its spirit. Likewise, the immigration policy of the UK counted its colonies outside its territory and the provisions in the Refugee Convention do not apply to immigration activities that take place there. The UK signed the Convention with this particular clause.[220] Similarly, illegal immigrants in Italy who came from Libya and North Africa after the war and the Arab spring have experienced the same racist treatment by members of "Roma communities".[221] States should reconsider their treatment of irregular immigrants and how to deal with asylum seekers who cross their borders. They should strive to protect their human rights after examining their claim instead of eliminating irregular immigration and

---

[218] David Scott FitzGerald (2019): Refuge Beyond Reach: How Rich Democracies Repel Asylum Seekers. Oxford Scholarship Online: March 2019. Oxford University Press. P. 228.

[219] David Scott FitzGerald, ibid. P. 229, 230.

[220] Ibid. P. 225.

[221] Alessandra Silveira, Mariana Canotilho, Pedro Madeira Froufe (eds) (2013): Citizenship and Solidarity in the European Union, from the Charter of Fundamental Rights to the Crisis, the State of the Art. Peter Lang. Brussels. P. 333.

combating it by detaining them in centers such as the "zero tolerance model regime" which is applied in the USA and Australia.[222] In other words, such detention would be extremely controversial because asylum seekers did not commit any offense when they crossed the borders, they were simply looking for a safe place where they could enjoy fundamental human rights without fear of persecution, armed conflict, or any serious threat to their lives. Conversely, States take aggressive measures against them without any clear justification. Detention should be as a punishment for constituting a certain risk to national security or public order, or even if the asylum seeker's application was rejected and he did not comply with the deportation decision, then detention would be justifiable to some extent.[223] It is important to mention that the US policy of 'mandatory detention and criminal prosecution' against asylum seekers was strictly adopted in 2018, in which the US government started "separating the children from their parents" as a deterrence for those who entered its territory without authorization seeking asylum. Consequently, the government has sent toddlers, infants, and children to "foster homes and government-run facilities" where they do not receive sufficient care, and a lot of them have been put in cages.[224]

The Absence of the Duty to Permit Entry in Host States:

The biggest challenge that the UNHCR has recently faced concerning the implementation of its resettlement program manifests in the flagrant difference in the way States contribute to resettle refugees in States that receive a large number of asylum seekers and the States that are still advocating their policy of closed borders such as the USA and many European States.[225]

States' sovereignty still controls the borders firmly and it largely influences the decision of accepting asylum seekers and, hence, who would be a

---

[222] Maurice Stierl: Migrant Resistance in Contemporary Europe, edited by Jenny Edkins and Nick Vaughan-Williams. New York: Routledge, 2019. P. 141.

[223] Julia Iliopoulos-Strangas, Michael Potacs, Elena Simina Tanasescu, Jacques Ziller (eds): Migration-Migration-Migrations. Neue Herausforderungen für die Staatssouveränität und für den sozialen Rechtsstaat- New challenges for Europe, for State Sovereignty and for the Rule of Law and the Welfare State- Nouveaux défis pour l'Europe, la souveraineté de l'Etat et l'Etat de droit social. Germany: Nomos Verlagsgesellschaft (11) 2017. P. 216. And see also, Serena Parekh: No Refugee: Ethics and the Global Refugee Crisis. Oxford University Press. 2010. P. 129-131.

[224] Serena Parekh, ibid. P. 132, 133.

[225] Marie Claire Foblets, Luc Leboeuf (eds): Humanitarian Admission to Europe, The Law between Promises and Constraints. 1 Edition, Nomos. Germany 2020. P. 250.

candidate to claim a right to stay. This approach considers that refugees will greatly affect 'economic prosperity', national security, social cohesion, and other aspects. Thus, States are keen on reaching a balance between their international obligations and their previous values.[226] It is no less certain that this right to permit or deny entry to asylum seekers is undeniable, even though it could not be an absolute right grounded on sovereignty because of the criteria defined in the Refugee Convention in accordance with human rights treaties. However, that does not deny the fact that there is no duty to be imposed on the States' shoulders to allow persons to enter their territories. Furthermore, this kind of control is implemented as extraterritorial control. Some countries implement measures on the high seas to surveil the boats of asylum seekers and attempt to prevent them from arriving at their territorial sea. Others, like some members of the EU, are obliged to apply uniform principles to control the external borders of the Schengen area respecting the right of free movement of any person who enters the area. According to Art. 3(2) of the Convention implementing the Schengen Agreement, The Schengen acquis (SIC): "The Contracting Parties undertake to introduce penalties for the unauthorized crossing of external borders at places other than crossing points or at times other than the fixed opening hours". Internal flights do not comply with such control. Nevertheless, external flights, including all the countries which are not members of the EU, such as the UK, would be considered third countries, and any movement from the nationals of third countries should be under the "external border control."[227] Thus, according to Art.6 of SIC, "cross-border movement at external borders" must be checked by examining all the person's travel documents and entry conditions to assess whether he constitutes a serious threat to national security and public order of the competent member State he wants to enter. The Schengen States have developed a common visa policy to protect all European Union States from any person who could threaten the national security of a member State, so that he would not be allowed to enter the Schengen area. Regarding asylum seekers who want to enter, they would not be subject to the visa policy because Art. 5 (2) of the Schengen acquis has stipulated that: "These rules shall not preclude the application of special

---

[226] Serena Parekh, ibid. P. 78.
[227] Hailbronner, Kay: Immigration and Asylum Law and Policy of the European Union. Kluwer Law International. The Hague/ London/ Boston. 2000. P. 130.

provisions concerning the right to asylum".[228] The provisions of Art. 63 of the Treaty Establishing the European Community (TEC) protect the human rights of third-country nationals in immigration issues by entitling the Council to take measures regarding the entry and the reception of asylum seekers in the competent State. It also safeguards their right not to be returned to their country if the circumstances are still dangerous for them. It has been considered that protecting the human rights of asylum seekers could overwhelm the "public policy interests". Nevertheless, granting the right to enter is not explicitly a duty of member States, but they should grant all asylum seekers an absolute right to enter or to stay in their territories.[229]

According to Art. (8) of the jurisprudence of the ECtHR, States have the sovereign right to control their borders and adopt the immigration policy that fits their interests. Moreover, refugees must meet the criteria set out by the UNHCR to be able to resettle, which implies clauses for the refugee status in which refugees should be in need of 'legal and physical protection' or be 'survivors of violence and torture', need 'medical treatment', or be "women at risk and refugees with lack of integration prospects."[230]

According to the Refugee Convention and the Council's Directive 2004/83/EC of 29 April 2004 (on Minimum Standards for the Qualification and Status of Third Country Nationals or stateless Persons as Refugees or as Persons who otherwise need International Protection and the Content of the Protection granted), the right to enter and resettle in a member State could be highly restricted because of national security and public order considerations. However, the European Court of Human Rights still needs to explain the accurate meaning of serious threat or danger to national security or public order. The main reason for this is that member States could abuse this limitation on the right to enter and stay of third-country nationals, and expel or extradite asylum seekers to a third country in case there are good reasons to consider them a danger to their national security. According to the Directive, "the concepts of danger to the community or to the security of member States" can limit the right to enter or the residence permits and

---

[228] Ibid. P. 125.
[229] Ibid. P. 88.
[230] Marie Claire Foblets, Luc Leboeuf (eds): Humanitarian Admission to Europe. Ibid. P. 251.

allows States to exclude, revoke or refoule third-country nationals.[231]

Nevertheless, the European Court of Justice (ECJ) still has to clarify the concepts of "danger to the community or danger to the security of member States" that the Directive has adopted, and the national security and public order which have been considered as limitations to the right to enter that enable member States to exercise their full discretion and not be imposed to allow asylum seekers to enter and stay within their territory. Despite this, the European Commission has affirmed the necessity of "respecting the human rights and democratic principles" in the process of entry or expulsion. This means that member States would be subject to "strict scrutiny" as well as "control by the institutions of the community" which should enshrine the human rights that are stipulated in the ECHR. The European Court of Human Rights also has to supervise these measures taken by member States to ensure that they are consistent with International Human Rights Law and human rights in Community Law. In addition, the decisions of entry and expulsions must balance the interests of individuals and States. The ECtHR has mentioned sthe lack of the right to enter or to reside in the host State after the violation of Art. 8 of the ECHR, which says:

"1. Everyone has the right to respect for his private and family life, his home, and his correspondence. 2. There shall be no interference by a public authority with the exercise of this right except such as is in accordance with the law and is necessary in a democratic society in the interests of national security, public safety or the economic well-being of the country, for the prevention of disorder or crime, for the protection of health or morals, or for the protection of the rights and freedoms of others". When French authorities delay in granting a residence permit to a Spanish national, this infringes the right to reside according to Community Law. Consequently, the right of a third country national to enter and reside in a host stay would also be a subject to the discretion of the host State. Although this right has been recognized in international as well as in European instruments, it still needs to be explicitly recognized as an obligation of member States towards asylum

---

[231] Maria- Teresa Gil-Bazo. New Issues in Refugee Research, Refugee status, subsidiary protection, and the right to be granted asylum under EC Law. Research Paper No. 136. Refugee Studies Centre. Oxford University. United Kingdom. November 2006. P. 24.

seekers who require international protection.[232] In other words, the rights of those persons who need international protection and which are addressed in the Refugee Convention should not be left to the interpretations of judges of member States. There should be an explanation of refugees' rights and a forcible implementation of their right to asylum by recognizing their right to stay, which should be granted without restrictions like the other human rights established in human rights treaties.[233]

Conclusion:

The remote-control policies of asylum and immigration affairs by some countries constitute an evident difference among States regarding the refugee plight. Especially since most of the resettlement countries are member States of the EU, despite the gap which manifests in the absent enforceability of the right to resettle for an indefinite time in the host State. At least European Countries take efficient measures to resolve this crisis by applying the principle of solidarity and the responsibility of burden-sharing among them to fulfill their commitments toward refugees globally. Although the Common European Asylum System does not entirely safeguard admitting asylum seekers in member States and granting them necessarily an absolute right to stay, member States have resisted their public interests many times to prefer the human rights of asylum seekers in accordance with protecting human rights and fundamental freedoms in the European Union. The Union has three basic objectives which are security, freedom, and justice. However, the right to stay cannot be an absolute right because of many considerations related to the national security and public order of the host States, as well as the concept of the nation-State. Receiving refugees can also increase the radical xenophobia within its community against refugees who want to associate themselves with nationals, who can correspondingly refrain from associating with refugees based on the right of self-determination. Thus, proportionality may play an essential role in finding a real solution to asylum seekers' plight internationally and not only in the European Union. A way to do this could be by attempting to balance the interests of asylum seekers and

---

[232] Ibid. P. 24, 25.
[233] Lamis Elmy Abdelaaty: Discrimination and Delegation. Oxford University Press. New York (2021). P. 191.

those of the countries. In this regard, an open borders policy could help to solve this problem because a "no borders policy" would entail significant dangers for the host States. Some of them might be threatening the welfare of the State and the cultural identity of the national community. However, closed borders would be the worst possible solution because this keeps un from fulfilling our moral obligations toward asylum seekers in terms of protecting their human dignity and their fundamental human rights. The international community needs a new treaty to expressly recognize the right to stay for refugees if they do not constitute any threat to the host State, and they are, indeed, active persons and contribute efficiently to the national economy to ease the burden on the State.

References:

1. Alessandra Silveira, Mariana Canotilho, Pedro Madeira Froufe (eds) (2013): Citizenship and Solidarity in the European Union, from the Charter of Fundamental Rights to the Crisis, the State of the Art. Peter Lang. Brussels.

2. Alexander Betts (2011): Global Migration Governance. Edited by Alexander Betts. First edition. Oxford University Press.

3. Andersson, Ruben (2014): Illegality, inc. Clandestine migration and the business of bordering Europe / Ruben Andersson. Oakland, CA: University of California Press (California series in public anthropology, 28).

4. Anette Faye Jacobsen (2008): Human Rights Monitoring, A Field Mission Manual. Martinus Nijhoff Publishers. Boston.

5. Anne Marie Baylouny (2020): When Blame Backfires: Syrian Refugees and the Citizen Grievances in Jordan and Lebanon. Cornell University Press. First published. Ithaca, New York.

6. Anne T. Gallagher (2013): Migration, Human Rights, and Development: A Global Anthology. International Debate Education Association. New York, NY 10010.

7. Antonio Di Marco, The Subsidiary Protection: The Discriminatory and Limited Protection of the "New Refugees" 20 (1-2 2015). Available online at Mediterranean Journal of Human Rights

8. Arash Abizadeh, 2006: Liberal Egalitarian Arguments for Closed Borders, Some Preliminary Critical Reflections. Ethics and Economics, 4 (1), Department of Political Science, McGill University

9. Bacaian, Livia Elena (2011): The protection of refugees and their right to seek asylum in the European Union Mémoire présenté pour l'obtention du Master en études européennes par Livia Elena Bacaian rédigé sous la direction de Nicolas Wisard Jurée : Master in European Studies, Geneva. INSTITUT EUROPÉEN DE L'UNIVERSITÉ DE GENÈVE.

10. Basem Mahmud (2022): Emotions and Belonging in Forced Migration, Syrian Refugees and Asylum Seekers. Routledge Advances in Sociology, First published. New York.

11. Blake, Nicholas; Husain, Raza (2003): Immigration, asylum and Human Rights. Oxford: Oxford University Press (Blackstone's Human Rights Act series).

12. Brian Opeskin, Richard Perruchoud, Jillyanne Redpath-cross. (2012): Foundations of International Migration Law:Cambridge University Press.

13. Carens, Joseph H. (1987): Aliens and Citizens: The Case for Open Borders. 2nd ed. 49 volumes: Cambridge University Press.

14. Carens, Joseph H. (2013 // 2015): The ethics of immigration. 1. issued as an Oxford Univ. Press paperback. New York: Oxford University Press; Oxford Univerisity Press (Oxford political theory).

15. Carl Ulrik Schierup, Peo Hansen, and Stephan Castles (2006): Migration, Citizenship, and the European Welfare State: A European Dilemma. Oxford Scholarship Online: May 2006.

16. Carol M. Swain (2018): Debating Immigration. Second edition, Cambridge University Press. New York, USA.

17. Chris Rumford (2014): Cosmopolitan Borders. Department of Politics and International Relations, Royal Holloway, University of London, UK: Palgrave Macmillan 2014.

18. Corinne Lewis. (2012): UNHCR and International Refugee Law. From treates to innovation. Great Britain: Tj International Ltd, Padstow, Cornwall.

19. Crawley Heaven, Castles Stephen, Loughna Sean, States of Conflict: Causes and Patterns of Forced Migration to the EU and Policy Responses. Report 2003.

20. David Miller, Christine Straehle (2020): The Political Philosophy of Refuge: Cambridge University Press.

21. David Scott FitzGerald (2019): Refuge Beyond Reach: How Rich Democracies Repel Asylum Seekers. Oxford Scholarship Online: March 2019. Oxford University Press.

22. Derek Heater: Does Cosmopolitan Thinking Have a Future? Review of International Studies. British International Studies Association (2000). 26179-197.

23. Edward Shizha, Rosemary Kimani Dupuis, Priscilla Broni (eds): Living Beyond the Borders. Essays on Global Immigrants and Refugees. Peter Lang. New York, 2018.

24. Elspeth Guild, Jan Niessen (eds): Immigration and Asylum Law and Policy in Europe. Digital Borders and Real Rights, Effective Remedies for Third-Country Nationals in the Schengen System. Vol 15, Evelien Brouwer. Martinus Nijhoff Publishers 2008. Leiden, Boston.

25. Elspeth Guild, Jan Niessen (eds): Immigration and Asylum Law and Policy in Europe. European Asylum Law and International Law. Hemme Battjes. Vol 8, Koninklijke Brill NV, Netherlands, 2006.

26. Elspeth Guild, Jan Niessen (eds): Institutional and Policy Dynamics of EU Migration Law, Immigration and Asylum Law and Policy in Europe. Vol 10, Georgia Papagianni. Martinus Nijhoff Publishers 2006. Leiden, The Netherlands.

27. Elspeth Guild, Paul Minderhoud (eds): Security of Residence and Expulsion, Protection of Aliens in Europe. 2000. Kluwer Law international / The Hague/ London/ Boston.

28. Ernst Hirsch Ballin, Emina Ćerimović, Huub Dijstelbloem, Mathieu Segers: European Variations as a Key to Cooperation. The Netherland Scientific Council for Government Policy (WRR). Published by Springer Nature Switzerland, 18 September 2020.

29. Fiddian-Qasmiyeh, Elena; Loescher, Gil; Long, Katy; Sigona, Nando (2014): The Oxford handbook of refugee and forced migration studies. First edition. Oxford: Oxford University Press.

30. Fine, Sarah; Ypi, Lea (eds) (2016): Migration in political theory. The ethics of movement and membership. First edition. Oxford: Oxford University Press.

31. Gilbert H. Gornig, Hans-Detlef Horn (2017): Migration, Asyl, Flüchtlinge und Fremdenrecht. Deutschland und seine Nachbarn in Europa vor neuen Herausforderungen. Staats- und völkerrechtliche Abhandlungen der Studiengruppe für Politik und Völkerrecht, Volume 31. Dunker& Humblot. Berlin. Germany.

32. Gordon Brown (ed.), The Universal Declaration of Human Rights in the 21st Century: A Living Document in a Changing World. Cambridge, UK: Open Book Publishers, 2016. http://dx.doi. org/10.11647/OBP.0091

33. Guys S. Goodwin- Grill, Jane McAdams (2007): the refugee in International Law. Third edition. New York, Oxford University Press.

34. Guy S. Goodwin-Gill, Article 31 of the 1951 Convention relating to the Status of Refugees: Non-penalization, Detention and Protection. A paper prepared of the Department of International Protection for the UNHCR Global Consultations. University of Oxford. October 2001.

35. Guild, Elspeth; Minderhoud, P. E. (2001): Security of residence and expulsion protection of aliens in Europe. The Hague, London: Kluwer Academic Publishers (Immigration and asylum law and policy in Europe, v.1).

36. Hailbronner, Kay (2000): Immigration and Asylum Law and Policy of the European Union. Kluwer Law International. The Hague/ London/ Boston.

37. Hailbronner, Kay; Thym, Daniel (Eds.) (2016): EU immigration and asylum law. A commentary. Second edition. München, Oxford: C.H. Beck; Hart.

38. Handbook on European law relating to asylum, borders and immigration (2013). Luxembourg: Publications Office of the European Union.

39. Hathaway, James C.; Foster, Michelle (2014): The law of refugee status. Second edition. Cambridge United Kingdom: Cambridge University Press.

40. Hannum, M: The right to leave and Return in International law and Practice (1987): The Strasburg Declaration on the right to leave and Return, 81 American Journal of International Law 1987.

41. James C. Hathaway, Michelle Foster (2014): The Law of Refugee Status. Cambridge University Press.

42. Jasmin Lilian Diab (2017): International Migration and Refugee Law: Does Germany Migration Policy towards Syrian Refugees Comply? Anchor Academic Publishing. Hamburg.

43. Jason Hart (2010): Years of conflict, Adolescence, Political Violence and Displacement. Edited by Jason Hart. First edition. Berghahn Books (New York. Oxford).

44. Jeff Crisp, Damtew Dessalegne (2002): New Issues in Refugee Research, Refugee Protection and Migration Management: The challenge for UNHCR. Working paper No.64. August 2002. UNHCR Evaluation and Policy Analysis Unit. Geneva.

45. Jose Jorge Mendoza: Does Cosmopolitan Justice Ever Require Restrictions of Migration? Article in Public Affairs Quarterly. Volume 29, Number 2, April 2015. P. 175- 186.

46. Julia Iliopoulos-Strangas, Michael Potacs, Elena Simina Tanasescu, Jacques Ziller (eds) (2017): Migration-Migration-Migrations. Neue Herausforderungen für die Staatssouveränität und für den sozialen Rechtsstaat- New challenges for Europe, for State Sovereignty and for the Rule of Law and the Welfare State-Nouveaux défis pour l'Europe, la souveraineté de l'Etat et l'Etat de droit social. Germany: Nomos Verlagsgesellschaft (11).

47. Kamilia Rostom (2020): Integrating Syrian Refugees in Eastern Germany. A Cultural Textbook. Peter Lang. NewYork.

48. Karim Atassi (2018): Syria, the Strength of an Idea, the Constitutional Architectures of Its Political Regimes. Preface by Jean Marcou. Translated from the French by Christopher Sutcliffe. Cambridge University Press first published. United Kingdom.

49. Kay Hailbronner (2000): Immigration and Asylum Law and Policy of the European Union. Kluwer Law International. The Hague, Netherlands.

50. Kay Hailbronner, Daniel Thym (2016): EU Immigration and Asylum Law, A Commentary. Second edition. C.H. Beck. Hart. Nomos. Germany.

51. Lambert, Hélène (1995): Seeking asylum. Comparative law and practice in selected European countries / by Hélène Lambert. Dordrecht, London: M. Nyhoff.

52. Lamis Elmy Abdelaaty (2021): Discrimination and Delegation. Oxford University Press. New York.

53. Laura Affolter (2021): Asylum Matters on the Front Line of Administrative Decision-Making. Palgrave Socio-Legal Studies. University of Bern, Springer Nature Switzerland.

54. Laura Westra, Satvinder Juss, Tillio Scovayzzi(2015): Towards a refugee Oriented Right of Asylum. United Kingdem , Dorest Pess.

55. Maciej Duszczyk, Marta Pachocka, Dominika Pszczolkowska (eds) (2020): Relation between Immigration and Integration Policies in Europe, Challenges, Opportunities and Perspectives in Selected EU Member States. First published, Routledge. London and New York.

56. Manuel R. Garcia-Mora (1956): International Law and Asylum as a Human Right. 1st ed. United States of America: Public Affairs Press.

57. Marie Claire Foblets, Luc Leboeuf (eds): Humanitarian Admission to Europe, The Law between Promises and Constraints. 1 Edition, Nomos. Germany 2020.

58. Maria- Teresa Gil-Bazo. New Issues in Refugee Research, Refugee status, subsidiary protection, and the right to be granted asylum under EC Law. Research Paper No. 136. Refugee Studies Centre. Oxford University. United Kingdom. November 2006.

59. Markus Kotzur / David Moya / Ulkü Sezgi Sözen / Andrea Romano (eds): The External Dimension of EU Migration and Asylum Policies, Border Management, Human Rights and Development Policies in the Mediterranean Area. 1st Edition. Nomos Verlagsgesellschaft, Baden-Baden, Germany 2020.

60. Martin, David A. (1988): The new asylum seekers. Refugee law in the 1980's: 9th Sokol colloquium on international law: Papers / edited by David A. Martin. Dordrecht, Boston: M. Nijhoff.

61. Massimo Condinanzi, Alessandra Lang, Bruno Nascimbene (2008): Citizenship of the Union and Freedom of Movement of Persons. Immigration and Asylum Law and Policy in Europe, Band: 14. Martinus Nijhoff Publishers.

62. Maurice Stierl: Migrant Resistance in Contemporary Europe, edited by Jenny Edkins and Nick Vaughan-Williams. New York: Routledge, 2019.

63. Maurizio Ferrera: The Boundaries of Welfare: European Integration and the New Spatial of Social Protection, New Boundaries, New Structuring? On the Future of Social Protection in the European Union. Oxford University Press Scholarship Online: February 2006.

64. Mendoza, José Jorge; Mendieta, Eduardo (2011): Neither a State of Nature nor a State of Exception. In *Radical Philosophy Review* 14 (2), pp. 187–195. DOI: 10.5840/radphilrev201114222.

65. Nuala Mole, Catherine Meredith: Asylum and the European Convention on Human Rights, Council of Europe publishing, 2010.

66. Pauline Kleingeld. Kant's Cosmopolitan Law World Citizenship for a Global Order, Kantian Review, Volume 2, 1998. Washington University, St Louis.

67. Peers, Steve, und Nicola Rogers. EU Immigration and Asylum Law. Martinus Nijhoff, 2006.

68. Phil Orchard 2014: A Right to Flee (Refugees, States, and the construction of International Cooperation). Cambridge, United Kingdom.

69. Rainer Bauböck (ed) (2006): Migration and Citizenship. Legal Status, Rights and Political Participation. Amsterdam University Press, Amsterdam.

70. Rosemary Byrne, Gregor Noll, and Jens Vedsted -Hansen (Eds) (2002): New Asylum Countries? Migration Control and Refugee Protection in an Enlarged European Union. Kluwer Law International. Netherlands.

71. Rumford, Chris; Geiger, Martin (2014): Cosmopolitan borders. Houndmills, Basingstoke, Hampshire, New York, NY: Palgrave Macmillan.

72. Samer N. Abboud (2016): Syria. Polity press, Cambridge CB2 1UR, UK.

73. Serena Parekh (2020): No Refugee: Ethics and the Global Refugee Crisis. Oxford University Press.

74. Shah, Prakash (2005): The challenge of asylum to legal systems. London: Cavendish.

75. Shelly Wilcox, Journal Compilation, Philosophy Compass 4/1 (2009). The open Borders Debate on Immigration. San Francisco State University. Blackwell publishing.

76. Sieglinde Rosenberger, Verena Stern, Nina Merhaut (eds) (2018): Protest Movements in Asylum and Deportation. Switzerland: Springer Open.

77. Societas Iuris Publici Europaei, Julia Iliopoulos-Strangas, Michael Potacs, Simina Elena Tănăsescu, Jacques Ziller: Migration - Migration - Migrations. Neue Herausforderungen für Europa, für die Staatssouveränität und für den sozialen Rechtsstaat. New Challenge for Europe, for State Sovereignty and for the Rule of Law and Welfare State. 1. Auflage. Nomos, 2017. https://dx.doi.org/10.5771/9783845285368.

78. T. Alexander Aleinkoff, Vincent Chctail(2003): Migration And International Legal Norms. T. M. C. Asser Press, The Hage, Netherlands.

79. Teresa Hayter (2004): Open Borders, The Case Against Immigration Controls. Second Edition, Pluto Press. London.

80. THE UNITED NATIONS HIGH COMMISSIONER FOR REFUGEES (2003): Agenda for protection.

81. Thomas Gammeltoft- Hansen (2011): Access to Asylum: International Refugee Law and the Globalization of Migration Control. Cambridge University Press, New York.

82. Thomas Hobbes: Leviathan, English/ Deutsch. Reclams Universal Bibliothek Nr. 18595. Germany (2013).

83. Thomas Riggs and Kathleen J. Edgar, eds. *In Context Series* Farmington Hills, MI: Gale, 2018. 988 pp. 2 vols.

84. Todea, Diana Virginia. "Libertarianism and Immigration". Libertarian Papers2, no. a30 (2010): 1-21.

85. United Nations General Assembly. Making migration work for all, report of the Secretary-General. Seventy- second session, Agenda items 14 and 117. A/72/ 643. 12 December 2017.

86. UNHCR Resettlement Handbook, Division of International Protection. Geneva, revised edition July 2011.

87. Vanessa Agnew, Kader Konuk, Jane O. Newman (eds) 2020: Refugee Routes, Telling, Looking, Protesting, Redressing. Vol,1. Transcript Verlag, Bielefeld.

88. Vicki Squire: Europe's Migration Crisis, Borders Deaths and Human Dignity. University of Warwick. New York, Cambridge University Press, first published 2020.

89. Wellman, Christopher Heath; Cole, Phillip (2011): Debating the ethics of immigration. Is there a right to exclude? / Christopher Heath Wellman and Phillip Cole. New York, Oxford: Oxford University Press.

90. Whittaker, David J. (2006): Asylum seekers and refugees in the contemporary world. London: Routledge (The making of the contemporary world).

91. Willem van Schendel. Spaces of Engagement, How Borderland, Illegal Flows, and Territorial States Interlock. 2005.

www.ingramcontent.com/pod-product-compliance
Lightning Source LLC
Chambersburg PA
CBHW031428180326
41458CB00002B/487